Geology of Passive Continental Margins:

History, Structure and Sedimentologic Record (With Special Emphasis on the Atlantic Margin)

For the AAPG Eastern Section Meeting and Atlantic Margin Energy Conference

Education Course Note Series #19

A. W. Bally
A. B. Watts
J. A. Grow
W. Manspeizer
D. Bernoulli
C. Schreiber
J. M. Hunt

Acknowledgements

These papers were prepared for the 1981 Atlantic Margin Energy Conference. They were compiled by A. W. Bally, of Rice University's Department of Geology, and their presentation made in conjunction with The American Association of Petroleum Geologists Eastern Section Meeting.

Extra copies of this, and all other books in the AAPG Education Course Note Series, are available from:

AAPG Bookstore
P.O. Box 979
Tulsa, Oklahoma 74101

Published in October, 1981

ISBN: 0-89181-168-0

GEOLOGY OF PASSIVE CONTINENTAL MARGINS:
HISTORY, STRUCTURE AND SEDIMENTOLOGIC RECORD
(WITH SPECIAL EMPHASIS ON THE ATLANTIC MARGIN)

TABLE OF CONTENTS

ATLANTIC-TYPE MARGINS

A. W. Bally
Department of Geology
Rice University
P. O. Box 1892
Houston, Texas   77001

Introduction

This introduction is only a general frame of reference for the short course. The other papers in this notebook cover a selection of topics that are relevant for an understanding of the hydrocarbon habitat of the U.S. Atlantic margin. The scope of a short course does not permit a comprehensive treatment; therefore, we focused on aspects that would provide useful background to explorationists who are actively engaged in the difficult task of evaluating hydrocarbon prospects on the U.S. Atlantic margin.

We have tried to provide selected but reasonably up-to-date reference lists that may enable the reader to look into many aspects of the development of the North American Atlantic margin. At the end of this introduction are a number of reference lists that were included for the convenience of the reader. Reference List I cites papers listed in this introduction and a number of other recently published papers that may be of interest. Reference List II(a) cites books and maps that provide useful background for passive margin studies. Reference List II(b) cites passive margin related papers that are in preparation for a volume on the AAPG sponsored Hollis Hedberg Conference, which was held last January in Galveston. Finally, Reference List III cites volumes that describe passive margin related holes that were drilled under the auspices of the Deep Sea Drilling Project. On lists I and II an asterisk marks papers concerned with the Canadian Atlantic margin. That margin, because of early favorable legislation, has been the subject of much more intensive exploration than its U.S. counterpart. Therefore, the Canadian margin and its petroleum potential is somewhat better understood, and more drilling information is published.

What are Atlantic-type margins?

Lithospheric plates (Fig. 1) are circumscribed by three types of boundaries, i.e.:

(1) Extensional rifts (the mid-ocean ridges) associated with shallow focus earthquakes; (2) transform fault zones associated with shallow focus earthquakes and characterized by strike-slip first motions; (3) predominantly compressional subduction zones that are associated with shallow-intermediate and deep focus earthquakes of the Benioff zones.

LITHOSPHERIC PLATES

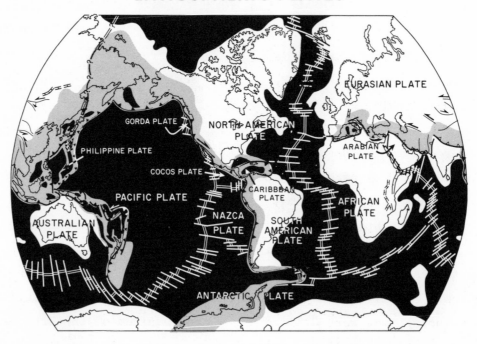

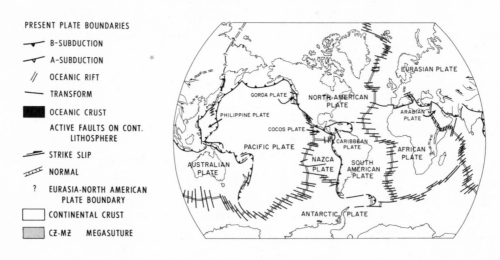

Fig. 1. Distribution of lithospheric plates. Lower inset shows
plate names without differentiating crustal types.
(From Bally and Snelson, 1980, with permission of the
Can. Soc. Petrol. Geol.)

Continental margins straddle the ocean crust boundary. They can be grouped into three classes that are related to plate boundaries (Figs. 2 and 3).

1. Atlantic-type margins which are also often called passive or divergent continental margins. Passive, because today these margins have little or no significant seismic and volcanic activity. Divergent, because they are margins where lithospheric plates due to ocean spreading move away, or diverge, from the mid-ocean ridge, which forms at an extensional plate boundary. In this notebook we will use the terms Atlantic-type, passive and divergent margins interchangeably.

2. Transform margins which may be associated with either passive or else with active margins.

3. Active margins are associated with intensive earthquake activity and spectacular volcanism. They are also often called convergent margins because they form at convergent plate boundaries, where cold rigid lithosphere is sinking deep into the hotter, less viscous asthenosphere. Island arcs, forearc basins and marginal basins on their concave side are characteristic of active margins.

The reader should keep in mind that passive margins may often be offset by extensive transform segments that formed early in their history. It also may be useful to point out that the marginal or back-arc basins associated with island arcs have many similarities with Atlantic-type margins. The main difference, however, is that they are behind a volcanic arc, that most of them are young (late Paleogene and Neogene), and that they are not as geologically long-lived as Atlantic-type margins.

This course is focusing on the U.S. Atlantic margin, and only occasionally we will refer to other Atlantic-type margins.

Morphology and surface sediments

Atlantic-type continental margins are typically subdivided into four major sub-provinces:

(1) The coastal plain, an onshore extension of the continental shelf, and the coastal zone itself, including its intertidal zones, large estuaries, lagoons, barrier islands, etc. Large amounts of sediments are trapped in this

CONTINENTAL MARGINS

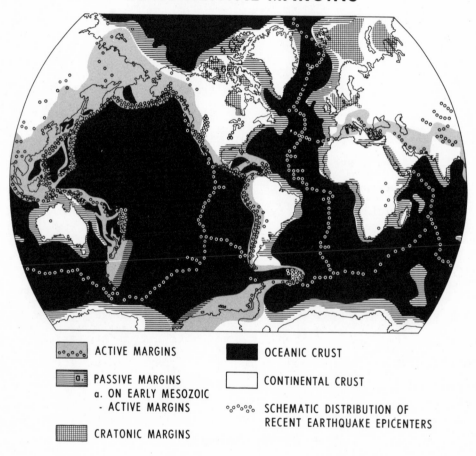

ACTIVE MARGINS		OCEANIC CRUST	
PASSIVE MARGINS a. ON EARLY MESOZOIC - ACTIVE MARGINS		CONTINENTAL CRUST	
CRATONIC MARGINS		SCHEMATIC DISTRIBUTION OF RECENT EARTHQUAKE EPICENTERS	

Fig. 2. Passive and active continental margins and submarine cratonic basins. The grey zone includes all Mesozoic-
Cenozoic mountain ranges and intramontane sedimentary
basins. (Megasuture of Bally and Snelson, 1980, with
permission of the Can. Soc. Petrol. Geol.)

1-5

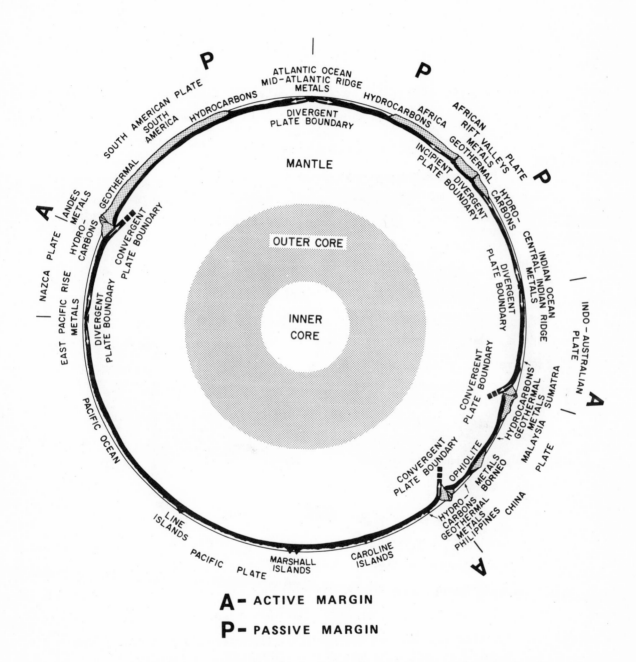

Fig. 3. Schematic great circle through the equator of the earth showing lithospheric plates, plate boundaries and occurrences of energy and mineral resources. For clarity, the thickness of the lithosphere is expanded by a factor of approximately 3. (From Rona, 1977, with permission of the Amer. Geophys. Union.)

zone. Typical clastic environments of the coastal zone are shown on Figure 4. Clastic bodies deposited in coastal environments may well form some attractive hydrocarbons reservoirs on Atlantic-type margins (in stratigraphic as well as in structural traps).

Note also that the coastline is, geological speaking, ephemeral. An example of the Delaware coastal zone is illustrated on Fig. 5. Note particularly the details of the coastal onlap sequence that is associated with the Holocene sequence.

(2) The continental shelf, usually 60-100 km wide, but which may extend as far as 1200 km. Water depths are around 130 m, but may go as deep as 550 m. Gradients generally do not exceed 1°. The boundary between the shelf and the slope is called the shelf break. Typical morphological elements of a portion of the U.S. Atlantic shelf are shown on Figure 6. Milliman et al. (1972) illustrated the nature of the surficial sediments on the U.S. Atlantic shelf (Fig. 7). To the north of Cape Hatteras clastics prevail, whereas to the south of that cape clastics in the nearshore segment of the shelf are replaced by carbonates farther offshore (see also Enos, 1974; Ginsburg, 1974; and Milliman, 1974). Note also that substantial portions of the shelf are not covered by recent sediments; instead, the surface is formed by glacial and relict sediments, while most modern river sediments are trapped within the coastal zone. Thus, the Atlantic shelf has yet to reach equilibrium since the beginning of the rapid sea level rise some 15 million years ago.

The submergence of the North and Central Atlantic margins due to the melting of the northern ice sheets is illustrated on Figure 8. Recent theoretical studies by W. R. Peltier (1980) have shown that some six different postglacial regimes may influence the morphology of the continental shelves of the world (Fig. 9). It is commonly accepted that the Pleistocene development of continental shelves is an unusual geological event; and, therefore, present sedimentation on passive margins is not necessarily a key to the depositional patterns of earlier times.

(3) The continental slope is typically some 15-100 km wide, and from the shelf edge ranges to about 5000 m depth, with gradients between 2° and 6°. The continental slope of the U.S. Atlantic margin north of Cape Hatteras is covered with fine grained sediments: sandy silts on the upper slope and silty

COASTAL ENVIRONMENTS AND MODELS
OF CLASTIC SEDIMENTATION

ENVIRONMENTS				DEPOSITIONAL MODELS
CONTINENTAL	ALLUVIAL (FLUVIAL)	ALLUVIAL FANS (APEX, MIDDLE & BASE OF FAN)	CHANNELS (WASHES): SHEETFLOOD, STREAMFLOOD (MUD-FLOWS), STREAMS (WATER-LAID); PAVEMENT: GULLIES	BRAIDED CHANNELS (WASHED) AND ABANDONED CHANNELS — EDGE OF MOUNTAINS — ALLUVIAL FAN — PAVEMENT
		BRAIDED STREAMS	CHANNELS & BARS; FLOODBASINS	BRAIDED STREAM — CHANNELS
		MEANDERING STREAMS (ALLUVIAL VALLEY)	MEANDER BELTS: CHANNELS, NATURAL LEVEES, POINT BARS; FLOODBASINS: STREAMS, LAKES & SWAMPS	MEANDER BELT, FLOOD BASIN, ALLUVIAL VALLEY, MEANDER BELT, NATURAL LEVEE, POINT BAR, CHANNEL, CREVASSE, DIRECTION OF POINT BAR ACCRETION
	AEOLIAN	DUNES	COASTAL DUNES, DESERT DUNES, OTHER DUNES; TYPES: TRANSVERSE, SEIF (LONGITUDINAL), BARCHAN, PARABOLIC, DOME-SHAPED	BEACH, WIND DIRECTION, OCEAN, COASTAL DUNES, OLDER DEPOSITS, BARCHANS & SAND SHEETS, SEIF DUNES, DESERT DUNES
TRANSITIONAL	DELTAIC	UPPER DELTAIC PLAIN	MEANDER BELTS: CHANNELS, NATURAL LEVEES, POINT BARS; FLOODBASINS: STREAMS, LAKES & SWAMPS	ALLUVIAN PLAIN, FLOOD BASIN, SWAMPS, LAKE, MARSH, DELTAIC PLAIN ENVIRONMENTS MEANDER BELT, UPPER DELTAIC PLAIN, LOWER DELTAIC PLAIN, DISTRIBUTARY CHANNEL, BIRDFOOT DELTA, RIVER MOUTH BARS, SUB-AQUEOUS PORTION OF DELTA, INNER FRINGE, OUTER FRINGE
		LOWER DELTAIC PLAIN	DISTRIBUTARY CHANNELS: CHANNELS, NATURAL LEVEES; INTER-DISTRIBUTARY AREAS: MARSH, LAKES, TIDAL CHANNELS & TIDAL FLATS	NARROW SHELF, MARINE CURRENTS, ARCUATE DELTA, COASTAL SAND BARRIERS
		FRINGE — FLUVIOMARINE DELTA FRONT — INNER / OUTER; DISTAL	RIVER MOUTH BARS, BEACHES & BARRIERS, TIDAL FLATS	NARROW SHELF, RATE OF SUBSIDENCE GREATER THAN RATE OF DEPOSITION, WIDE RANGE IN TIDES, DISTRIBUTARIES EMPTY INTO ESTUARIES. ESTUARINE DELTA
	COASTAL INTER-DELTAIC	COASTAL PLAIN (SUBAERIAL)	BARRIER ISLANDS: BACK BAR, BARRIER, BEACH, BARRIER FACE, SPITS & FLATS, WASH-OVER FANS; CHENIER PLAINS: BEACH & RIDGES, TIDAL FLATS; TIDAL: TIDAL FLATS, TIDAL DELTAS	TIDAL STREAMS, TIDAL FLATS, BAY, MARSH, LAGOON, TIDAL CHANNEL, CURRENT, MARINE ENVIRONMENT, BARRIER IS. COMPLEX
		SUB-AQUEOUS	LAGOONS: SHOALS & REEFS; TIDAL CHANNELS; SMALL ESTUARIES	BEACH RIDGES, RIVER, MUDFLATS, CURRENT, MARINE ENVIRONMENT, CHENIER PLAIN

(TYPES OF DELTAS)

AFTER R. LEBLANC, 1972

Fig. 4. Coastal environments and models of clastic sedimentation (after LeBlanc, 1972).

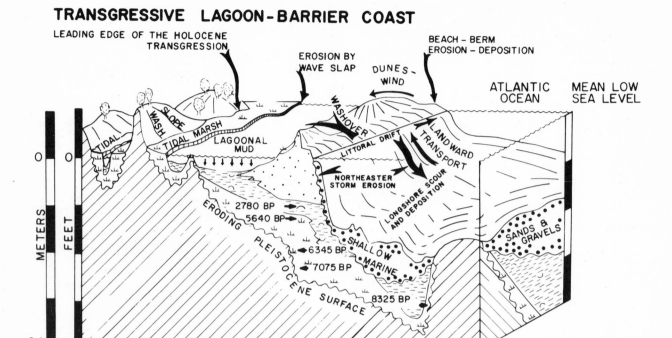

TRANSGRESSIVE LAGOON-BARRIER COAST

Fig. 5. Three-dimensional representation of the Delaware coastal
zone, showing both modern environments and those detected
by subsurface analysis (slightly modified after Kraft et
al., 1973).

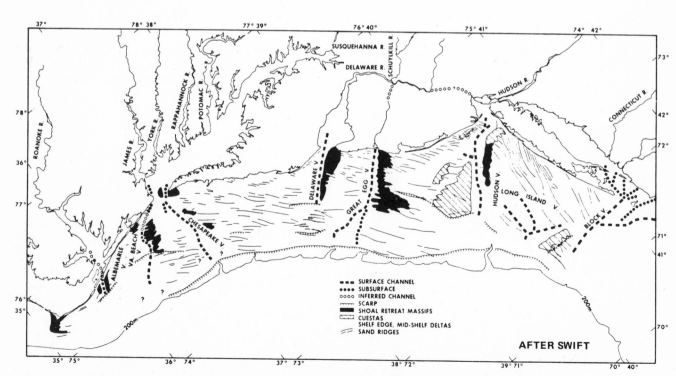

Fig. 6. Morphological elements of the Middle Atlantic Bight,
North America. (From Swift, 1974.)

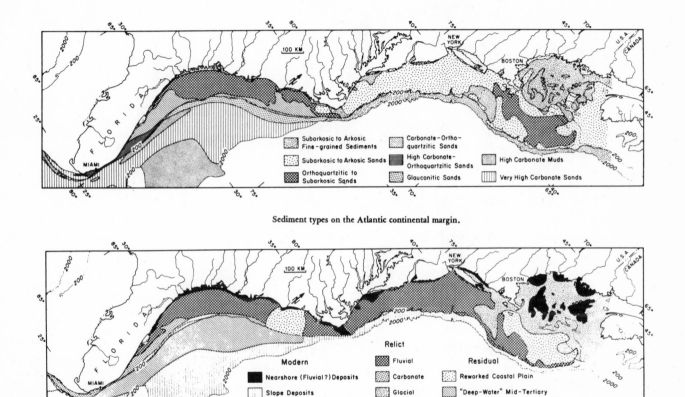

Sediment types on the Atlantic continental margin.

Source and age of the Atlantic continental margin sediments.

Fig. 7. Top: Sediment types of the Atlantic continental margin
off the eastern United States. Bottom: Source and age
of the Atlantic continental margin sediments off the eastern United States (after Milliman, 1972; reprinted from
the Bull. of the Geol. Soc. of America).

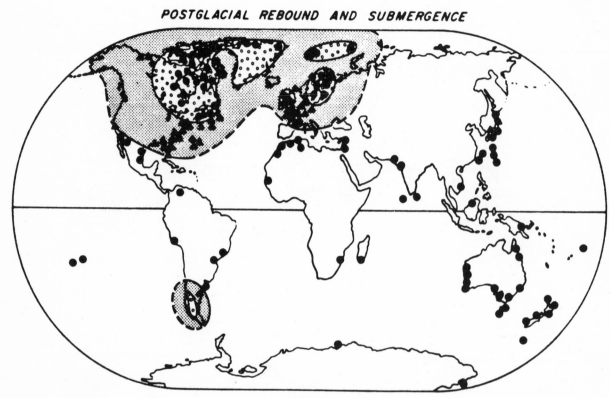

POSTGLACIAL REBOUND AND SUBMERGENCE

LEGEND

- REGION OF POSTGLACIAL REBOUND
- PERIPHERAL ZONE OF SUBMERGENCE
● - DATED MARINE SHELLS ABOVE PRESENT SEA LEVEL
▲ - DATED TERRESTRIAL PEATS BELOW PRESENT SEA LEVEL

Fig. 8. Distribution of radiocarbon-dated specimens in the age range 2500-5000 years BP as related to sea level (after Walcott, 1972).

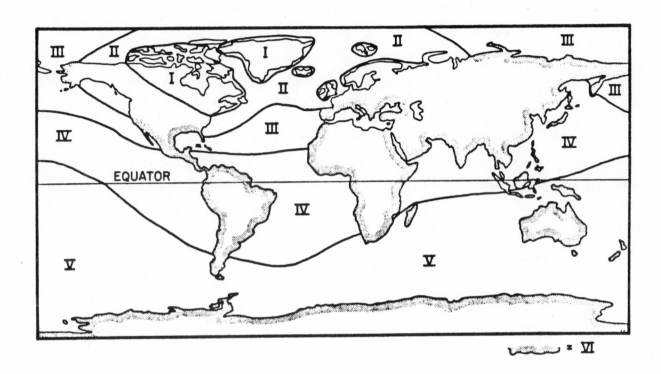

Fig. 9. The global extent of six regions, in each of which the
relative sea level curve has a characteristic signature.
This diagram is based on a theoretical model developed
by W. R. Peltier (1980), with permission of the Amer.
Geophys. Union.

Region I: Monotonic sea-level record showing the continuous fall of sea level in
regions that were covered with ice. In these regions the earth surface is uplifted
first quickly and then slowly.
Region II: Monotonic sea-level record with continuous submergence (see also Fig. 8).
Region III: Very slight amount of emergence at present.
Region IV: No raised beaches and continuous submergence.
Region V: Raised beaches begin to form as soon as glacial melting is complete.
However, while water is being added to the oceans, the rate of increase is insuffi-
cient to keep pace with the increase in water depth, so that no raised beaches can
form. Once melting is complete, the local bathymetry becomes stationary, land
rises above the surface, and new beaches are cut into older beaches.
Region VI: Areas where raised beaches are produced by the upward tilting of the
land in response to the increased water load immediately offshore.

clays on the lower slope. Planktonic remains increase towards the ocean. Calcium carbonates increase offshore and to the south and dominate the Florida-Hatteras slope. In addition to Holocene sediments, relicts of older Pleistocene sediments are found on the slope, and there are numerous outcrops of much older sedimentary rocks. For instance, south of Cape Hatteras Miocene outcrops dominate the Florida-Hatteras scarp. On the Blake plateau Miocene lime and phosphatic sands form outcrops. There is a need for outcrop maps of the U.S. Atlantic margin. Such maps have been published for portions of the Canadian Atlantic margin (King and MacLean, 1976).

(4) The continental rise is not always present and generally coincides with the distribution of clastic deep sea fans. Clastics of these fans have been deposited by turbidity currents and slumps, but also by geostrophic currents that parallel the topographic contours of the rise. The occurrence of high latitude sands found on the rise off the southern United States, where clastic influx from the mainland is limited, is due to such geostrophic currents. Continental rises are from 0-600 km wide, with depths of 1400-5000 m.

One of the difficulties arising from the anomalous glacial and interglacial depositional and erosional conditions is that they do not permit easily to apply recent models to understand the more ancient sediments of the Atlantic margin. Therefore, depositional models for the older Mesozoic and Cenozoic sequences have to be developed independently as seismic exploration and drilling proceeds.

The global development of Atlantic-type margins

A modern understanding of Atlantic-type margins has to begin with the reconstruction of the Pangean supercontinent, which was completed by mid-Triassic times. Fig. 10 shows one of many published reconstructions of that supercontinent and a number of stages that illustrate the subsequent breakup of Pangea. Notice on that sequence of diagrams that during Triassic times the outside of Pangea was rimmed by active margins, including an active margin that forms the southern boundary of the Asian continent. During Triassic the only Atlantic-type or passive margin extends from northwest Australia over India to the Arabian Gulf and North Africa. That passive margin had developed already during Paleozoic times. Much of it was later engulfed in the collisions of the Afro-Arabian and Indian continents with Eurasia. Thus, former passive margins of Gondwana underlie much of

THE BREAKUP OF PANGEA

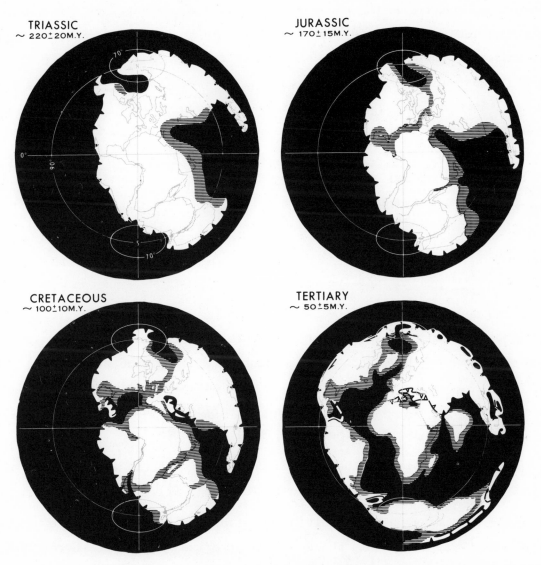

TRIASSIC
~ 220±20 M.Y.

JURASSIC
~ 170±15 M.Y.

CRETACEOUS
~ 100±10 M.Y.

TERTIARY
~ 50±5 M.Y.

RECONSTRUCTION SIMPLIFIED AFTER BRIDEN, DREWRY AND SMITH 1974

LAMBERT EQUAL AREA PROJECTION

MODIFIED TO SHOW INFERRED

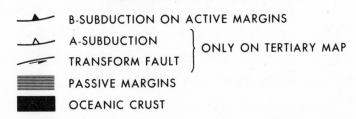

B-SUBDUCTION ON ACTIVE MARGINS

A-SUBDUCTION

TRANSFORM FAULT

} ONLY ON TERTIARY MAP

PASSIVE MARGINS

OCEANIC CRUST

Fig. 10. The breakup of Pangea (from Bally and Snelson, 1980, with permission of the Can. Soc. of Petrol. Geol.).

the Middle East, or else they were uplifted and are outcropping in the high ranges of the Himalayas. Only in northwest Australia are we seeing today an area that has been a passive margin since Paleozoic times.

A consequence of the conversion of a world dominated by one continent and one ocean into a world with several of each is that Atlantic-type margins become increasingly more widespread. Needless to say, the breakup of Pangea also led to substantial climatic changes (for an overview, see Hay, 1974; Berggren and Hollister, 1974; and Thiede, 1981). A rough estimate suggests that more than half of the volume of sedimentary rocks younger than 200 m.y. have been deposited on Atlantic-type margins since the breakup of Pangea. These rocks provide a unique and continuous log of the structural and paleoenvironmental evolution of the oceans and the adjacent continents. Relatively speaking geologists have barely started unraveling the stratigraphic evolution of the Atlantic-type margins of the world.

Model for the evolution of passive margins

The development of plate tectonics has generated a number of models that aim at explaining the subsidence history of passive margins. Two recent summaries of this work have been given by Turcotte (1980) and Bott (1980). The paper by A. B. Watts (this volume) gives a more detailed review of the subject as it relates to the U.S. Atlantic margin. Additional models are described by Falvey and Middleton, 1981; and Meissner, 1981.

Today there seems to be a broad consensus that the evolution of a passive margin occurs in three main phases (see Fig. 11), as follows:

(1) A rifting phase, involving stretching of the lithosphere and thermal uplift of the mantle. This phase is characterized by complex horst and graben tectonics (phases I and II of Fig. 11).

(2) The onset of drifting involving the separation of continental lithosphere. Ocean crust is for the first time emplaced, and accretion by ocean spreading across mid-ocean ridges begins in the gap between attenuated continental blocks (III and IV of Fig. 11). The onset of drifting may be dated by magnetic seafloor anomalies and corresponds simply to the oldest oceanic crust adjacent to a continent. On the continental crust, which has been attenuated by lithospheric stretching, the onset of drifting is often dated by an unconformity which is called the "breakup unconformity" (after Falvey, 1974).

EVOLUTION OF PASSIVE MARGIN

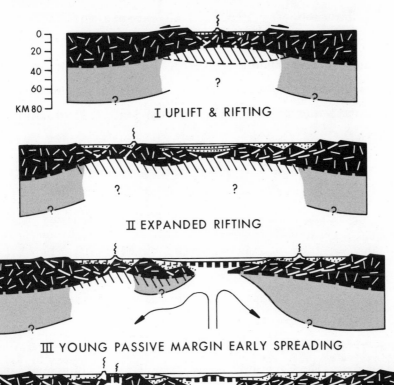

I UPLIFT & RIFTING

II EXPANDED RIFTING

III YOUNG PASSIVE MARGIN EARLY SPREADING

IV YOUNG PASSIVE MARGIN JUMP OF SPREADING CENTER

V OLD PASSIVE MARGIN

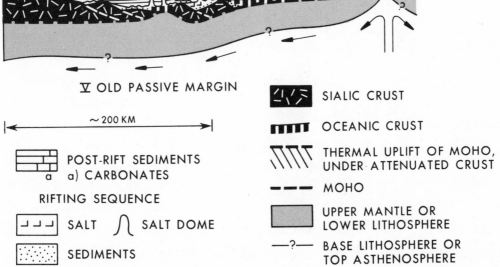

~ 200 KM

POST-RIFT SEDIMENTS
a) CARBONATES
RIFTING SEQUENCE

SALT   SALT DOME

SEDIMENTS

SIALIC CRUST

OCEANIC CRUST

THERMAL UPLIFT OF MOHO, UNDER ATTENUATED CRUST

MOHO

UPPER MANTLE OR LOWER LITHOSPHERE

—?— BASE LITHOSPHERE OR TOP ASTHENOSPHERE

Fig. 11. Evolution of passive margins (from Bally and Snelson, 1980, with permission of the Can. Soc. of Petrol. Geol.).

(3) The main drifting phase is dominated by massive subsidence, with rates of subsidence that decrease exponentially from the date of the onset of drifting. Typically the rate of sedimentation exceeds the rate of subsidence and leads to the accumulation of thick prograding sedimentary sequences (V of Fig. 11). These sequences are frequently separated by unconformities. These in turn determine the sequence boundaries which circumscribe the units that are used by Vail et al. 1977; Vail and Todd, 1981; and Hardenbol, 1981, in their seismic stratigraphic work.

In some cases, particularly where horst blocks are so far away and separated from the mainland that they cannot be covered by a terrigenous supply, a sediment supply deficiency leads to the formation of starved margins.

As developed earlier and illustrated on Fig. 10, all of today's passive margins formed as part of the breakup of Pangea. Different segments of the ocean opened at different times. The preceding rifting phase is in some cases fairly short-lived and may involve only one rifting event; in other cases the duration of the rifting is prolonged and may involve several rifting phases (i.e., east coast of Greenland or northwest Australia). Approximately, one can separate the rifting sequence from the drifting sequence on different continental margins (or the position of the breakup unconformity) as follows:

> Mid-Jurassic (about 180 Ma): North America-Africa (Pitman and Talwani, 1972);

> Lower Cretaceous (about 130 Ma): South America-Africa (Larson and Ladd, 1973) and India-Antarctica-Australia (Markl, 1974, 1978);

> Mid-Cretaceous (about 90 Ma): Newfoundland-British Isles (Srivastava, 1978);

> Late Cretaceous (about 75 Ma): Greenland-North America (Srivastava, 1978); (about 80-90 Ma): India-Madagascar (Norton and Sclater, 1979);

> Lower Paleocene (about 60-65 Ma): Norwegian Sea and Baffin Bay (Talwani and Eldholm, 1977; Srivastava, 1978);

> Eocene (about 50 Ma): Australia-Antarctica (Weissel and Hayes, 1972);

Upper Miocene (about 10 Ma): Red Sea and Gulf of Aden
(Laughton et al., 1970);

Late Miocene (about 5 Ma): Gulf of California (Larson et
al., 1968; Moore, 1973).

Figs. 12, 13 and 14 are line drawings of seismic lines on the U.S. Atlantic margin published by the USGS. Note the interpreted rift sequence (shaded) and the
overlying drifting sequence. Figs. 15 and 16 are segments of seismic reflection
lines that display the rifted sequence and the breakup unconformity.

Overlying the rifted sequence and the breakup unconformity is the thick
sequence associated with the drifting phase. In some areas carbonates are dominant, i.e., the Florida-Blake Plateau Bahamas area; in other areas clastics are
the main deposits, i.e., the Niger Delta and southern Australia; but in most areas
a mix of carbonates and clastics occurs. Figs. 12 and 13 are typical for the Baltimore Canyon area (see also Grow, this volume). Note the prograding Jurassic carbonates and the Jurassic-Lower Cretaceous shelf edge. Evaporites may occur both as
rift fill (Orpheus Basin, Nova Scotia) or at the base of the rifting sequence (e.g.,
Gabon; Brink, 1974). Lithologies in the drifting sequence are controlled by the
morphology of the hinterland and the climate.

The structural contrast between the crustal half-grabens of the rifting
sequence and the gravity controlled tectonics of the drifting sequence is often
quite striking. The latter is often characterized by listric normal growth faults
that are limited to the soft sediments and/or by salt tectonics.

The complex progradation process of the drifting sequence determines
the basic morphology of Atlantic-type margins with their flat, relatively stable
shelves, unstable slopes, and the deep-sea fans of the rise.

In this notebook the papers of Manspeizer and Bernoulli focus on the
geological evidence for rifting that may be relevant for an understanding of the
U.S. Atlantic margin. The reason for our emphasis on this subject is that the
quality of available reflection seismic data is relatively poor for an adequate
understanding of the late Triassic-Mid-Jurassic rifting on the U.S. Atlantic
margin. Consequently, it may be helpful to indicate what geological options are
possible. The issue is important in view of the association of major hydrocarbon provinces with rifting (i.e., Sirte Basin, the Suez Basin, the North Sea
Basin and the new discoveries on the northern Grand Banks). It is important to

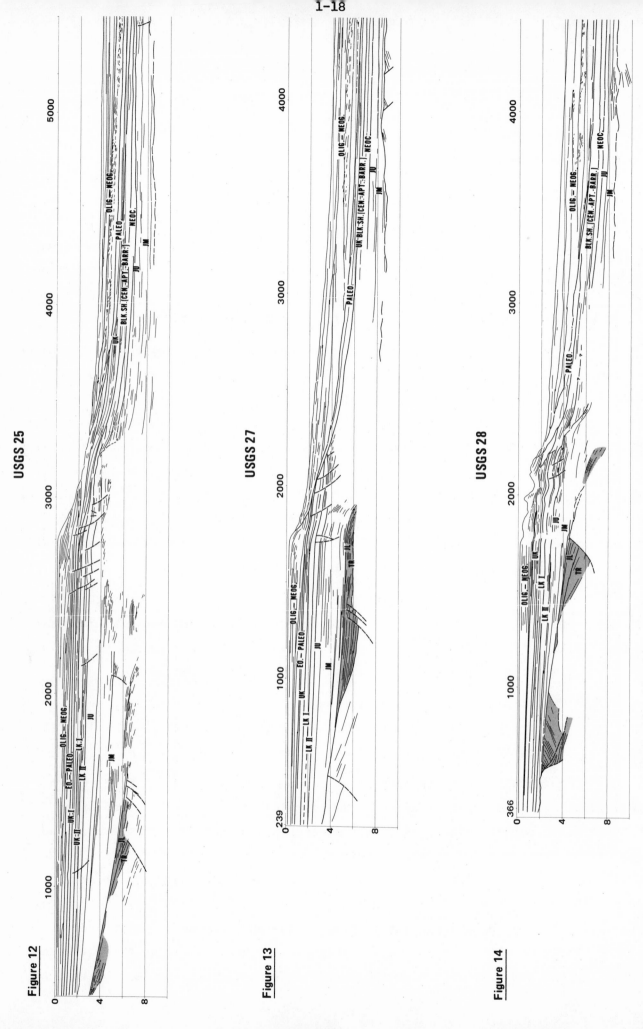

Figs. 12, 13, 14. Baltimore Canyon - USGS 25, 27, 28; Upper Triassic-Lower Jurassic rift sediments shaded.

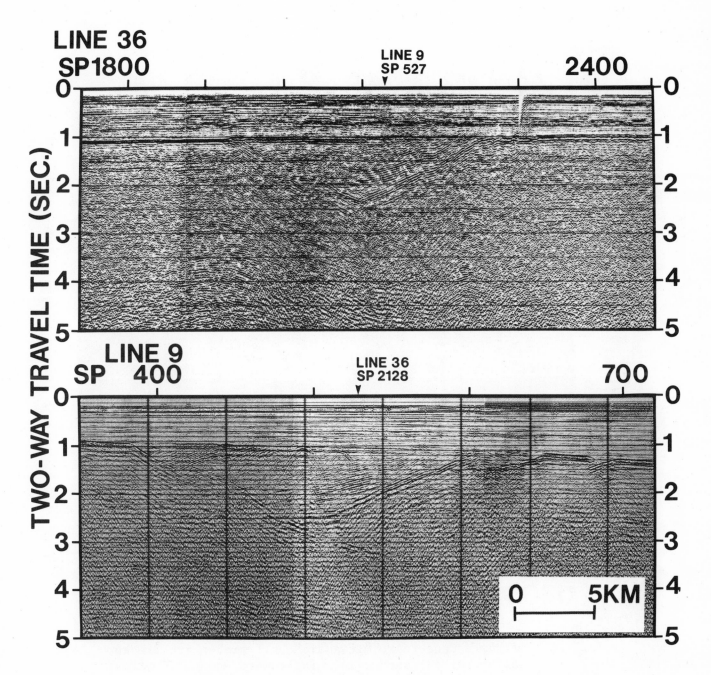

Fig. 15. Georges Bank, "Triassic" half-graben and breakup unconformity; boundary fault dipping toward ocean. Courtesy
D. Hutchinson and J. Grow, U.S. Geol. Survey.

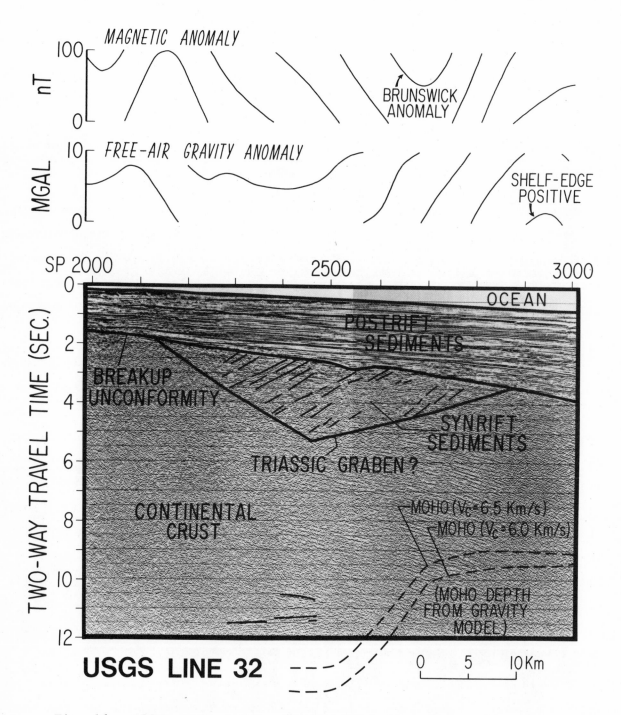

Fig. 16.   Offshore Cape Fear, "Triassic" half-graben and breakup
unconformity; boundary dipping toward ocean. Courtesy
D. Hutchinson and J. Grow, U.S. Geol. Survey.

contrast what little we know about grabens on the U.S. Atlantic margin with these basins.

The paper of Grow reviews the whole regional picture of the U.S. Atlantic shelf, but it is easily noted that much of the evidence is in reality illustrating the geology of the drifting phase of the U.S. Atlantic shelf. The geology of the shelf, the slope and the rise is quite variable. Correlations from the rise to the shelf are particularly difficult because of Tertiary and possibly earlier erosion on the slope.

Some aspects of rifting

To understand passive margins, we need to better understand rifting phenomena. Unfortunately, our state of knowledge is far from being adequate. A very short summary on the subject with references is contained in Bally and Snelson (1980) and also in Bott (1980). Here we will only focus on a few conceptual aspects which may turn out to be important.

Among proponents of rift tectonics there is a debate concerning the shape of normal fault planes. Are they planar or listric (i.e., curved)? A few simple and obviously naive drawings illustrate the geometric nature of the problem. Figure 17a shows that planar normal faults without folding will not show any antithetic rotation of beds into the fault plane. Such rotation can be achieved by folding or uplift prior to or concurrent with the faulting, but large angles of rotation typically imply unrealistically large uplifts. Note also that in both cases a deep keel develops under the graben system (the keystone-effect). On a crustal scale such keels have never been observed; instead, it appears that the Moho under graben systems is generally elevated. Figure 17b illustrates another model of planar faults which is often called the "domino model". The base of the blocks again show keels which are not observed on a crustal scale. Note the unrealistic position of the keystone block.

Figure 18a shows an alternative, involving listric normal fault planes. The blocks were assumed to move in a manner where the top of the bed remained undisturbed and in contact with the fault plane. Note that the problem of the deep keel becomes less important, although in the upper figure some elongate pointed keels are rotated to form part of the central uplift. The keels may virtually vanish with listric faults that have tight, almost circular radii, as shown on

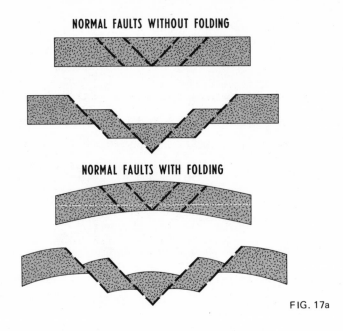

NORMAL FAULTS WITHOUT FOLDING

NORMAL FAULTS WITH FOLDING

FIG. 17a

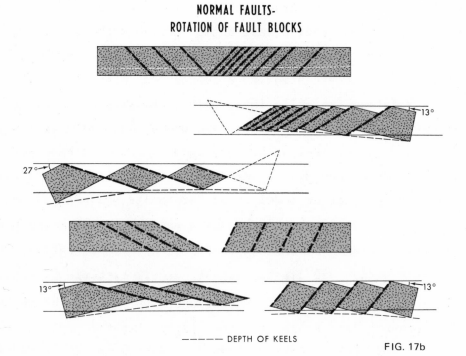

**NORMAL FAULTS-
ROTATION OF FAULT BLOCKS**

————— DEPTH OF KEELS

FIG. 17b

Fig. 17.   Planar normal faults.
           17a without folding, with folding.
           17b variation on the "domino" model.

the section below. Again, on both diagrams it becomes obvious that a relatively small rotation generates uplifts that appear to be in excess of what is observed in nature. An obvious problem is the wedge-like opening in the central block.

Figure 18b indicates how some of the problems arising in the preceding diagram may be alleviated. The problem of excessive uplift and rotation of pointed keels is solved with the aid of small compensatory faults that dip towards the listric master fault. Also, the wedge-like gap in the center diagram is eliminated. The second diagram from the top appears to be the most realistic simplification, because one frequently can observe compensatory faults, as shown on the diagram. The two lower diagrams are not very realistic.

Bally et al. (1981) have reviewed much of the evidence supporting the listric shape of normal faults. Based on that review, a reasonable case can be made that a number of listric normal faults that intersect the brittle upper crust actually can be detected with the help of reflection seismic lines. Probably the best case for the existence of listric normal faults has been made by Montadert et al. in the Gulf of Biscay (Figs. 19 and 20). However, much more crustal seismic information is needed to firm up the concept. Of course, it is not very likely that listric normal fault patterns are as simple as our diagrams imply.

In conclusion, normal fault systems that exhibit rotation of beds into the fault plane are likely to be listric fault systems. If such listric normal faults show updip convergence of the beds, we are dealing with growth faults that formed over longer periods of time. If, on the other hand, horizontal layers of sediments fill in the space between the rotated top of a fault block and the listric fault, we may be dealing with geologically instantaneous listric faulting, that is, faulting that took place over a very short time. Listric normal faults provide an easy structural mechanism for stretching the brittle upper crust over a ductile lower crust and mantle. For people interested in testing lithospheric attenuation by stretching, estimates of the amount of stretching of the upper brittle crust are important (see Royden et al., 1980; Royden and Keen, 1980; LePichon and Sibuet, 1981; and Watts, this volume).

Another important conceptual aspect that relates to rifting concerns the overall symmetry of graben systems. Traditionally we are used to visualizing

LISTRIC NORMAL FAULTS

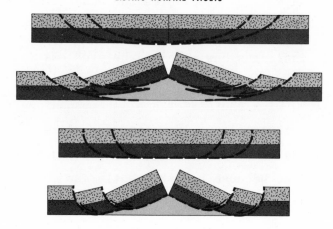

FIG. 18a

LISTRIC NORMAL FAULTS

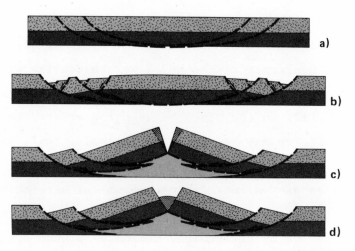

a)

b)

c)

d)

FIG. 18b

Fig. 18.   18a listric normal faults with uplift.
          18b second diagram from top shows listric normal faults
          without uplift and with compensating faulting.
          The two lower diagrams suggest that the central wedge may
          be filled by erosional processes.

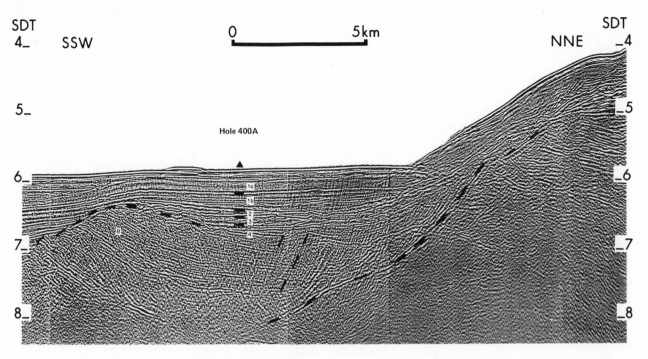

FIG. 19a

Fig. 19b. Northern Gulf of Biscay, line drawing of the section of
Fig. 19a converted to depth and migrated. Horizontal and
vertical scale, the same. Note listric normal fault
bounding the tilted blocks. Near the base of the listric
faults is a horizontal reflector corresponding to the
interface between 4.9 km/s and 6.3 km/s layers, as defined
by seismic refraction (Avedik and Howard, 1979). Moho
discontinuity is at 12 km. After Montadert et al., 1979.

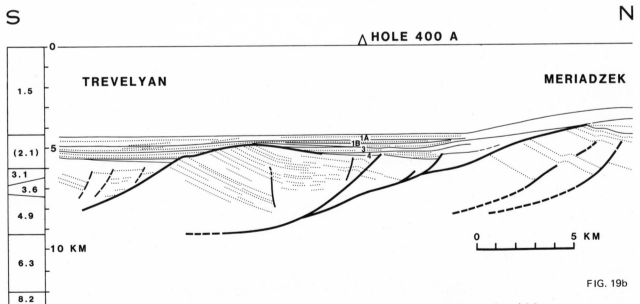

FIG. 19b

Fig. 19a. Northern Gulf of Biscay, section across IPOD Hole 400.
The acoustic basement (B) consists of layered sedimentary
rocks of probable Jurassic and early Mesozoic age. These
formerly continuous layers were faulted and tilted during
the early Cretaceous rifting phase. Vertical scale in
seconds, two-way travel time. Unit 1-A - Quaternary to
late Pliocene; 1-B - Pliocene to early Miocene; 2 - Miocene to late Paleocene; 3 - Maestrichtian-Campanian;
4 - late Albian, late Aptian. After Montadert et al.,
1979.

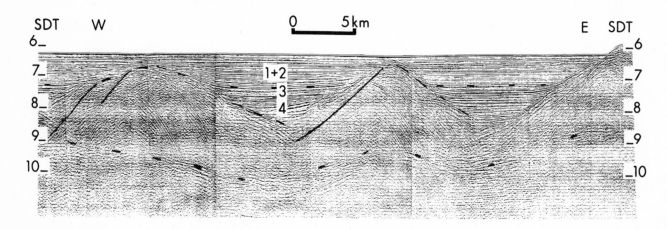

Fig. 20. Northern Bay of Biscay, seismic profile south of Goban
Spur showing tilted blocks with listric faults. Note the
horizontal reflector below the tilted blocks. It is
observed on the deepest part of the margin. On Trevelyan,
it corresponds to the boundary between a 4.9 km/s layer
and a 6.3 km/s layer only 3 km thick. The Moho is about
12.5 km below sea level. Profile CM 16 processed. After
Montadert et al., 1979.

rift systems as more or less symmetrical horsts and grabens, and the term rift
is often thought to be equivalent to "symmetrical graben". Fig. 21 illustrates
such a concept; the figure is adapted to plate tectonics (and actual observations!)
because it suggests that these grabens, in order to become a continuous, albeit
somewhat diffuse, plate boundary, have to be linked by small segments of transform faults.

The evidence of seismic reflection lines across graben systems (much
of it unpublished; but see Effimoff and Pinezich, 1981) suggests that few - if
any - symmetrical graben systems may exist. Instead, extensive systems of half-
grabens seem to dominate the scene. These are separated by rotated fault
blocks, and they are linked together by transform segments. The latter are often
very difficult to map. Fig. 22 shows an idealized block diagram of a graben region
where the polarity of a half-graben system changes across a transform zone without
major offset along the graben axis. Figures 23 and 24 illustrate an increased
offset of the graben axis along a transform zone. Note that these offsets compart-
mentalize the graben system and that each compartment may be easily separated
from the others when the sea level falls, thus setting up a possible cycle of
dessication and evaporite precipitation. This may well be an important structural reason for the coincidence of extensive evaporites within graben systems.

The half-graben concept becomes important for the understanding of
changes in basement depth along a continental margin such as the contrast between
the relatively high Georges Bank and the low Baltimore Canyon basements of the
U.S. continental margin. Figure 23 shows the development of an Atlantic-type
margin with listric fault systems that dip towards the ocean, while Figure 24
shows a similar development with listric normal faults that dip towards the continent, leading to different breakup patterns. The diagrams are intended to
show the basement surface, and the graben fill is not shown in the diagrams.
Both figures show a striking contrast across the transform fault: where there
is little crustal attenuation and consequently less subsidence due to the
ensuing cooling of the lithosphere, a relatively high basement platform remains
(i.e., Georges Bank); whereas rapid lithospheric cooling following the extensive attenuation of the crust by stretching will lead to the formation of a
thick sedimentary basin (e.g., Baltimore Canyon).

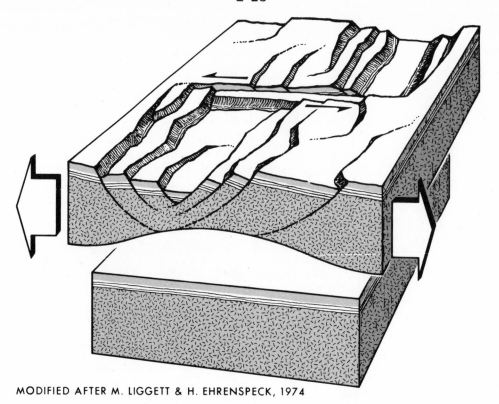

MODIFIED AFTER M. LIGGETT & H. EHRENSPECK, 1974

Fig. 21.   Sketch showing illustration of strike-slip faulting,
           listric normal faulting and crustal attenuation. Modi-
           fied after Liggett and Ehrenspeck (1974) and Liggett and
           Childs (1974).

TRANSFORM ZONE SEPARATING TWO HALF - GRABEN SEGMENTS

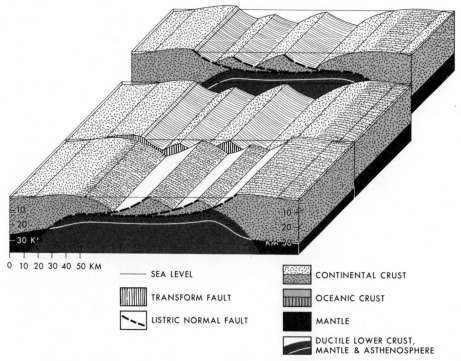

SEA LEVEL · CONTINENTAL CRUST · TRANSFORM FAULT · OCEANIC CRUST · LISTRIC NORMAL FAULT · MANTLE · DUCTILE LOWER CRUST, MANTLE & ASTHENOSPHERE

0 10 20 30 40 50 KM

Fig. 22.   Transform zone separating two half-graben segments with
           opposite polarity of listric normal faults. Note that
           the sedimentary fill of the half-graben is omitted from
           the drawing.

HALF - GRABEN AND TRANSFORM FAULT
LISTRIC FAULTS DIPPING TOWARD OCEAN

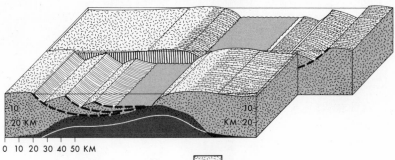

0 10 20 30 40 50 KM

—— SEA LEVEL

|||| TRANSFORM FAULT

LISTRIC NORMAL FAULT

CONTINENTAL CRUST

OCEANIC CRUST

MANTLE

DUCTILE LOWER CRUST,
MANTLE & ASTHENOSPHERE

PASSIVE MARGIN HALF - GRABEN AND TRANSFORM FAULT
LISTRIC FAULTS DIPPING TOWARD OCEAN

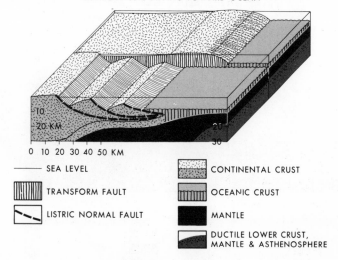

0 10 20 30 40 50 KM

—— SEA LEVEL

|||| TRANSFORM FAULT

LISTRIC NORMAL FAULT

CONTINENTAL CRUST

OCEANIC CRUST

MANTLE

DUCTILE LOWER CRUST,
MANTLE & ASTHENOSPHERE

Fig. 23. Half-graben system and transform fault with listric
faults dipping towards the ocean, on top. Rifting configuration at the inception of ocean spreading, below.
Note that in both diagrams the sediment fill of the
half-graben has been omitted from the drawing.

HALF-GRABEN AND TRANSFORM FAULT
LISTRIC FAULTS DIPPING TOWARD CONTINENT

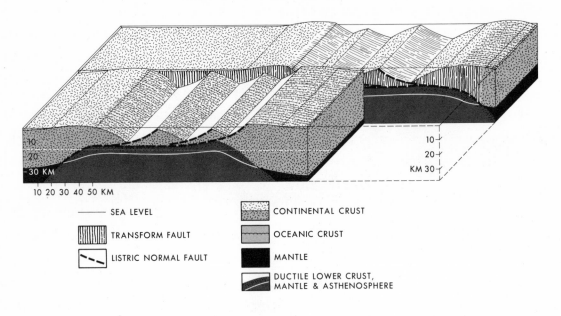

————— SEA LEVEL

▨ TRANSFORM FAULT

⟋ LISTRIC NORMAL FAULT

▨ CONTINENTAL CRUST

▨ OCEANIC CRUST

■ MANTLE

▨ DUCTILE LOWER CRUST, MANTLE & ASTHENOSPHERE

PASSIVE MARGIN HALF - GRABEN AND TRANSFORM FAULT
LISTRIC FAULTS DIPPING TOWARD CONTINENT

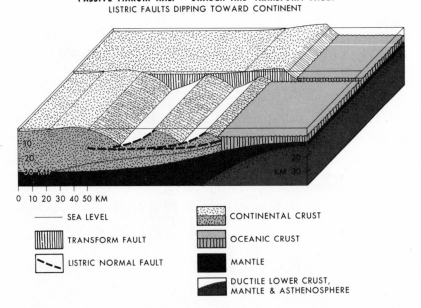

————— SEA LEVEL

▨ TRANSFORM FAULT

⟋ LISTRIC NORMAL FAULT

▨ CONTINENTAL CRUST

▨ OCEANIC CRUST

■ MANTLE

▨ DUCTILE LOWER CRUST, MANTLE & ASTHENOSPHERE

Fig. 24. Half-graben system and transform faults with listric faults dipping towards the continent, on top. Rifting configuration at the inception of ocean spreading, below.
Note that in both diagrams the sediment fill of the half-graben has been omitted from the drawing.

With regard to Figure 24, it should be pointed out that the regional seismic lines of the USGS (see Grow, this volume, and Figs. 12, 13, 14) suggest that the half-graben systems underlying much of the Baltimore Canyon area suggest a rotation along listric normal faults that dip towards the continent, in contrast to the polarity of the outcropping half-graben systems described by Manspeizer (this volume) and illustrated also on Figs. 15 and 16.

In looking for the reason for such changes in polarity, it may be useful to examine possible pre-existing structural weaknesses in the crust. Work in the Western Cordillera of North America has suggested that there late Paleogene and Neogene listric normal fault systems merge into the sole of a system of earlier décollement thrust faults that formed before and during the Laramide orogeny. The same concepts can be applied to the Appalachian system of the eastern U.S. There earlier work by oil companies in the fold belt and recent work by COCORP suggest that the Appalachian folded belt is carried westward on a décollement system of Alleghenian age (Cook et al., 1979). From this system a series of thrust faults emerge at the surface. A deep basement surface that underlies that system may extend well under the Piedmont province. The crude parallelism of the early Mesozoic half-graben systems with the strike of the Valley and Ridge folds of the foreland suggest that the listric normal faults responsible for the half-grabens merge into the underlying earlier Alleghenian sole fault system. The reason for the opposite polarity of the listric faults underlying the U.S. Atlantic margin would then be that they are more likely related to the décollement system that underlies the east verging Paleozoic décollement system of the Paleozoic Mauretanides of Africa.

Another consequence of the half-graben model is illustrated on Figure 25. Customarily it is often assumed that conjugate passive margins, i.e., margins that on a reconstruction across an ocean would fit against each other, should reveal a similar history. The diagram illustrates that this may not necessarily be the case if the highly attenuated crust remains on one side of an ocean, while the non-attenuated side stays on the other side of the ocean.

Note that the diagrams, Figs. 23 and 24 which were just discussed all show some kind of a marginal high against the oceanic crust. It should be emphasized that the high, as shown, was formed prior to the emplacement of the oceanic crust and that it ceased to be active following the rifting episode. As there appears to be near perfect peneplanation at the end of the rifting episode, the later drifting sequence following that episode is not affected in any significant

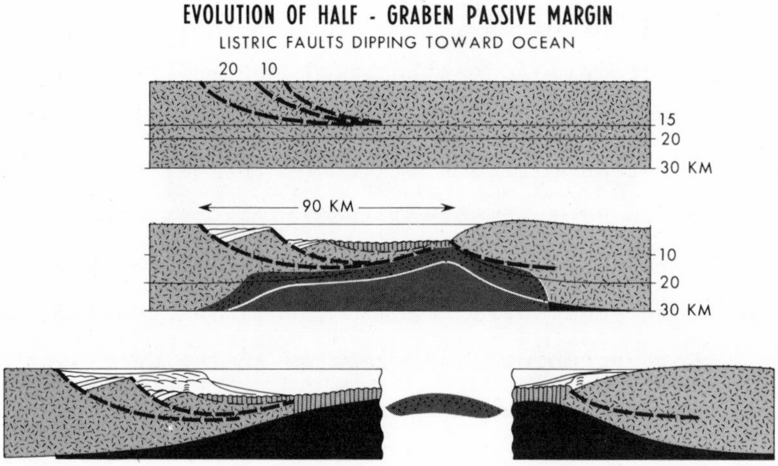

EVOLUTION OF HALF - GRABEN PASSIVE MARGIN
LISTRIC FAULTS DIPPING TOWARD OCEAN

Fig. 25. Evolution of half-graben model on conjugate passive
margins.

manner. As implied in the paper by Grow, the marginal high that was reported for many years to be associated with the East Coast magnetic anomaly today finds little observational support.

Stratigraphic evolution on Atlantic-type margins

Each passive margin segment has stratigraphic characteristics of its own. These are controlled by climatic fluctuations, the structural and physiographic evolution of the hinterland, and the subsidence history. Therefore, one cannot easily sum up stratigraphic principles in a few general statements. A great advance has been made by the seismic stratigraphic methodology which was developed by Exxon geologists under the leadership of P. Vail. Vail et al. (1977) have explained their methodology in considerable detail, and subsequent discussions have led to further refinements which are discussed in a recent paper (Vail and Todd, 1981). Figure 26 shows the Jurassic-Tertiary global cycles of relative changes in sea level as interpreted by Vail et al., 1977.

The overall worldwide correlatability of Vail's sequences and unconformities appears to be plausible to most workers interested in passive margins. However, there is some debate as to whether the cycles differentiated by Vail and his co-workers indeed reflect sea-level changes, or whether they may be caused by tectonically induced phenomena or a combination of the two. Watts (this volume) shows that sediment loading on a basement with a flexural rigidity that increases with time produces coastal onlap of the type used by Vail to estimate sea-level rises and that, therefore, the onlap may not be entirely due to a eustatic origin.

Bally (1980) points out that the subcrops of the "worldwide" unconformities which also can be correlated into cratonic areas and are often observed in mountain ranges may suggest tectonic events that separate one plate tectonic regime from another. They would be equivalent to unconformities that separate packages of sub-parallel magnetic stripes on the seafloor. This suggestion will remain vague until an effort is made to study on a worldwide basis the structural and plate tectonic regime preceding one unconformity with the regime that follows that regime. Care would be necessary to precisely document the paleontologic or else radiometric brackets that straddle these ubiquitous unconformities.

Be that as it may, there is little question that the methodology developed by Vail et al. is most helpful in predicting the age of seismic sequences on passive margins.

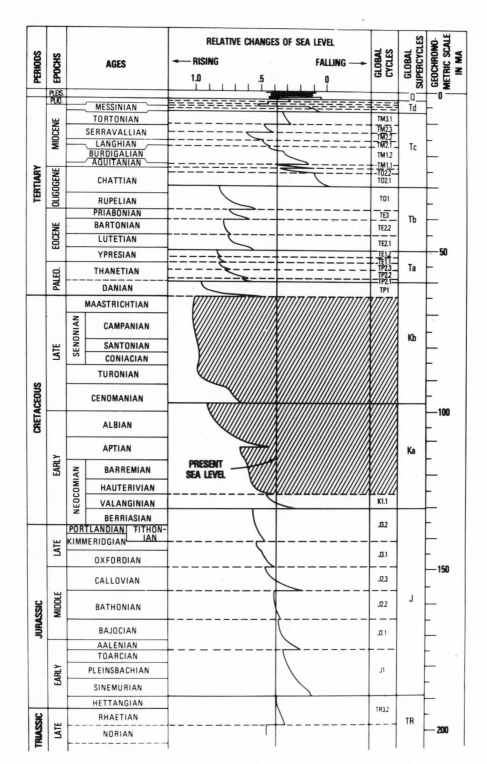

AFTER P.R.VAIL, ET AL, 1977

Fig. 26.   Jurassic-Tertiary global cycles of relative changes of
           sea level (from Vail et al., 1977a).

A quick glance at the line drawings of Figs. 12, 13 and 14 (see also Grow, this volume) will show that, like on many other passive margins, the slope on the Atlantic margin is dissected by submarine canyons and that substantial erosion takes place along the slope. The resulting slope unconformities are critical for an assessment of the hydrocarbons potential, because in some cases they may well erode pre-existing hydrocarbon traps. The stratigraphy of the rise, on the other hand, appears to be simpler and has been partially tested by a number of Deep Sea Drilling Project holes.

We would like to add a note of caution to our general observations. Published sections that are based on reflection seismic data or line drawings like Figs. 12, 13 and 14 convey the false impression that the interpretation and correlation of seismic reflectors from the rise into the slope and the adjacent shelf is relatively easy and unambiguous. In our experience, even with high quality multi-channel data, correlations are often very difficult to make. This is particularly true for the slope region, where multiple unconformities which often are ill defined disrupt the continuity of reflections. Thus, in the absence of deep stratigraphic tests, the quality of published correlations across the slope area may be questionable. Needless to say, this should not keep anybody from trying, but on the other hand one should not delude oneself that such correlations are very firm.

Hydrocarbon exploration

The main ingredients relevant for an appreciation of the hydrocarbon potential of the U.S. Atlantic margin have been summarized in the review of Hunt (this volume). Clearly it is too early to come up with a realistic assessment, that is, one based on adequate information. One needs only to remember the wildly fluctuating potential reserve forecasts for the U.S. Atlantic margin made by different groups at different times and to be aware of the wide spread in bids for single tracts in offshore lease sales. In this short course we will not concern ourselves with pure speculation concerning potential reserves.

To give a perspective to the relative importance of the established hydrocarbon reserves on passive margins, the following observations made by Bois et al. (1980) are interesting: Mesozoic formations contain 54% of the oil reserves and 44% of the gas reserves of the world. Of these only 1.5% of the oil and gas reserves occur on present passive margins. Of course, some 66% of the Mesozoic oil and 18% of the Mesozoic gas reserves occur in the Middle East, which until the upper Cretaceous was a passive margin. The Tertiary, on the other hand, is responsible for 32% of the oil and 27% of the gas reserves of the world, but only 10% of these Tertiary oil reserves and 27% of the Tertiary gas reserves occur on passive margins. The bulk of the Tertiary reserves are associated with the big deltaic provinces of the Gulf Coast and Nigeria.

From this it can be easily concluded that so far passive continental margins have, at least statistically and relative to other provinces, not been very good performers if one excepts the big deltas. On the other hand, it cannot be overemphasized that passive margins exploration is still in its infancy. There are some successes, i.e., northwestern Australia, Gabon, Cabinda and some of the Brazilian basins, all of which have economically attractive reserves; but there are also less successful ventures, e.g., the offshore areas of northwest Africa, Portugal, and Nova Scotia. Note also that the continental slopes and rises so far have been virtually unexplored, and while it is easy to rationalize that these provinces may not be all that hydrocarbon-rich, the obvious fact remains that we do not know enough about them to come up with a sound judgment. The exploration task in these provinces will be long and arduous and can only be justified in a climate where the cooperation between industry and governments is harmonious and permits industry to make profits that are commensurate with the high and essentially unpredictable risks of frontier exploration.

A last point may be a simple reminder that with a proposed Exclusive Economic Zone of 200 miles, practically all continental shelves and slopes of the world fall under national jurisdiction (Fig. 27). On the other hand, substantial portions of the continental rise may fall outside that jurisdiction. This is relevant for the future development of the continental rise of the U.S. Atlantic margin. Obviously, there is no point in giving the rights for mineral exploration on the U.S. continental rise away to an international agency. Even though the potential of the U.S. Atlantic rise is not all that exciting, the discussion of that potential is going to be pretty windy unless one gets on with the actual job of exploration. A few deep stratigraphic ocean margin tests will be informative, but in all likelihood do little to condemn the area for future exploration efforts.

It is furthermore doubtful that any single company can afford to explore the continental rise on its own, and it is even more doubtful - even given the

PROPOSED 200 MILE
EXCLUSIVE ECONOMIC ZONES

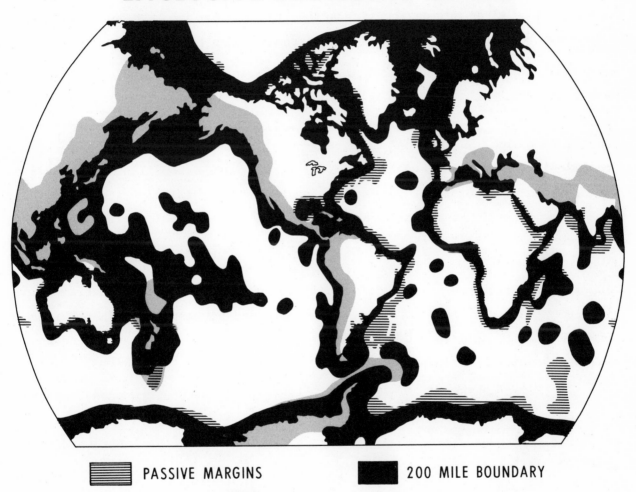

PASSIVE MARGINS   200 MILE BOUNDARY

CZ-MZ C-MEGASUTURE

Fig. 27. Proposed 200-mile Exclusive Economic Zones (EEZ's)
superimposed on continental margins. Compare with
Fig. 2 and note that in essence continental margins
and the 200-mile EEZ's coincide. Continental rises
are often excluded.

discovery of enormous reserves - that any single company will have access to all the capital that will be necessary to develop such reserves. If one indeed wants to go on with the job of exploration of the continental rise, the proposal made by Hedberg (1979) to undertake the exploration of these difficult areas in a consortium mode would make eminently good sense. A unique opportunity for constructive interaction between industry and government is thus available, and the sooner such a plan is given serious consideration, the earlier we will get a realistic understanding of the potential for hydrocarbons under the U.S. continental rise.

A.W.Bally:JC
July 6, 1981

REFERENCES - LIST I

* Amoco Canada Petroleum Company Ltd. and Imperial Oil Limited, 1973, Regional geology of the Grand Banks: Bull. Canadian Petroleum Geol., v. 21, no. 4, p. 479-503.

Bally, A. W., and S. Snelson, 1980, Realms of subsidence, Canadian Soc. Petroleum Geol. Mem. 6, p. 1-94.

_____, D. Bernoulli, G. A. Davis, and L. Montadert, 1981, in press, Listric normal faults: Oceanologica Acta.

Berggren, W. A., and C. D. Hollister, 1974, Paleogeography, paleobiogeography and the history of circulation in the Atlantic Ocean, in W. W. Hay, ed., Studies in Paleo-oceanography, Soc. Econ. Paleontol. Mineral. Spec. Pub. 20, p. 126-186.

Bois, C., P. Bouche, and R. Pelet, 1980, Histoire geologique et repartition des reserves d'hydrocarbures dans le monde: Inst. Francais Petrole Rev., v. 25, no. 2, p. 273-298.

Bott, M. H. P., 1980, Mechanisms of subsidence at passive continental margins, in Dynamics of Plate interiors, Amer. Geophys. Union Geodynamics Ser., v. 1, p. 27-32.

Brink, A. H., 1974, Petroleum geology of Gabon Basin: AAPG Bull., v. 58, p. 216-235.

Buffler, R. T., F. J. Schaub, R. Huerta, A. B. Ibrahim, and J. S. Watkins, 1981, in press, A model for the early evolution of the Gulf of Mexico Basin: Oceanologica Acta.

Cochran, J. R., 1981, in press, Simple models of diffuse extension and the pre-seafloor spreading development of the continental margin of the Northeastern Gulf of Aden: Oceanologica Acta.

Cook, F. A., D. S. Albaugh, L. D. Brown, S. Kaufman, J. E. Oliver, and R. D. Hatcher, Jr., 1979, Thin-skinned tectonics of the crystalline Appalachians: COCORP seismic reflection profiling of the Blue Ridge and Piedmont: Geology, v. 7, p. 563-567.

Crowell, J. C., 1981, in press, Juncture of San Andreas transform system and Gulf of California rift: Oceanologica Acta.

Effimoff, I., and Pinezich, A. A., 1981, in preparation, Tertiary structural development of selected valleys based on seismic data - Basin and Range Province, northeastern Nevada: Paper for Roy. Soc. meeting, London.

Eldholm, O., and L. Montadert, 1981, in press, The main types of passive margins: An introduction: Oceanologica Acta.

Enos, P., 1974, Surface sediment facies of the Florida-Bahama Plateau: Geol. Soc. America Map MC-5, 2 p., scale 1:3,168,000.

_____

* (Asterisk denotes papers specifically concerned with Canada's Atlantic margin.)

Falvey, D. A., 1974, The development of continental margins in plate tectonic theory: Australian Petroleum Explor. Assoc. Jour., v. 14, p. 95-106.

_____ and M. F. Middleton, 1981, in press, Passive continental margins: evidence for a pre-breakup deep crustal metamorphic subsidence mechanism: Oceanologica Acta.

Ginsburg, R. N., 1974, Introduction to comparative sedimentology of carbonates: AAPG Bull., v. 58, no. 5, p. 781-786.

* Given, M. M., 1977, Mesozoic and Early Cenozoic geology of offshore Nova Scotia, Bull. Canadian Petroleum Geol., v. 25, no. 1, p. 63-91.

* Grant, A. C., 1980, Problems with plate tectonics: the Labrador Sea: Bull. Canadian Petroleum Geol., v. 28, no. 2, p. 252-278.

Grow, J. A., and R. E. Sheridan, 1981, in press, Structure and evolution of the U.S. Atlantic continental margin: Oceanologica Acta.

Hardenbol, J., P. R. Vail, and J. Ferrer, 1981, in press, Interpreting paleoenvironments, Subsidence history and sea-level changes of passive margins from seismic and biostratigraphy: Oceanologica Acta.

Hay, W. W., ed., 1974, Studies in paleo-oceanography: Soc. Econ. Paleontol. Mineral. Mem. 20, 218 p.

Hedberg, H. D., 1979, Hedberg proposes offshore drilling consortium: AAPG Explorer, v. 1, no. 2, November, p. 1.

Hinz, K., H. Dostmann, and J. Fritsch, 1981, in press, The continental margin of Morocco: seismic sequences, structural elements and the geological development: Oceanologica Acta.

* Jackson, H. R., C. E. Keen, R. K. H. Falconer, and K. P. Appleton, 1979, New geophysical evidence for sea-floor spreading in central Baffin Bay: Canadian Jour. Earth Sci., v. 16, no. 11, p. 2122-2135.

* Jansa, L. F., 1981, in press, Mesozoic carbonate platforms and banks of the eastern North American margin: Marine Geology.

* _____, J. P. Bujak, and G. L. Williams, 1980, Upper Triassic salt deposits of the western North Atlantic: Canadian Jour. Earth Sci., v. 17, no. 5, p. 547-559.

* _____ and J. A. Wade, 1975, Geology of the continental margin off Nova Scotia and Newfoundland, in Offshore geology of eastern Canada: Geol. Surv. Canada, Paper 74-30, v. 2, p. 51-105.

* Keen, C. E., 1979, Thermal history and subsidence of rifted continental margins - evidence from wells on the Nova Scotian and Labrador shelves: Canadian Jour. Earth Sci., v. 16, p. 505-522.

* _____, C. Beaumont, R. Boutilier, 1981, in press, Preliminary results from a thermo-mechanical model for the evolution of Atlantic-type continental margins: Oceanologica Acta.

* King, L. H., and B. MacLean, 1976, Geology of the Scotian shelf: Marine Sciences Paper 7, Geol. Surv. Canada, Paper 74-31.

Kraft, J. C., R. B. Briggs, and S. D. Halsey, 1973, Coastal Geomorphology, Publ. State Univ. of New York, p. 321-354.

Larson, R. L., H. W. Menard, and S. M. Smith, 1968, Gulf of California: a result of ocean-floor spreading and transform faulting: Science, v. 161, p. 781-784.

_____ and J. W. Ladd, 1973, Evidence for the opening of the South Atlantic in the early Cretaceous: Nature, v. 246, p. 227-266.

Laughton, A. S., R. B. Whitmarsh, and M. T. Jones, 1970, The evolution of the Gulf of Aden: Royal Soc. London Philos. Trans., v. 267, p. 227-266.

LeBlanc, R. J., 1972, Geometry of sandstone reservoir bodies, from Underground Waste Management and Environmental Implications: AAPG Mem. 18, p. 133-189.

LePichon, X., J. C. Sibuet, and J. Francheteau, 1977, The fit of the continents around the North Atlantic Ocean: Tectonophysics, v. 38, p. 169-209.

_____ and J. C. Sibuet, 1981, Passive margins: A model of formation: Jour. Geophys. Res., v. 86, p. 3708-3720.

Liggett, M. A., and H. E. Ehrenspeck, 1974, Pahranagat shear system, Lincoln County, Nevada: Argus Explor. Co., Rept. of Inv., NASA-CR-136388, E74-10206, 10 p.

_____ and J. F. Childs, 1974, Crustal extension and transform faulting in the southern Basin Range Province: Argus Explor. Co., Rept. of Inv., NASA-CR-137256, E74-10411, 28 p.

Loutit, T. S., and J. P. Kennett, 1981, in press, Australasian Cenozoic sedimentary cycles, global sea level changes and the deep-sea sedimentary record: Oceanologica Acta.

Markl, R., 1974, Evidence for the breakup of eastern Gondwanaland by the early Cretaceous: Nature, v. 251, p. 196-200.

_____, 1978, Further evidence for the early Cretaceous breakup of Gondwanaland off southwestern Australia: Marine Geology, v. 26, p. 41-48.

Meissner, R., 1981, in press, Passive margin development: A consequence of specific convection patterns in a variable viscosity upper mantle: Oceanologica Acta. .

Milliman, J. D., 1974, Recent sedimentary carbonates - part 1: marine carbonates: New York, Springer-Verlag, 375 p.

_____, O. N. Pilkey, and D. A. Ross, 1972, Sediments of the continental margin off the eastern United States: Geol. Soc. America Bull., v. 83, p. 1315-1334.

Montadert, L., D. G. Roberts, O. de Charpal, and P. Guennoc, 1979a, Rifting and subsidence of the northern continental margin of the Bay of Biscay, in L. Montadert and D. G. Roberts, eds., Initial Reports of the Deep-Sea Drilling Project, p. 1025-1060: Washington, D.C., U.S. Govt. Printing Office.

_____ O. de Charpal, D. G. Roberts, P. Guennoc, and J. C. Sibuet, 1979b, Northeast Atlantic passive margins: Rifting and subsidence processes, in M. Talwani, W. W. Hay, and W. B. F. Ryan, eds., Deep-Drilling results in the Atlantic Ocean, Maurice Ewing Ser. 3, p. 164-186: Washington, D.C., Amer. Geophys. Union.

Norton, I. D., and J. G. Sclater, 1979, A model for the evolution of the Indian Ocean and the breakup of Gondwanaland: Jour. Geophys. Res., v. 84, B-12, p. 6803-6830.

Peltier, W. R., 1980, Models of glacial isostasy and relative sea level, in Dynamics of Plate Interiors, Amer. Geophys. Union Geodynamics Ser., v. 1, p. 111-128.

Petters, S. W., 1981, in press, Paleoenvironments of the Gulf of Guinea: Oceanologica Acta.

Pitman, W. C., III, and M. Talwani, 1972, Sea floor spreading in the North Atlantic: Geol. Soc. America Bull., v. 83, p. 619-646.

Roper, P. J., 1980, Post-Jurassic tectonism in eastern North America: Tectonophysics, v. 67, p. 61-80.

Royden, L., J. G. Sclater, and R. P. von Herzen, 1980, Continental margin subsidence and heat flow: important parameters in formation of petroleum hydrocarbons: AAPG Bull., v. 64, p. 173-187.

* _____ and C. E. Keen, 1980, Rifting process and thermal evolution of two continental margins of eastern Canada determined from subsidence curves: Earth Planet. Sci. Lett., v. 51, p. 343-361.

Schlee, J., J. C. Behrendt, J. A. Grow, J. M. Robb, R. E. Mattick, P. T. Taylor, and B. J. Lawson, 1976, Regional geologic framework of northeastern United States: AAPG Bull., v. 60, no. 6, p. 926-951.

* _____ and L. F. Jansa, 1981, in press, The paleoenvironment and development of the eastern North American continental margin: Oceanologica Acta.

* Srivastava, S. P., 1978, Evolution of the Labrador Sea and its bearing on the early evolution of the North Atlantic: Royal Astron. Soc. Geophys. Jour., v. 52, p. 313-357.

Swift, D. J. P., 1974, Continental shelf sedimentation, in C. A. Burk and C. L. Drake, eds., The Geology of Continental Margins: New York, Springer-Verlag, p. 117-135.

Talwani, M., and O. Eldholm, 1977, Evolution of the Norwegian-Greenland Sea: Geol. Soc. America Bull., v. 88, p. 969-999.

_____, J. Mutter, and O. Eldholm, 1981, in press, The initiation of opening of the Norwegian Sea: Oceanologica Acta.

Thiede, J., 1981, in press, Late Mesozoic and Cenozoic sedimentation along oceanic island margins: analog to continental margins: Oceanologica Acta.

Turcotte, D. L., 1980, Models for the evolution of sedimentary basins, in Dynamics of Plate Interiors, Amer. Geophys. Union Geodynamics Ser., v. 1, p. 21-33.

Vail, P. R., 1977, Sea level changes and global unconformities from seismic sequence interpretation, a report of the JOIDES Subcommittee on the Future of Scientific Ocean Drilling, Woods Hole, Mass., Mar. 7-8, unpublished.

_____ R. M. Mitchum, Jr., R. G. Todd, J. M. Widmier, S. Thompson, III, J. B. Sangree, J. N. Bubb, and W. G. Halelid, 1977, Seismic stratigraphy and global changes of sea level, in C. E. Payton, ed., Seismic Stratigraphy - Applications to Hydrocarbon Exploration: AAPG Mem. 26, p. 49-212.

_____ and R. G. Todd, 1981, Northern North Sea Jurassic unconformities chronostratigraphy and sea-level changes from seismic stratigraphy, in L. V. Illing and G. D. Hobson, eds., Petroleum geology of the continental shelf of north-west Europe: London, Heyden & Son Ltd., p. 216-235.

Walcott, R. I., 1972, Late Quaternary vertical movements in eastern North America: Quantitative evidence of glacial-isostatic rebound: Rev. Geophys. Space Phys., v. 10, p. 849-884.

Watts, A. B., and M. S. Steckler, 1981, in press, Subsidence and tectonics of Atlantic-type continental margins: Oceanologica Acta.

Weissel, J. K., and D. E. Hayes, 1972, Magnetic anomalies in the southeast Indian Ocean, in D. E. Hayes, ed., Antarctic Oceanology II: The Australian-New Zealand Sector: Am. Geophys. Union, Ant. Res. Ser. 19, p. 165-196.

Wilson, R. C. L., and C. A. Williams, 1979, Oceanic transform structures and the development of Atlantic continental margin sedimentary basins - a review: Jour. Geol. Soc. London, v. 136, p. 311-320.

REFERENCES - LIST II(a)

Books and maps that provide useful background
for passive margin studies.

Australian Petroleum Association Limited, 1970-81, The APEA Journal. This journal contains numerous articles describing the Australian passive margins.

Bally, A. W., P. L. Bender, T. R. McGetchin, and R. I. Walcott, eds., 1980, Dynamics of Plate Interiors, Amer. Geophys. Union Geodynamics Ser., v. 1: Washington, D.C., Amer. Geophys. Union, 162 p.

Bouma, A., G. T. Moore, and J. M. Coleman, 1978, Framework, facies and oil-trapping characteristics of the Upper Continental margin, Continental margin studies no. 7: Tulsa, Oklahoma, Amer. Assoc. of Petrol. Geol., 326 p.

Burk, C. A., and C. L. Drake, eds., 1974, The geology of continental margins: New York, Springer-Verlag, 1009 p.

Cohee, G. V., M. F. Glaessner, and H. D. Hedberg, eds., 1978, Contributions to the geologic time scale: AAPG Studies in Geology, No. 6, 388 p.

Emery, K. O., and E. Uchupi, 1972, Western North Atlantic Ocean: Topography, rocks, structure, water, life and sediments, AAPG Mem. 17: Tulsa, Oklahoma, Amer. Assoc. of Petrol. Geol., 532 p.

Esso Production Res. and Humble Oil & Refining, 1970, Bathymetric maps, Eastern Continental margin, U.S.A., 3 sheets, scale, 1:1,000,000: Tulsa, Oklahoma, Amer. Assoc. of Petrol. Geol.

Heezen, B. C., M. Tharp, and M. Ewing, 1959, Physiographic diagram of the North Atlantic Ocean, in The floors of the oceans, Pt. I, the North Atlantic: Geol. Soc. America Spec. Paper 65, 122 p.

Keen, C. E., 1979, Crustal properties across passive margins: Tectonophysics, v. 59, 390 p.

Lamont-Doherty Geol. Observatory, 1978, Argentine continental margin, a suite of four maps (free-air gravity, magnetic, sediment isopach and bathymetry): Tulsa, Oklahoma, Amer. Assoc. of Petrol. Geol.

_____ 1979, Brazil continental margin, a suite of four maps (free-air gravity, magnetic, sediment isopach and bathymetry): Tulsa, Oklahoma, Amer. Assoc. of Petrol. Geol.

Manspeizer, W., ed., 1980, Field studies of New Jersey geology and guide to field trips: 52nd annual meeting of the New York State Geological Association: Newark, NJ, Rutgers University, 398 p.

McFarlan, E., Jr., C. L. Drake, and L. S. Pittman, organizers, 1977, Geology of continental margins: AAPG Continuing Education Course Note Ser. 5.

Miall, A. D., ed., 1980, Facts and principles of world petroleum occurrence: Canadian Soc. Petroleum Geologists, 1003 p.

Nairn, A. E. M., and F. G. Stehli, eds., 1973, Ocean basins and margins, v. 1, The South Atlantic: New York, Plenum, 583 p.

_____ and _____, eds., 1974, Ocean basins and margins, v. 2, The North Atlantic: New York, Plenum, 598 p.

_____ and _____, eds., 1975, Ocean basins and margins, v. 3, The Gulf of Mexico and the Caribbean: New York, Plenum, 706 p.

_____ and _____, eds., 1977, Ocean basins and margins, v. 4A, The Eastern Mediterranean: New York, Plenum, 503 p.

_____, W. H. Kanes, and F. G. Stehli, 1978, Ocean basins and margins, v. 4B, The Western Mediterranean: New York, Plenum, 447 p.

_____, M. Churkin, Jr., and F. G. Stehli, 1979, Ocean basins and margins, v. 5, The Arctic Ocean: New York, Plenum, 610 p.

National Research Council, Continental margins, geological and geophysical research needs and problems: Washington, D.C., National Acad. of Sciences, 302 p.

Payton, C. E., ed., 1977, Seismic stratigraphy - applications to hydrocarbon exploration, AAPG Mem. 26: Tulsa, Oklahoma, Amer. Assoc. of Petrol. Geol., 516 p.

* Pelletier, B. R., W. J. M. van der Linden, and J. A. Wade, 1975, Offshore geology of eastern Canada, v. 1. Concepts and applications of environmental marine geology; v. 2, Regional geology: Geol. Survey Canada Paper 74-30.

Perry, R. K., H. S. Fleming, N. Z. Cherkis, R. H. Feden, and J. V. Massingill, 1977, Bathymetry of the Norwegian-Greenland and western Barents Seas: Geol. Soc. America Map MC-21, scale 1:2,333,230.

Rona, P. A., 1980, The central North Atlantic Ocean basin and continental margins: Geology, geophysics, geochemistry, and resources, including the Trans-Atlantic Geotraverse (TAG) NOAA, Atlas no. 3, U.S. Dept. of Commerce, 99 p.

Talwani, M., C. G. Harrison, and D. E. Hayes, eds., 1979, Deep drilling results in the Atlantic Ocean: ocean crust: Amer. Geophys. Union Maurice Ewing Ser., v. 2, 431 p.

_____, W. Hay, and W. B. F. Ryan, eds., 1979, Deep drilling results in the Atlantic Ocean: continental margins and paleoenvironment: Amer. Geophys. Union Maurice Ewing Ser., v. 3, 437 p.

Watkins, J. S., L. Montadert, and P. W. Dickerson, eds., 1979, Geological and geophysical investigations of continental margins, AAPG Mem. 29: Tulsa, Oklahoma, Amer. Assoc. of Petrol. Geol., 472 p.

Wones, D. R., ed., 1980, The Caledonides in the U.S.A., I.G.C.P. Proj. 27: Caledonide orogen: Virginia Polytechnic Inst. and State Univ. Mem. 2, 329 p.

Yarborough, Y., K. O. Emery, W. R. Dickinson, D. R. Seely, W. G. Dow, J. R. Curray, and P. R. Vail, 1977, Geology of continental margins, AAPG Course Note no. 5: Tulsa, Oklahoma, Amer. Assoc. of Petrol. Geol., 122 p.

* Yorath, C. J., E. R. Parker, and D. J. Glass, eds., 1975, Canada's continental margins and offshore petroleum exploration, Canadian Soc. Petroleum Geologists Mem. 4, 898 p.

REFERENCES - LIST II(b)

Watkins, J. S., ed., 1981, in preparation, Continental margin processes, AAPG Mem., selected papers on passive margins:

Bacoccoli, G., Offshore Brazil - Twelve years of oil exploration.

Barker, C., Oil and gas on passive continental margins.

Brice, S. E., M. D. Cochran, G. Pardo, and A. D. Edwards, Tectonics and sedimentation of the South Atlantic rift sequence: Cabinda, Angola.

Bouma, A. H., Intraslope basins in northwest Gulf of Mexico: A key to ancient submarine canyons and fans.

Cloetingh, S. A. P. L., M. J. R. Wortel, and N. J. Vlaar, State of stress at passive margins and initiation of subduction zones.

Dillon, W. P., P. Popeno, J. A. Grow, K. D. Klitgord, B. A. Swift, C. K. Paull, and K. V. Cashman, Growth faulting and salt diapirism: Their relationship and control in the Carolina trough, eastern North America.

Fournier, G. R.. Neogene palynostratigraphy of the southern Mexico margin, DSDP Leg 66.

Gerrard, I., and G. C. Smith, The Post-Palaeozoic succession and structure of the South-Western African continental margin.

Grachev, A. F., Geodynamics of the transitional zone from the Moma rift to the Gakkel ridge.

Hutchinson, D. R., J. A. Grow, K. D. Klitgord, and B. A. Swift, Deep structure and evolution of the Carolina trough.

Ibrahim, Abou-Bakr, and E. Uchupi, Continental/oceanic crustal transition in the Gulf Coast geosyncline.

Katz, B. J., and R. N. Pheifer, Characteristics of Cretaceous organic matter in the Atlantic.

Keen, C. E., C. Beaumont, and R. Boutiller, A summary of thermo-mechanical model results for the evolution of continental margins based on three rifting processes.

Kvenholden, K. A., Hydrates of natural gas in continental margins.

LePichon, X., J. C. Sibuet, and J. Angelier, Subsidence and stretching.

Naini, B., and M. Talwani, Structural framework and the evolutionary history of the continental margin of western India.

Nunns, A., The structure and evolution of the Jan Mayen microcontinental fragment and surrounding regions.

Sawyer, D. S., A. Swift, M. N. Toksoz, and J. G. Sclater, Thermal evolution of the Georges Bank and Baltimore Canyon basins.

Schlee, J. S., and J. Fritsch, Seismic stratigraphy of the Georges Bank basin complex, offshore New England.

Seibold, E., and M. Sarnthein, Climatic indicators in margin sediments off Northwest Africa.

Seiglie, G., and M. Baker, Foraminiferal zonation of the Cretaceous off Zaire and Cabinda, West Africa, and its geological significance.

Sobolev, S. V., and E. V. Artyushkov, Mechanism of passive margins and inland seas formation.

Tucholke, B. E., and E. P. Laine, Neogene and Quaternary development of the lower continental rise off the central U.S. East Coast.

van Hinte, J. E., Synthetic seismic sections from biostratigraphy: An aid in continental margin exploration.

Vierbuchen, R. C., R. P. George, and P. R. Vail, A thermal-mechanical model of rifting with implications for outer highs on passive continental margins.

von Rad, U., and N. F. Exon, Mesozoic-Cenozoic sedimentary and volcanic evolution of the starved passive continental margin off NW Australia.

Willumsen, P. S., R. P. Cote, et al., Tertiary sedimentation in the southern Beaufort Sea, Canada.

REFERENCES - LIST III

A selected list of Deep Sea Drilling Project Reports
that contain information relevant to passive margins.

Deep Sea Drilling Project, National Ocean Sediment Coring Program, National Science Foundation: Washington, D.C., U.S. Govt. Printing Office.

Vol. I   - Orange, Texas, to Hoboken, N.J., Aug.-Sept. 1968, Leg 1.

Vol. II   - Hoboken, N.J., to Dakar, Senegal, Oct.-Nov. 1968, Leg 2.

Vol. III   - Dakar, Senegal, to Rio de Janeiro, Brazil, Dec. 1968 to Jan. 1969, Leg 3.

Vol. IV   - Rio de Janeiro, Brazil, to San Cristobal, Panama, Feb.-Mar. 1969, Leg 4.

Vol. X   - Galveston, Texas, to Miami, Florida, Feb.-Apr. 1970, Leg 10.

Vol. XI   - Miami, Florida, to Hoboken, N.J., Apr.-June 1970, Leg 11.

Vol. XII   - Boston, Mass., to Lisbon, Portugal, June-Aug., 1970, Leg 12.

Vol. XIII   - Lisbon, Portugal, to Lisbon, Portugal, Aug.-Oct. 1970, Leg 13. (In 2 parts.)

Vol. XIV   - Lisbon, Portugal, to San Juan, Puerto Rico, Oct.-Dec. 1970, Leg 14.

Vol. XXI   - Suva, Fiji, to Darwin, Australia, Nov. 1971 to Jan. 1972, Leg 21.

Vol. XXIII   - Colombo, Ceylon, to Djibouti, F.T.A.I., Mar.-May 1972, Leg 23.

Vol. XXIV   - Djibouti, F.T.A.I., to Port Louis, Mauritius, May-June 1972,
                Leg 24.

Vol. XXV   - Port Louis, Mauritius, to Durban, South Africa, June-Aug. 1972,
                Leg 25.

Vol. XXVI   - Durban, South Africa, to Fremantle, Australia, Sept.-Oct. 1972,
                Leg 26.

Vol. XXVII   - Fremantle, Australia, to Fremantle, Australia, Nov.-Dec. 1972,
                Leg 27.

Vol. XXVIII   - Fremantle, Australia, to Christchurch, New Zealand, Dec. 1972 to
                Feb. 1973, Leg 28.

Vol. XXIX   - Lyttleton, New Zealand, to Wellington, New Zealand, Mar.-Apr.
                1973, Leg 29.

Vol. XXXVI   - Ushuala, Argentina, to Rio de Janeiro, Brazil, Apr.-May 1974,
                Leg 36.

Vol. XXXVII   - Rio de Janeiro, Brazil, to Dublin, Ireland, May-July 1974, Leg
                37.

Vol. XXXVIII - Dublin, Ireland, to Amsterdam, The Netherlands, Aug.-Sept. 1974,
                Leg 38.

Vol. XXXIX   - Amsterdam, The Netherlands, to Cape Town, South Africa, Oct.-
                Dec. 1974, Leg 39.

Vol. XL   - Cape Town, South Africa, to Abidjan, Ivory Coast, Dec. 1974 to
                Feb. 1975, Leg 40.

Vol. XLI   - Abidjan, Ivory Coast, to Malaga, Spain, Feb.-Apr. 1975, Leg 41.

              - Supplement to Vols. XXVIII, XXXIX, XL, and XLI, 1978.

Vol. XLIII   - Istanbul, Turkey, to Norfolk, Virginia, June-Aug. 1975, Leg 43.

Vol. XLIV   - Norfolk, Virginia, to Norfolk, Virginia, Aug.-Sept. 1975, Leg 44.

Vol. XLVII   - Part 1 - Las Palmas, Canary Islands, to Vigo, Spain, Mar.-Apr.
                1976, Leg 47.

Vol. XLVII   - Part 2 - Vigo, Spain, to Brest, France, Apr.-May 1976, Leg 47.

Vol. XLVIII   - Brest France, to Aberdeen, Scotland, May-July 1976, Leg 48.

Vol. L   - Funchal, Madeira Islands, to Funchal, Madeira Islands, Sept.-
                Nov. 1976, Leg 50.

THE U.S. ATLANTIC CONTINENTAL MARGIN:

SUBSIDENCE HISTORY, CRUSTAL STRUCTURE AND THERMAL EVOLUTION

by

A. B. Watts

Lamont-Doherty Geological Observatory
and Department of Geological Sciences
of Columbia University
Palisades, New York 10964

June, 1981
Submitted to the
American Association Petroleum Geologists
Short Course
To be held in conjunction with the
Atlantic Margin Energy Conference
Atlantic City, New Jersey
October 4-6, 1981

THE U.S. ATLANTIC CONTINENTAL MARGIN:
SUBSIDENCE HISTORY, CRUSTAL STRUCTURE AND THERMAL EVOLUTION

by

A. B. Watts

Abstract

The U.S. Atlantic continental margin contains substantial thicknesses of generally seaward dipping Mesozoic to Cenozoic sediments. Multichannel seismic reflection profiling show that these sediments reach thicknesses >14 km under the continental shelf off New Jersey and >7 km under the slope and rise. Commercial exploration wells and the Continental Offshore Stratigraphic Test (COST) No. B-2 and B-3 wells in the shelf and slope off New Jersey show that most of the sediments were deposited in continental or shallow water (marine) environments. Such large thicknesses of shallow water sediments cannot be caused by sedimentary loading alone and other factors must be involved. A useful approach to the problem is to isolate these factors by "backstripping" sediment as well as water loads for different intervals of time during margin evolution. "Backstripping" studies in which the effects of compaction, paleobathymetry, sea-level changes and the flexural strength of the basement are included have been carried out using downhole geological and geophysical logs from the COST B-2 and B-3 wells. The resulting tectonic subsidence at the wells can be satisfactorily explained by a simple thermal model in which the lithosphere undergoes a passive extension at the time of rifting. In this model, extension causes stretching or thinning of the lithosphere, which subsequently cools and subsides with time. The model assumes isostatic equilibrium during and after the extension so that there is an initial subsidence which depends on the initial crustal thickness, followed by a thermal subsidence determined by the amount of heating. Based on the model the best fitting estimates of the amounts of extension at the margin are between 250 and 300% (β =3.5 to 4.0). Simple mechanical models have been constructed, using these estimates of β and a flexural strength of the basement which increases with time, in which sediments infill the subsiding margin. The thermal and mechanical modelling imply an equal proportion of sediments accumulating during the period of initial subsidence (pre- and syn-rift sediments) and the period of thermal subsidence (post-rift sediments). Unfortunately, there is presently too little seismic and lithologic information on the actual proportion of pre- and syn-rift to post-rift sediments off New Jersey to constrain these models. The models predict a coastal plain sequence in which younger sediments progressively overstep older sediments due to the increase in flexural strength of the basement with age. The coastal onlap, which is observed at many margins, may therefore be due at least partly to tectonic rather than eustatic effects. The tectonic subsidence at the COST B-2 and B-3 wells off New Jersey has been used to estimate the paleotemperature in the sediments and the amount of crustal thinning that has occurred at the margin. The well data indicate that up to about 20 km of crustal thinning has occurred beneath the outer part of the shelf. This estimate is in general agreement with gravity and geoid data across the margin but is poorly constrained by heat flow and seismic data. Future studies based on multichannel seismic reflection profiling and continental shelf and slope drilling should provide better observational constraints on both the extent and amount of crustal thinning that has occurred off New Jersey. These studies, in conjunction with the development of more refined thermal and mechanical models, offer the most promise of determining the origin and evolution of U.S. margin during the next decade.

Introduction

The origin and evolution of continental margins of Atlantic-type is a subject of considerable current interest in the Earth Sciences. Continental margins are characterized during their evolution by epeirogenic or vertical movements (uplift and subsidence) of the Earth's crust. Their study is therefore of interest to plate tectonics which successfully explains the horizontal movements of the Earth's major lithospheric* plates. Furthermore, continental margins are associated with some of the largest accumulations of sedimentary rocks on the Earth's surface and therefore are of interest to the petroleum industry since most of the world's gas and oil production is from sedimentary basins.

The U.S. Atlantic continental margin (defined here as extending off-shore from New England to Florida) has been the site of extensive geologic and geophysical investigations by academic, government and industry groups during the past few decades. The early seismic refraction surveys by M. Ewing and colleagues showed that the margin was comprised of a wedge of Mesozoic and Tertiary sedimentary rocks that thinned beneath the outer part of the continental shelf over a buried "basement ridge" (Ewing and Ewing, 1959; Drake et al., 1959). The evidence for a ridge was based mainly on high compressional wave velocities (>5.0 km/sec, Drake et al., 1959) at shallow depths (3 to 5 km) beneath the outer part of the shelf. This evidence was subsequently supported by a positive magnetic anomaly over the outer part of the shelf and slope (Taylor et al., 1968), inferences from single channel seismic reflection profiles (Emery et al., 1970) and, positive Airy isostatic gravity anomalies over the outer shelf and slope (Rabinowitz, 1974). The importance of the early seismic surveys though, were that they led to the first comparison between continental margin structure and conceptual models for sedimentary basin development inferred from the geological record. Drake et al. (1959), for example, compared the structure of the shelf-ridge-slope region to the miogeosynclinal and eugeosynclinal concepts of Kay (1947) and others.

During the past decade, knowledge of the shallow structure of the U.S. continental margin has progressed rapidly, mainly because of technological

*We define here the lithosphere as the seismic lithosphere which includes the crust.

advances in seismic reflection profiling techniques and the dynamical positioning of drilling ships at sea. These advances have led to an improved understanding of the structure and evolution of the margin.

Seismic reflection profiling of the U.S. continental margin between 1973 and 1978 using multichannel hydrophone streamers (Schlee et al., 1976; Grow and Markl, 1977; Grow et al., 1979; Schlee, 1981) have shown substantial thicknesses of sediments beneath shelf (up to about 14 km) and slope (up to about 8 km) regions. These sediments occur in a series of "basins" separated by "platforms" that underlie the shelf and slope of the margin (Klitgord and Behrendt, 1979). The largest of these basins, the Baltimore Canyon Trough, occurs off New Jersey and contains in excess of 14 km of sediments.

More recent multichannel seismic reflection profiling (MCS) using 48 channels and improved processing techniques (note added in proof: Grow et al., 1979; Grow, 1980) revealed deeper sedimentary reflectors than any of the previous MCS lines. These profiles showed reflectors at depths >10 km beneath the outer shelf suggesting an absence of a buried ridge at the margin. The relatively high P wave velocities (>5 km/sec) at depths of 3 to 5 km were interpreted as due to consolidated sedimentary rocks rather than crystalline basement. Grow (1980) interpreted the magnetic anomaly over the outer shelf, previously interpreted by Klitgord and Behrendt (1979) as due to thickened oceanic basement, as in part due to the transition between oceanic and continental crust and in part due to secondary volcanic events such as dykes and sills within the sediments. The Airy isostatic gravity anomalies over the outer shelf have been interpreted (Karner and Watts, in press) as due to loading of sediments on a basement with a flexural rigidity that increases with time.

The Continental Offshore Stratigraphic Test (COST) No. B-2 and B-3 test wells and exploratory drilling (Scholle, 1977, 1980; Fig. 1) provided new information on the stratigraphy and age of seismic reflectors underlying the outer part of the shelf. These wells show a sedimentary section composed almost entirely of sands and shales with subordinate amounts of coal and lignite. Biostratigraphic studies indicate that most of these sediments are Jurassic to Quaternary age and were deposited in continental or shallow-marine (neritic to outer shelf) environments. The shallow water depths ($\lesssim$ 500 m) suggest that sedimentary loading is not the only cause of the subsidence of

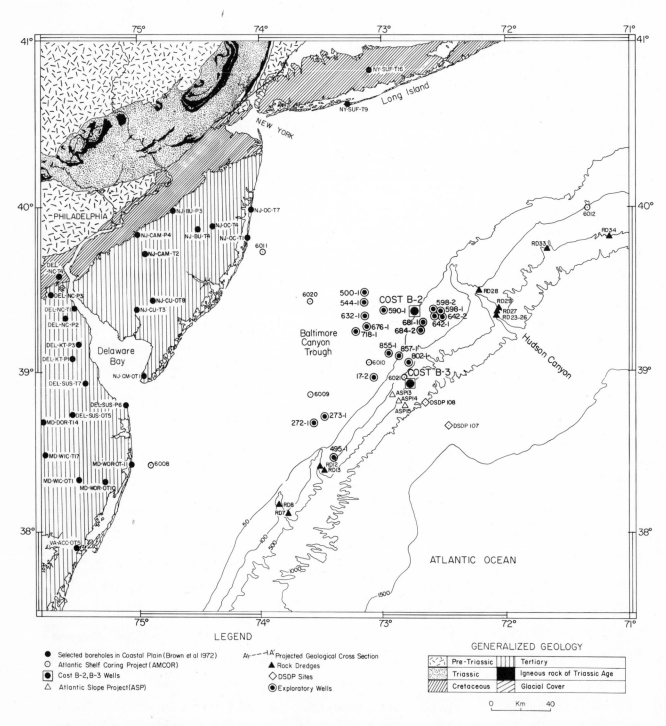

Figure 1. Summary geology map showing location of COST B-2 and B-3 wells and exploratory wells off New Jersey. The location of the wells is based mainly on Mattick and Bayer (1980) and Mattick and Hennessy (1980).

the U.S. margin (for example, Watts and Ryan, 1976) and other factors must be involved.

The acquisition of new seismic reflection profiling and drilling data has been accompanied, during the past decade, by the development of new models for the origin of continental margins. A number of models, in fact, have now been proposed to explain the large thicknesses of shallow water sediments which exist at margins. These include:

1) Stress based models in which differential loading produces seaward creep of lower crustal rocks and subsidence on the shelf (Bott, 1973).

2) Deep crustal metamorphism in which subsidence is produced by an increase in the density of rocks in the lower crust (Falvey, 1974; Spohn and Neugebauer, 1978).

3) Models in which subsidence is the result of thermal contraction following crustal thinning at the time of rifting. The thinning results from either uplift and erosion (Sleep, 1971; Kinsman, 1975; Turcotte et al., 1977), extension and necking of the crust (Artemjev and Artyushkov, 1971; McKenzie, 1978) or pervasive dike intrusion (Royden et al., 1980).

A useful approach to the problem of continental margins has been to quantitatively account for the effects of sedimentary loading during margin evolution, allowing the "tectonic subsidence" of the margin to be isolated (Watts and Ryan, 1976; Steckler and Watts, 1978). The tectonic subsidence is that part of the subsidence of a margin not caused by the weight of sediment and water loads through time.

The subsidence history of the U.S. continental margin has now been examined in some detail, using downhole geological and geophysical logs from the COST wells (Steckler and Watts, 1978; Watts and Steckler, 1979; Angevine and Turcotte, 1981; Sawyer et al., in press). These studies suggest that large amounts of crustal thinning have occurred along the margin. For example, Watts and Steckler (1979) have shown that the magnitude of the tectonic subsidence at the COST B-2 well requires, on isostatic grounds, that up to about 20 km of crustal thinning has occurred beneath the outer continental shelf off New Jersey. This amount of thinning is consistent with the results of gravity and geoid studies of the margin (Watts and Steckler, 1979; Grow et al., 1979; Hutchinson and Grow, personal communication).

Thermal models for the origin of continental margins predict that the thinning occurs at or close to the time of initial rifting (Sleep, 1971; McKenzie, 1978). The main differences between the models are in the processes by which thinning occurs. Sleep (1971) proposed that thinning occurs by sub-aerial erosion of thermally uplifted lithosphere while McKenzie (1978) proposed that thinning occurs by a passive stretching of the lithosphere. The detailed extent of the thinned crust along the U.S. margin is not fully known at present. Seismic experiments such as the Large Aperture Seismic Experiment (LASE) may, in the future, provide constraints on the magnitude and extent of the thinning at the margin.

The purpose of this paper is to review current models for the origin and evolution of the U.S. Atlantic continental margin. We will discuss these models in terms of geological and geophysical data from a portion of the margin, off New Jersey. This region has been selected because:

1) There is now an extensive geological and geophysical data base off New Jersey, including gravity (surface-ship and satellite radar altimeter data), magnetic, single-channel and multichannel seismic reflection profiles, dredge hauls, and piston cores.

2) Two deep COST wells (No. B-2 and B-3) and more than 20 exploratory wells have now been drilled in the outer part of the shelf and slope off New Jersey.

3) The available geological and geophysical data indicate the continental margin has built out by greater than 150 to 200 km seaward of the hinge zone (Watts and Steckler, 1979). The sediments underlying the outer part of the shelf off New Jersey therefore contain a valuable record of the subsidence history of crust that is "transitional" in nature between oceanic and continental crust.

4) A number of inter-institutional geological and geophysical programs are planned in the future for the margin off New Jersey, including LASE, the North American Continent-Ocean Transects Program and possibly, the Ocean Margin Drilling (OMD) project

Geological Setting

The geological setting of the U.S. continental margin has been exten-

NEWARK BASIN

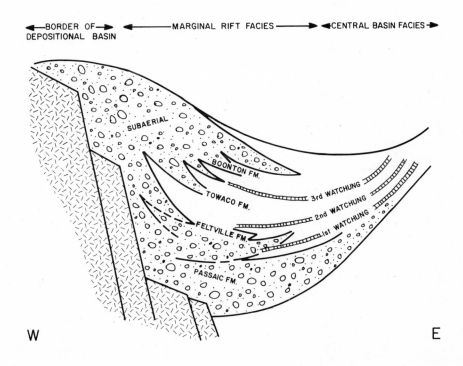

Figure 2. Summary stratigraphic section showing the distribution of facies in the Newark basin (from Manspeizer, 1980). The formations are Late Triassic (Passaic fm.) to Early Jurassic (Feltville, Towaco and Boonton fm.) in age. They are described as "Marginal rift facies" by Manspeizer (1980) and are comprised mainly of fanglomerates interbedded with black shales, deep water turbidites and alluvial fans.

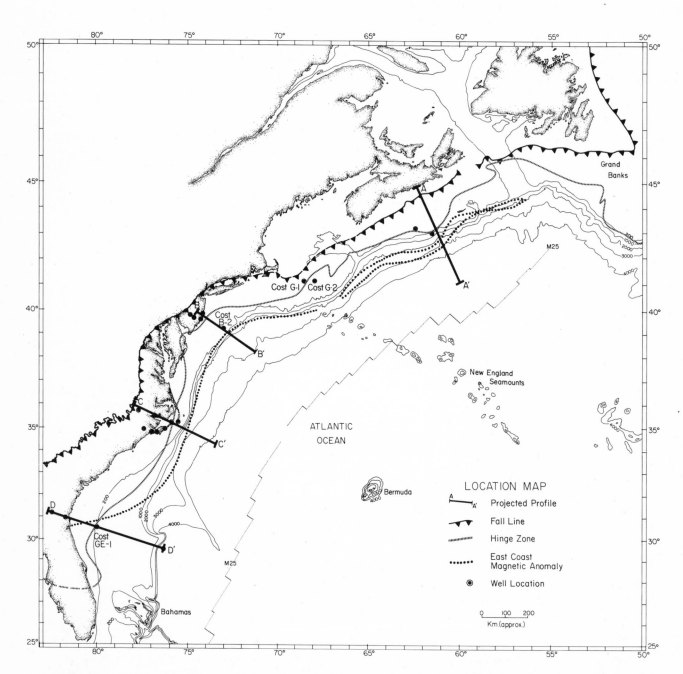

Figure 3. Location map of profiles off eastern North America. The position of the fall line is based on King (1969) on land and, Jansa and Wade (1975) and Austin et al. (1980) offshore. The location of the crest of the East Coast magnetic anomaly is from Rabinowitz (1974) and magnetic anomaly M-25 (155 m.y.B.P.) is from Schouten and Klitgord (1977). The position of the hinge zone is based on Maher and Applin (1971), Jansa and Wade (1975), Dillon et al. (1979) and Austin et al. (1980). Bathymetry is from Uchupi (1971). The heavy lines locate the geological cross-sections in Fig. 4.

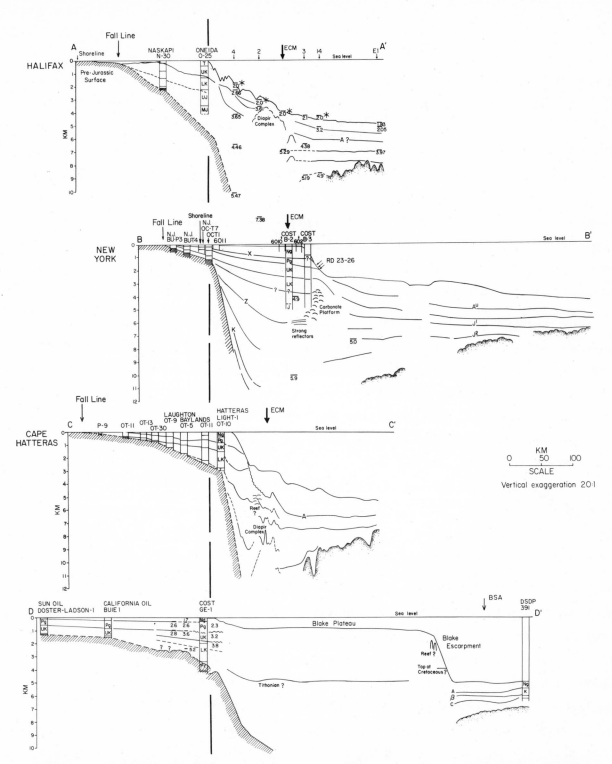

Figure 4. Summary geologic cross sections along the continental margin off North America aligned along the hinge zone (heavy dashed line). The stratigraphy of the land boreholes are from Brown et al. (1972). The stratigraphy of the wells offshore from Nova Scotia are from Williams (1975), the COST B-2 well from Scholle (1977), the COST GE-1 well from Amato and Bebout (1978) and DSDP site 391 from Scientific Party (1976). The solid lines in the four sections indicate prominent seismic reflectors identified on nearby multi-channel seismic profiles (Given, 1977; Grow et al., 1979; Grow and Markl, 1977; Buffler et al., 1979; Dillon et al., 1979; Sheridan, 1976). The arrow labeled ECM refers to the position of the East Coast Magnetic Anomaly and BSA to the Blake Spur Anomaly.

sively discussed in the literature (for example, Emery et al., 1970; Mayhew, 1974; Schlee et al., 1976; Poag, 1980; Austin et al., 1980). These studies indicate that the margin formed by rifting and subsequent separation of the African and North American plates in Late Triassic to Early Jurassic times. The margin is characterized by a substantial thickness of gently dipping Mesozoic to Tertiary sediments which overlie an igneous and metamorphic basement of Precambrian to Palaeozoic age. The sediments form a series of basins beneath the margin, one of which off New Jersey reaches thicknesses of more than 14 km. The basins are separated by a series of platforms, characterized by thin sediments and relatively shallow basement.

The Precambrian to Paleozoic basement of North America contains rift features, such as the Newark and Connecticut grabens (for example, Manspeizer, 1980; this volume), which probably formed in response to the extension at the time of rifting. These grabens contain in excess of 5 km of fanglomerates, flood plain deposits and lacustrine deposits (Fig. 2). The Precambrian to Paleozoic basement dips gently seaward along most of the U.S. margin towards a hinge zone* (Fig. 3), beyond which it rapidly increases in depth. Grabens have been recognized landward of the hinge zone beneath both the coastal plain (Brown et al., 1972) and the continental shelf (for example, Hutchinson et al., in press). They have not been recognized unequivocally seaward of the hinge zone, due mainly to the large sedimentary cover.

Mesozoic and Tertiary sediments uncomformably overlie the Precambrian to Paleozoic basement along much of the U.S. continental margin. The sediments comprise a gently dipping coastal plain sequence which are bounded by a fall-line* from the basement rocks (Fig. 4). The fall-line extends offshore across Georges Bank, the Laurentian channel and the Scotian basin. The coastal plain sediments are Late Cretaceous to Recent in age and have been extensively sampled in land and offshore regions. The Jurassic does not outcrop in the coastal plain and has only been recovered in a few deep wells

*The hinge zone is a broad region characterized by a rapid change of thickness of Mesozoic/Tertiary sediments.

*The fall-line is a line in the eastern U.S. connecting waterfalls on successive rivers. The fall-line is therefore not strictly a tectonic term although it may be considered as a flexural nodal point that separates a region of subsidence from one of uplift.

in the coastal plain. Jurassic sediments have been sampled in deep wells in the offshore regions and are presumed to underlie much of the continental shelf, slope and rise regions along the margin. The available data indicates the Jurassic thins rapidly toward the hinge zone and that there was an extensive widening of the basin in Early Cretaceous times.

The sedimentary history of the U.S. continental margin is now reasonably well known, due mainly to the new seismic and well data (for example, Schlee et al., 1976; Austin et al., 1980; Grow, this volume). The first marine transgression occurred in Late Triassic to Early Jurassic times on a rapidly subsiding shelf. In nearshore regions sands and shales were deposited while in offshore regions limestones accumulated. Limestones have been sampled in deep wells off Nova Scotia and on Georges Bank. Along some parts of the margin (probably in slope regions) reefs formed, acting as a partial barrier to sediments infilling the newly formed basin. Reef growth may have continued until early Cretaceous times when they became buried by prograding sands and shales. The margin continued to prograde during the Late Cretaceous and Tertiary with sediments accumulation in both shelf and slope marine environments. The full extent of the prograding shelf was significantly reduced by Mid-Tertiary bottom counter-currents. Further erosion of the shelf occurred during a Late Pliocene and Pleistocene lowering of sea-level, restricting the transport of sediment to a number of deeply incised canyons in the slope.

The major structural feature of the U.S. continental margin, that significantly controlled the post-rift sedimentary history of the margin, is the hinge zone (Fig. 3). The hinge zone, which marks a zone of rapid increase in depth of continental basement, has been recognized in MCS reflection profiles (for example, Horizon K of Schlee et al., 1976) and seismic refraction data along much of the margin (Fig. 3). The hinge zone trends generally parallel to the fall-line and the East Coast Magnetic Anomaly (ECMA), at least north of 34° North. Fig. 4 shows four geological and geophysical profiles of the U.S. and Canada margin, aligned along the hinge zone. There is no obvious relation between the location of the hinge zone and the position of the shelf break (Fig. 4). For example, the hinge zone is located at or near the shelf break off Cape Hatteras and Halifax but is about 150 km landward of the shelf break off New Jersey.

The geological and geophysical setting of part of the U.S. continental

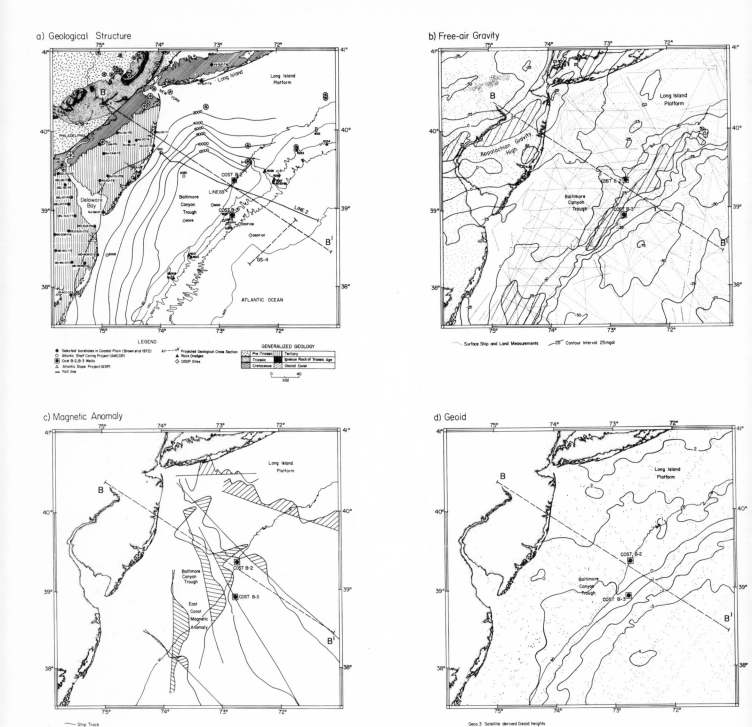

Figure 5. Geological and geophysical setting of the U.S. continental margin off New Jersey. a). Geological structure. The solid contour lines indicate the thickness of sedimentary rocks from the sea-floor to "acoustic basement" based on Grow and Klitgord (1980). The contour interval is 2000 m. The location lines indicate Lamont-Doherty multichannel seismic line 69 and the dashed line the location of projected profile BB' in Fig. 4. b). Free air gravity anomaly. The sources of the data are Defense Mapping Agency (land areas) and Lamont-Doherty Geological Observatory, Woods Hole Oceanographic Institution and U.S.G.S. (J. Grow, pers. comm.) (sea areas). The contour interval is 25 mgal and regions >+25 mgal have been shaded. c). Magnetic anomaly. The magnetic anomaly is shown along selected ship tracks. Positive anomalies are shaded. d). Geoid. The data represent geoid heights derived from GEOS-3 satellite altimeter data between 1975 and 1978. The contour interval is 1 meter.

margin off New Jersey is summarized in Fig. 5. MCS reflection profiles show that more than 14 km of sediments occur in the assymetric Baltimore Canyon trough beneath the shelf off New Jersey (Fig. 5a). The trough which is bounded to the northeast by the Long Island platform and to the southwest by the Carolina platform thins towards the hinge zone but is open-ended in a seaward direction. Gravity and geoid anomalies (Figs. 5b, 5d) show little correlation with the extent of the trough, indicating that the shelf region is generally in isostatic equilibrium. The largest gravity anomalies (an "edge effect" free-air gravity anomaly and a "step" in the geoid) are associated with the shelf break and probably reflect the transition between oceanic and continental crust although isostatic gravity anomaly profiles of the margin, based on an Airy crustal model, show large amplitude positive anomalies over the shelf break. These anomalies were originally interpreted by Rabinowitz (1974) as caused by a buried ridge but Karner and Watts (in press) have attributed them, in part, to sedimentary loading of a strong rigid basement. The East Coast Magnetic Anomaly (ECMA) generally follows the shelf break off New Jersey (Fig. 5c). The magnetic anomaly was originally interpreted as caused by a shallow basement ridge at depths of about 5 to 8 km beneath the outer shelf. Recent MCS profiles have shown evidence for seismic layering at greater depths (Grow et al., 1979 note added in proof; Grow, 1980). Grow et al. (1979) therefore interpreted the ECMA as caused at least in part by "minor secondary volcanic events" in the sediments such as dykes or sills. Most authors still agree that the main cause of the ECMA is in some way related to the boundary separating oceanic and transitional crust or oceanic and continental crust.

The COST B-2 and B-3 wells (Scholle, 1977; 1980) were drilled in the northeast part of the Baltimore Canyon Trough. The lithology of the B-2 well is summarized in Fig. 6, along with a summary geological column and part of the MCS reflection profile 69 (Fig. 5a). The upper 650 m of the well consists of sandy shallow marine to non-marine sediments overlying about 1250 m of deeper water finer grained sands and clays. The lower 3000 m of the well consists mainly of sandstones and shales of shallow marine to non-marine origin. The COST B-3 well (Scholle, 1980) contains more marine deposits than the B-2, and includes mainly limestones.

The MCS reflection profiles and well data have been combined into a

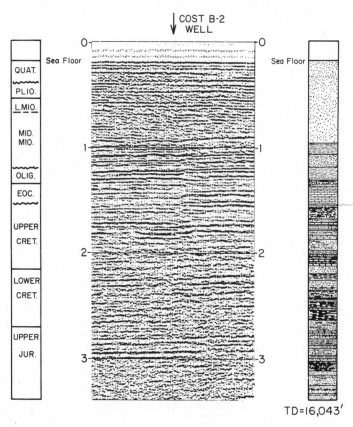

Figure 6. Lamont-Doherty Geological Observatory multi-channel Seismic Line 69 of over the continental shelf off New Jersey in the vicinity of the COST B-2 well. The MCS profile shows 24-fold, stacked Common Depth Point (CDP) data. The data is displayed with time varying gain and has had a bandpass filter applied with Low Cut 15 Hz and High Cut 45 Hz. The two-way travel time in seconds is indicated on either side of the profile. The column on the right is the summary lithology in the well and the column on the left is the summary geological interpretation (Smith et al., 1976; Scholle, 1977).

number of stratigraphic correlation studies and seismic facies studies off New Jersey (for example, Poag, 1980; Schlee, 1981). Schlee (1981) has discussed the stratigraphy of the margin in terms of a number of units, each character-ized by continuity of reflectors, intensity and the configuration of reflectors. Units B and C can be recognized on MCS profile 69 although it is difficult to identify all the units of Schlee (1981) on the profile.

Subsidence History

The sediments which have accumulated at the U.S. continental margin record the vertical movements of the crust (uplift and subsidence) that have occurred during its evolution. The stratigraphy of a margin is the consequence of a number of geological processes which interact with each other through time. These include sedimentary processes such as compaction (or diagenesis), eustasy, transport and sedimentary loading and, other tectonic processes.

A number of studies have shown that substantial thicknesses of sediments can form at a margin simply as a result of sedimentary loading (Gunn, 1943; Dietz, 1963; Walcott, 1972; Cochran, 1973; Turcotte et al., 1977). The sedi-ments that are transported to a margin represent a load on the margin which should sag due to their weight. Walcott (1972) and Cochran (1973) have shown, using oceanic estimates for the flexural rigidity of the lithosphere, that substantial thicknesses of sediments (>12 km) can form at a margin due to sediment loading since sediments at margins (in contrast to intra-cratonic basins) can always prograde seaward. There are, however, two main problems with the loading models. First, in order to produce large thicknesses of sediments the margin (which includes the shelf and slope) must prograde sea-ward by up to 200 to 500 km. Second, since most of the sediments are deposited in a slope rather than a shelf environment a large proportion of deep-water to shallow-water sediments is produced. The margin off New Jersey, for example, is only about 150 km wide and most of the sediments in the outer shelf and slope appear to have formed in shallow-water environments.

Although a number of hypotheses have been proposed to explain the subsi-dence of margins (for example, Sleep, 1971; Falvey, 1974; McKenzie, 1978) most are in agreement that sedimentary loading contributes in some way to the subsidence. A useful approach to the problem, therefore, has been to backstrip (Watts and Ryan, 1976; Steckler and Watts, 1978) sediment as well as water loads for different intervals of geological time during margin evolution. The objective of "backstripping" is to isolate that part of the subsidence of the margin caused by sedimentary factors from other tectonic factors. The resulting tectonic subsidence* at a margin can then be compared to predictions based on geological and geophysical models.

The procedures for "backstripping" (Fig. 7) have been discussed by Watts and Ryan (1976), Steckler and Watts (1978) and Watts and Steckler (1981). The procedure first requires that the stratigraphy of a margin is reconstructed for different intervals of time by including the effects of compaction, eustasy and paleobathymetry. The reconstructed stratigraphy is then "backstripped" or "unloaded" from the margin using different models for the response of the basement to sediment and water loads.

The present day thickness of older sedimentary strata measured, for example, in a deep well does not correspond to the actual thickness of sediments that were deposited because of the effects of compaction. As the weight of younger sediments increases, older sediments expel pore fluids and compact. The measure of the amount of compaction in sediments is the porosity, which is defined as the ratio of the pore volume to the total sediment volume.

In order to correct the stratigraphy for effects of compaction it is necessary to know how the porosity varies with depth during the evolution of the margin. Lithologic logs (sonic, density, porosity) only provide information on the present day variation of porosity with depth. The actual procedures required to correct for compaction are complicated since the processes by which sediments compact are not fully understood. The compaction of sediments is not only a mechanical process, which depends on the depth of burial of the sediments. Chemical processes of mineral solution and recrystallization play an increasingly larger role with depth. These processes, like the mechanical process, gradually cause a reduction in the

---

*This definition of tectonic subsidence at a margin was used by Keen (1979). Prior to this, Watts and Ryan (1976) referred to the tectonic subsidence as the "driving force" and Steckler and Watts (1978) referred to the tectonic subsidence as the "tectonic driving force".

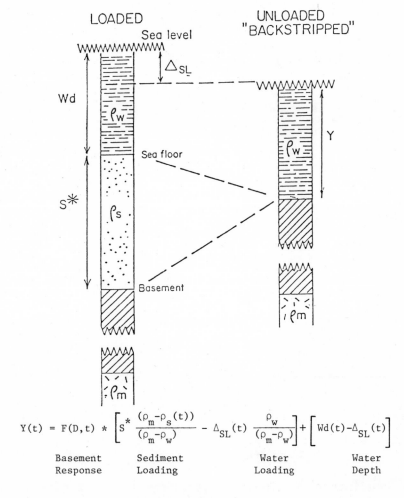

$$Y(t) = F(D,t) * \left[S^* \frac{(\rho_m - \rho_s(t))}{(\rho_m - \rho_w)} - \Delta_{SL}(t) \frac{\rho_w}{(\rho_m - \rho_w)} \right] + \left[Wd(t) - \Delta_{SL}(t) \right]$$

| Basement
Response | Sediment
Loading | Water
Loading | Water
Depth |

Figure 7. Schematic diagram summarizing the "backstripping" of a sedimentary interval at some time t during basin evolution (from Steckler and Watts, 1978). Δ_{SL} = variations in sea-level with respect to present. Wd = water depth of deposition. S^* = sediment thickness corrected for compaction. ρ_s = mean density of sediments. ρ_w = mean density of water. Y = tectonic subsidence. D = flexural rigidity. F = basement response function.

pore volume of sediments.

Steckler and Watts (1978) assumed a simple model of a constant porosity versus depth profile through geological time. The thickness of sediments at any time during the past was calculated by removing sediments younger than the age considered and sliding them up the porosity profile. The thickness is then simply calculated for each stratigraphic horizon from the porosity prior to and after sliding up the curve (for example, Watts and Steckler, 1981). Sclater and Christie (1980) and Royden and Keen (1980) used a similar approach but allowed each lithology to slide up its own porosity versus depth curve. Because the porosity data for each lithology in an individual well is limited, they fitted exponential curves to the data and used these curves to correct for compaction. There is observational evidence, in fact, suggesting an exponential decrease in porosity with depth for sandstones and chalks. Plots of porosity versus depth curves for shales, in contrast, show considerable scatter.

Watts and Steckler (1981) illustrated the effect of using different porosity versus depth curves in the calculation of sediment thicknesses at the COST B-2 well off New Jersey. They showed, using porosity versus depth curves that enveloped the data in the well, that the size of the compaction correction is significant and can exceed 1 km for sediments of Early Cretaceous age or older at the well. Fig. 8 shows porosity versus depth curves for the COST B-2 and B-3 wells. The solid line indicates the "smoothed" curve that was used in the "backstripping" calculations.

The tectonic subsidence at a margin provides a depression in which sediments infill. The sediments do not necessarily fill the depression to sea-level. The water depth that remains is therefore an important part of the subsidence of the margin.

Unfortunately, estimates of the water depth through time, or paleobathy-metry, are difficult to obtain because there is a general absence of depth indicators in the fossil record. Estimates are made either by direct comparisons to present day occurrences of certain species or assemblages, or by quantitatively determining the relative abundance of, for example, benthonic/planktonic forams and radiolarians or ostracods. In general, estimates of water depths are most accurate in regions where recent faunal assemblages are well known (for example, U.S. Gulf Coast, eastern Mediterranean) and in

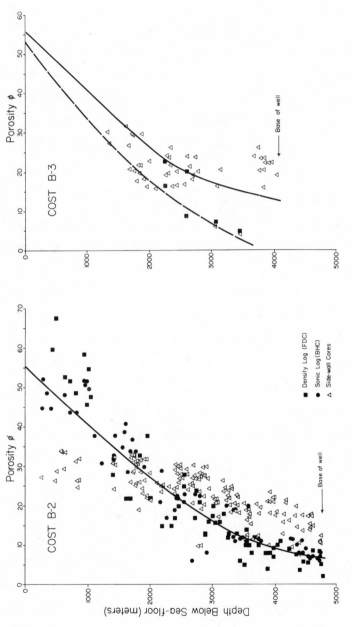

Figure 8. Porosity-depth curves for the COST B-2 and B-3 wells based on data compilations by Rhodehammel (1977), Smith et al. (1976) and Wu and Nichols (1980). The heavy line indicates the "smoothed" curve assumed in the "backstripping" calculations. The dashed line for the COST B-3 well is the curve used by P. Heller (personal comm.) in their "backstripping" studies at the well.

sediments formed in shallow-water environments (neritic and/or shelf facies). Estimates are less precise in older sediments and in sediments formed in deep-water environments.

Fig. 9 summarizes estimates of the paleobathymetry for the COST B-2 and B-3 wells off New Jersey as well as other wells off eastern North America. Early in the history of the margin off New Jersey, during the most rapid subsidence, the sediment supply seems to have been adequate to keep the water depths relatively shallow (100-250 meters). Later in margin history, large water depths developed (up to 500 meters) and sediments could not generally keep up with sea-level.

The variations in sea-level that occur through time (for example, Hays and Pitman, 1973; Vail et al., 1977; Pitman, 1978) contribute in two main ways to the tectonic subsidence of a margin. The height of sea-level is the reference surface for paleobathymetry and sediment thickness estimates. Thus changes in sea-level with respect to the present day are required in order to provide a reference surface for the tectonic subsidence. In addition, the excess water associated with a highstand in sea-level acts as a load on the basement and depresses it. Steckler and Watts (1978) and Watts and Steckler (1979) modelled this effect by assuming the basement responds to the water load as an Airy-type crust. This is justified in the case of the Late Cretaceous sea-level highstand because of its large areal extent although near the shoreline flexural effects may be important and should be taken into account.

The magnitude of sea-level changes through time is a subject of considerable controversy at the present time (Vail et al., 1977; Pitman, 1978; Watts and Steckler, 1979; Bond, 1978; Fig.10). Pitman (1978) estimated that sea-level has fallen by about 350 meters since the Late Cretaceous based on changes in the volume of mid-ocean ridges through time. This estimate appears to agree with that of Sleep (1976), based on the present elevation of Cretaceous sediments in a tectonically undisturbed region of the U.S. continental interior. Watts and Steckler (1979) ,in contrast, estimated that sea-level has fallen by less than about 200 meters since the Late Cretaceous using well data off eastern North America. Their method yields a minimum estimate, but their values are in better agreement with the magnitudes of sea level changes estimated from percentage of continental flooding estimates (Wise, 1974; Bond, 1978).

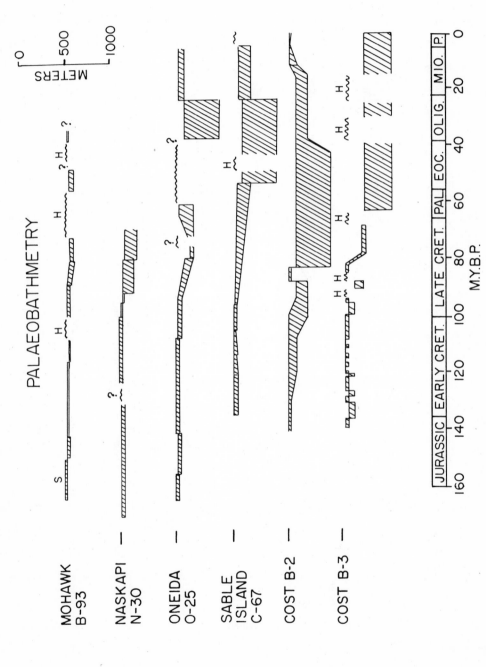

Figure 9. Paleobathymetry estimates for off-shore wells off eastern North America. Data for the Nova Scotian wells are described in Watts and Steckler (1979). The COST B-2 well is based on Smith et al. (1976) and the COST B-3 well is based on Valentine (1980).

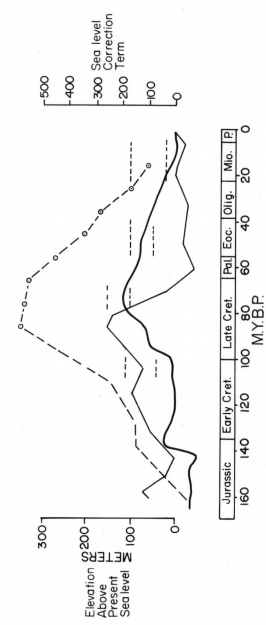

Figure 10. Sea-level changes through geological time. The dashed curve is the sea-level change estimated by Pitman (1978) from estimates of changes in the volume of mid-ocean ridge crests. The scale on the left is sea-level which represent to present day and scale on the right is the sea-level correction term ($\Delta_{SL} \times \rho_m / (\rho_m - \rho_w)$) used in "backstripping The horizontal dashed line is the adjusted sea-level curve of Bond (1978) based on estimates of continental flooding and different hypsometric curves for each continent. The fine curve is based on the Schuchert-Wise estimates of percentage flooding of North America and on an hypsometric curve for North America (Wise, 1974). The heavy curve is the sea-level change estimated by Watts and Steckler (1979) based on least squares fitting an exponential curve to the subsidence data from wells off eastern North America.

Watts and Steckler (1979) and Woods (in preparation) have shown the effect of using different sea-level curves on the tectonic subsidence for wells off eastern North America and in the North Sea basin. These studies show that sea-level can contribute in a major way to the subsidence at a well. There is not a consensus at present on the best sea-level to use in the calculations although Watts and Steckler (1979) and Woods (in press) have shown in their studies that the Watts and Steckler (1979) curve generally gives a better overall exponential fit to the tectonic subsidence than does the Pitman (1978) curve.

The final procedure in "backstripping" is to unload the reconstructed stratigraphy progressively through time. Unfortunately, the manner the basement responds to sediment loads through time is not well known. Studies of the response of the lithosphere due to surface loads such as, seamounts and oceanic islands, ice sheets, and oceanic or continental lithospheric plates as they approach a convergent plate boundary suggest that two models of isostasy, Airy and flexure, are probably important in the loading of sediments at a margin. These models are similar in the sense that a surface load is supported by crustal thickening. They differ, however, in the role assumed by the strength of the crust. In the Airy model, the crust cannot support vertical shear stresses and a surface load is supported by buoyancy of the underlying mantle material. The flexure model, in contrast, includes vertical shear stresses so that a load is supported partly by buoyancy and partly by the strength of the crust.

There is stratigraphic evidence from continental margins of different ages that both Airy and flexure models are probably important during margin evolution. Geological cross-sections, based on seismic reflection profiling and well data, show that the Brazil, Australia, Canada and Biscay margins generally consist of a lower sequence of strongly faulted sediments overlain unconformably by an upper sequence of gently dipping sediments (Ponte and Asmus, 1976; Boeuf and Boust, 1975; Given, 1977; de Charpal et al., 1978). These observations have been interpreted (Watts and Ryan, 1976; Watts and Steckler, 1981) as indicating that the Airy model, in which sediments are locally supported by the basement, is most applicable early in margin evolution while the flexure model, in which sediments load a broader region (forming for example, a coastal plain) is most applicable later in margin evolution.

The main problem in the application of the <u>flexure</u> model at continental margins is in estimating the appropriate value of the <u>flexural rigidity</u>* of the lithosphere during the evolution of a margin. A number of estimates of the flexural rigidity have now been obtained for surface loads in both oceans and continents. The flexural rigidity is in the range 7×10^{26} to 1×10^{31} dyne-cm for oceanic lithosphere (for example, McKenzie and Bowin, 1976; Watts et al., 1975; Watts and Cochran, 1974; Walcott, 1970c; McNutt and Menard, 1978; Caldwell, 1979; Cochran, 1980; McNutt, 1980) and $>5 \times 10^{27}$ to 4×10^{31} dyne-cm for continental lithosphere (for example, Haxby et al., 1976; Banks et al., 1977; McNutt and Parker, 1978; Cochran, 1980). Thus, a large range of values have been determined, particularly for the continents.

Fig. 11 summarizes all recent estimates of the effective <u>elastic thickness</u>* of oceanic lithosphere, T_e as a function of age of the oceanic lithosphere at the time of loading. The solid circles are based on seamount and oceanic island loads and the triangles and squares are based on the sea-floor topography at deep-sea trench - outer rise systems and mid-ocean ridge crests. This plot shows that the effective elastic thickness of oceanic lithosphere is a function of its age. Surface loads formed on young oceanic lithosphere, such as the western Walvis ridge, are associated with small values of the elastic thickness while loads formed on old oceanic lithosphere, such as the Hawaiian Islands, are associated with larger values. In addition, Fig. 11 suggests that the elastic thickness corresponds to the 300 to 600°C oceanic isotherms, based on the cooling plate model. Thus as oceanic lithosphere increases in age and cools, it becomes more rigid in its response to surface loads.

In most current models, (Sleep, 1971; McKenzie, 1978) the tectonic subsidence of continental margins is caused by thermal contraction following

---

*The <u>flexural rigidity</u> is a measure of the resistance of a plate to bending. It is defined as the product of Young's modulus of the plate and the Moment of Inertia in a plane of the cross-section of a plate.

*The <u>elastic thickness</u> of oceanic lithosphere, T_e, corresponds to the <u>mechanical or rheological</u> thickness of the lithosphere and is determined by the flexural rigidity. $D = ET_e^3/12(1-\sigma^2)$ where E = Young's Modulus and σ = Poisson's ratio.

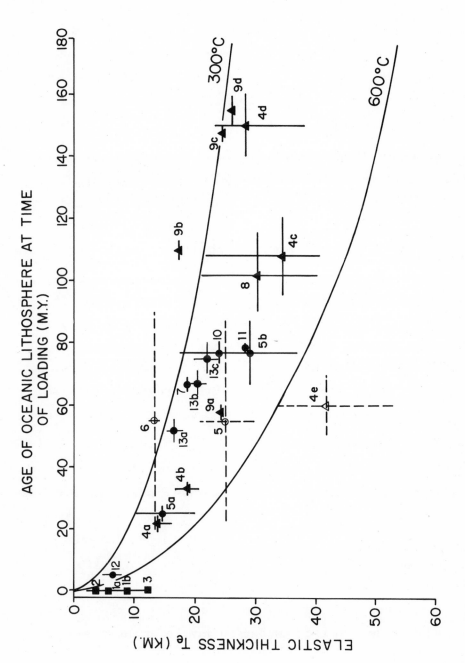

Figure 11. Plot of effective elastic thickness T_e of oceanic lithosphere against age of the lithosphere at the time of loading (from Watts et al., 1980). The estimates of T_e are based on oceanic crustal topography (solid squares), seamounts and oceanic islands (solid circles) and deep-sea trench – outer rise systems (solid triangles). The heavy lines are the 300°C and 600°C oceanic isotherm based on the cooling plate model.

heating and thinning of the lithosphere at the time of rifting. This suggests, on the basis of Fig. 11, that the flexural rigidity at a margin should increase through time as the lithosphere cools. Watts and Steckler (1981) discussed the results of a simple model in which the first 2/3 of the sediments at a margin load a relatively weak elastic plate (T_e = 5 km) while the remaining 1/3 load a more rigid plate (T_e = 25 km). They showed that a flexure model, in which the elastic thickness increases with age, explains a number of stratigraphic features at a margin including a coastal plain sequence in which younger sediments progressively onlap basement rocks and stratigraphic high in the region of the outer shelf.

Fig. 12 shows two simple models (Karner and Watts, in press) in which sediments either build up or out (prograde) at a relatively old continental margin. For both models the tectonic subsidence is assumed to decrease exponentially with time, based on the results of "backstripping" studies. The up-building model shows a stratigraphic high at the shelf break, similar to the model discussed by Watts and Steckler (1981). The outer high is a consequence of the loading history and the increase in flexural rigidity of the lithosphere with time. Thus it is most pronounced in the younger strata because most of the loading occurs in the region of the shelf on a relatively weak plate. The out-building model (Fig. 12), in contrast, does not show an outer high. This is because the main load progrades seaward causing a flexural depression of the strata in the region of the trailing shelf. Both models show a coastal plain in which younger sediments progressively onlap the basement.

The main features predicted by the flexure models in Fig. 12 can be recognized in the observed stratigraphy of the continental margin off New Jersey. For example, the U.S. coastal plain is characterized by younger Cretaceous to Tertiary sediments which progressively overstep older Jurassic sediments near the hinge zone (Fig. 4). Furthermore, buried reef complexes occur beneath the outer part of the shelf off New Jersey. Thus both the coastal plain and reef growth off New Jersey may be at least partly flexurally controlled.

These considerations suggest that flexure probably is a significant factor in the development of the U.S. continental margin, particularly following initial rifting. Unfortunately, only a few studies have included

a) Up-building

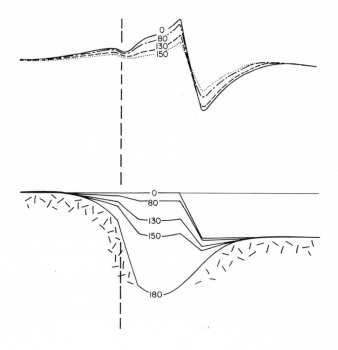

b) Out-building

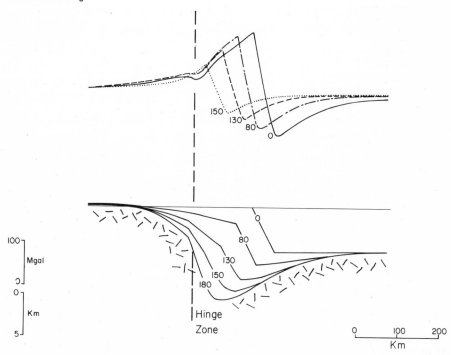

Figure 12. Simple models for the development of a continental margin based on either up-building (a) or out-building (b) of sediments (from Karner and Watts, in press). The stratigraphy has been calculated assuming an effective elastic thickness T_e that increases with age (Fig. 11) and a tectonic subsidence that decreases exponentially with time. The calculated free-air gravity anomaly profiles are shown above each model. Note that each model is associated with a gravity anomaly high over the shelf edge and a flanking low over the slope. The "hinge zone" is not associated with a prominent gravity anomaly.

flexure in "backstripping". <u>Flexural backstripping</u> requires a knowledge of both the loading history of the margin and the flexural rigidity as a function of time. If the stratigraphy of a margin is known (and corrections have been applied for the effects of compaction, palaeobathymetry, and eustasy) then the loading history can be estimated once the flexural ridigity is defined either iteratively (in which the load that explains a given flexure is found by trial and error) or directly (Watts and Ryan, 1976; Steckler, 1981). The main problem though is in estimating the flexural rigidity as a function of time.

The observations in Fig. 10 suggest an approach to estimating the flexural rigidity as a function of time. If the post-rift sedimentary sequence is complete then individual sedimentary horizons can be backstripped using values of the elastic thickness given by the depth to the 450 ± 150°C oceanic isotherm. The elastic thickness would increase, for example, from zero at rifting to 25 km at 60 m.y. following rifting. This, of course, pre-supposes at a margin that the temperature distribution in the lithosphere is similar to that of a mid-ocean ridge. A ridge model may not be applicable at a margin (for example, Steckler and Watts, 1978). Therefore some estimate of the flexural rigidity of a margin is required that is independent of a particular thermal model.

A possibility is the free-air gravity anomaly at a continental margin, since it is sensitive to both the loading history and the variation of flexural rigidity as a function of time (Fig. 12). The main limitation is that the gravity anomaly provides information only on the <u>average flexural response</u> at a margin. That is, it is sensitive to a flexural rigidity intermediate between a low value, associated with the youngest sediments, and a high value, associated with the oldest sediments. Karner and Watts (in press) have used the gravity anomaly to estimate the average response for margins of different ages. These results are summarized in Table 1 which shows that the average response of a margin generally increases with age, although precisely how the average response would vary with age for each margin is unclear. A complicating factor, of course, is that each margin has a different loading history and the proportion of young to old sediments may vary widely.

The procedure used in this paper will be to flexurally backstrip the sediments at the COST B-2 and B-3 wells using three different models for the

Table 1

Summary of Elastic Thickness Estimates For Atlantic Type Continental Margins*

Margin	Age m.y.B.P.	Elastic Thickness T_e
Coral Sea/ Lord Howe	~60	<5 km
Southwest Africa	~110	5-10 km
U.S. Atlantic margin	~195	10-20 km

*based on Karner and Watts (in press). Note the elastic thickness is based on an assumed mean crustal thickness of 32 km at the shoreline.

variation of flexural rigidity with time. The simplest model is an Airy model (Fig. 13, curve a) which is equivalent to using a zero flexural rigidity through time. This model assumes all the sediments formed on a relatively weak plate. The other models (Fig. 13, cuve b and c) are flexure models in which the flexural rigidity increases with age. In curve b the elastic thickness is given by $0.72 \times t^{1/2}$ where t is the time since rifting in m.y., consistent with the data in Table 1 for the average response to sediment loads for the U.S. margin. In curve c the elastic thickness is given by $3.0 \times t^{1/2}$, which assumes all the sediments loaded a relatively rigid plate. The differences between the curves are significant (Fig. 13), illustrating the importance of flexure even for the relatively wide margin off New Jersey. We cannot really distinguish between curves a, b, c (Fig. 13) without knowledge of the thermal model that describes margin evolution. In view of the lack of other observational constraints the average response curve for "backstripping" will be used since it is the only curve constrained by the gravity data.

The results of "backstripping" sediment and water loads for the COST B-2 and B-3 wells are summarized in Fig. 14. A number of assumptions have been made in the calculations. The stratigraphy at the wells has been reconstructed using the porosity data in Fig. 8, the palaeobathymetry data in Fig. 9, and the Watts and Steckler (1979) sea-level curve in Fig. 10 The sediment thickness corrected for compaction, average sediment density, paleo-bathymetry and sea-level is summarized for each well in Tables 2 and 3. The reconstructed stratigraphy was then backstripped from the margin assuming a total sediment thickness beneath the wells and an average response of the basement to sediment loads. The lightly shaded area of Fig. 14 illustrates the contribution of sediment and water loading to the subsidence at each well. The shaded region indicates that part of the subsidence which cannot be attributed to sedimentary processes and is termed the tectonic subsidence of the margin.

Thermal and mechanical evolution

The "backstripping" procedures outlined in the last section allows the tectonic subsidence of a U.S. Atlantic Continental margin to be isolated. Specifically, these procedures correct the stratigraphy at the margin for the effects of sedimentary processes such as compaction, palaeobathymetry, eustasy

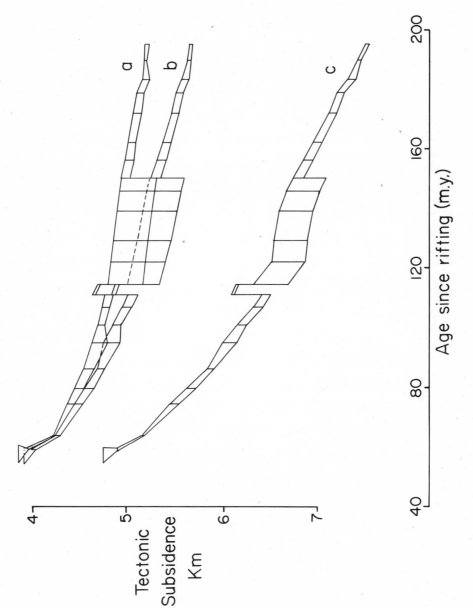

Figure 13. Tectonic subsidence at the COST B-2 well obtained by "backstripping" the well data using the smooth porosity-depth curve in Fig. 8, the paleobathymetry in Fig. 9, the Watts and Steckler (1979) sea-level curve and, different assumptions for the response of the lithosphere to the sediment loads. a) Airy model, b) and c) Flexure model with a flexural rigidity that increases with age.

Table 2

Summary of parameters at COST B-2 well

Strati-graphic Horizon Depth D meters	Age m.y.B.P.	S* meters	$\overline{\rho_s}$ g/cm³	Water Depth W_d meters	Sea-level Δ_{SL} meters
0	0	12802	2.46	0-27	0
159	5.0	12728	2.46	0-15	-6
239	11.4	12690	2.46	0-91	7
966	15.7	12299	2.45	91-183	11
978	22.5	12292	2.45	91-183	26
1104	32.5	12215	2.45	91-183	47
1126	38.0	12202	2.45	91-183	58
1163	44.0	12179	2.45	91-457	68
1293	49.0	12098	2.45	91-457	71
1395	55.0	12033	2.45	91-457	77
1406	65.0	12026	2.45	91-457	100
1436	72.5	12006	2.45	91-457	109
1630	80.0	11878	2.45	91-457	100
1730	83.0	11810	2.45	0-15	73
2014	88.0	11610	2.44	91-183	60
2201	94.0	11472	2.44	91-183	58
2360	100.0	11352	2.44	0-183	5
2594	108.0	11171	2.43	0-91	5
2930	115.0	10904	2.43	0-91	-6
3235	120.0	10652	2.42	0-91	0
3539	131.0	10388	2.42	0-15	23
4332	135.0	9677	2.40	0-15	26
4772	141.0	9270	2.39	0-15	-20

S* is based on assumed grain density = 2.65 g/cm³ and porosity versus depth curves in Fig. 8.

Δ_{SL} is from Watts and Steckler (1979) sea-level curve.

Table 3

Summary of parameters at COST B-3 well

Strati-graphic Horizon Depth D meters	Age m.y.B.P.	S* meters	$\overline{\rho}_s$ g/cm^3	Water Depth W_d meters	Sea-level Δ_{SL} meters
329	0.0	12194	2.35	800	0
604	24.0	12037	2.35	200-500	27
677	37.0	11993	2.35	200-500	57
738	40.0	11955	2.35	200-500	61
951	49.0	11819	2.35	200-500	71
1009	67.3	11781	2.35	178-225	101
1058	70.0	11748	2.35	178-225	107
1140	78.0	11692	2.35	178-225	101
1314	82.0	11570	2.35	0-50	86
1436	87.0	11481	2.35	100-200	60
1676	92.0	11299	2.34	100-200	59
1881	100.0	11135	2.34	0-50	5
2167	108.0	10895	2.34	0-50	5
2526	121.0	10580	2.34	0-50	0
3039	131.0	10108	2.33	0-50	23
3267	135.0	9891	2.33	50-100	26

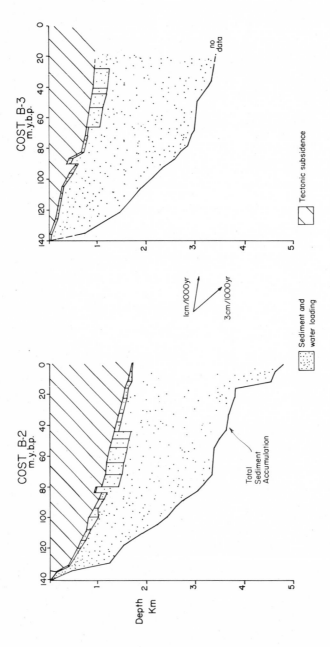

Figure 14. Tectonic subsidence and sediment accumulation at the COST B-2 and B-3 wells through time. The tectonic subsidence has been computed assuming an average response of the basement to sedimentary loads (Curve (b), Fig. 13). Note the tectonic subsidence is generally smoother than the total sediment accumulation curve suggesting that "backstripping" adequately accounts for sedimentary processes at the margin.

and sedimentary loading. The resulting tectonic subsidence can then be interpreted in terms of different geophysical models for the origin of the margin.

Most authors now consider that the dominant mechanism affecting the tectonic subsidence of continental margins is thermal contraction following initial rifting (for example, Sleep, 1971; Falvey, 1974; McKenzie, 1978). Sleep (1971) corrected the subsidence data from a number of deep wells in the U.S. coastal plain for the effects of sediment loading, using the Airy model of isostasy, and showed the resulting tectonic subsidence was similar in form to a mid-ocean ridge. Watts and Ryan (1976), using backstripping techniques, corrected the subsidence in deep wells in the western Mediterranean and off the East Coast U.S. for the effects of sediment loading, using both Airy and flexure models, and included the effects of compaction and palaeobathymetry. They showed that, like the earlier study by Sleep (1971), that the resulting tectonic subsidence of the margin was exponential in form and similar to that of a mid-ocean ridge.

Sleep (1971) suggested the tectonic subsidence at a margin was caused by crustal thinning following uplift and erosion at the time of initial rifting. The subsidence in this model depends on the ratio of total eroded thickness to the initial uplift and the erosion time constant (Foucher and LePichon, 1972). For small erosion time constants (<1 m.y.) ratios of only 4 to 5 are obtained. This suggests that for an initial uplift of 1.5 km (which is a reasonable estimate of the amplitude of topographic swells associated with the East Africa rift system) the total erosion will reach only 7.5 km (Le Pichon et al., 1973). Isostatic considerations suggest that crustal thinning of these amounts would result in the formation of a relatively thin basin (about 2 to 3 km if infilled only by water or 5 to 7.5 km if infilled by sediments). Thus, the uplift and erosion model of Sleep (1971) does not appear to be able to explain the large sedimentary thicknesses observed at the U.S. margin.

Another difficulty with the model is that there is little stratigraphic evidence at margins for large amounts of uplift and erosion at the time of initial rifting (for example, Kent, 1973; 1976). Initial rifting at margins appears, in contrast, to be associated with subsidence and normal faulting.

Steckler and Watts (1978), Keen (1979), and Watts and Steckler (1979) carried out more detailed studies of the subsidence history of the U.S. and Canadian margin and showed that the tectonic subsidence could be explained by a cooling plate model, similar to that used by Parsons and Sclater (1977) to describe the subsidence of mid-ocean ridge crests. The main differences were in the values of the thermal parameters required to fit the well data. Steckler and Watts (1978), for example, obtained a slope of depth versus age $^{1/2}$ which was significantly larger than that obtained for a mid-ocean ridge.

As stated previously, the cooling plate model may not be applicable to a margin. The main problem is that the model implies too high temperatures in the upper part of the crust. The basement rocks which have been drilled or sampled at a margin that has undergone large amounts of rapid subsidence (for example, western Mediterranean, Biscay margin) do not appear to have been extensively heated.

McKenzie (1978) proposed a model, which addressed both the uplift and heating problems, in which the lithosphere undergoes a passive uniform extension or stretching at the time of rifting. The extension causes necking or thinning of the crust which subsequently subsides with time (Fig. 15). Initially, there is an isostatic adjustment of the crust, or initial subsidence, due to the rise of hot asthenosphere material. Following extension, there is a thermal subsidence as heat is conducted to the surface and the lithosphere cools.

Fig. 16 shows subsidence curves based on the McKenzie (1978) model for different values of the amount of stretching β. The value of β defines the amount of extension that occurs and 1/β defines the amount of thinning. An initial crustal thickness of T_i = 27.3 km was assumed so that the initial subsidence for β = ∞ (infinite extension) would correspond to the mean depth of a mid-ocean ridge crest (2.5 km).

There is now good observational evidence for crustal extension during the early rifting history of continental margins. de Charpal et al. (1979) have mapped a number of listric faults (faults that curve with depth) in the Biscay margin off Spain and France. Movement on these faults produces rotation of crustal blocks which is visible in multichannel seismic reflection profiles of the margin. Given (1977) and Schlee (1981) have mapped graben systems in the Scotian and Long Island platforms off eastern North America, similar to the Connecticut and Newark rift systems in land regions Finally, Ponte and Asmus

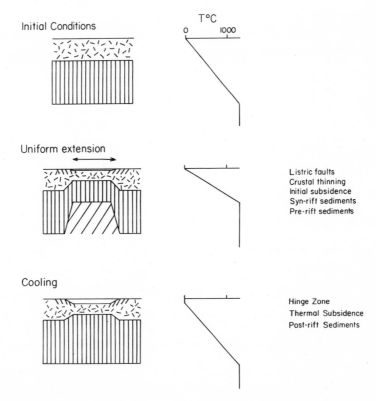

Figure 15. Schematic diagram showing the principal features of the
stretching model of McKenzie (1978). a). Initial conditions showing the
lithosphere (including a crust) in thermal equilibrium. b). Uniform
extension during which the lithosphere is extended and thinned. Since
isostatic equilibrium is assumed, the extension is associated with an
initial subsidence that depends on the initial crustal thickness
assumed. c). Cooling following the extension as the hot asthenosphere
cools. The cooling is associated with a thermal subsidence which decays
exponentially with time. The main geological features of the stretching
model are summarized to the right of the figure. Note that the uniform
extension model is associated with shallow crustal faulting and crustal
thinning. The location of the "hinge zone" (Fig. 4) is controlled by the
amount of heating of the margin, but probably continues to be an important
feature during the cooling.

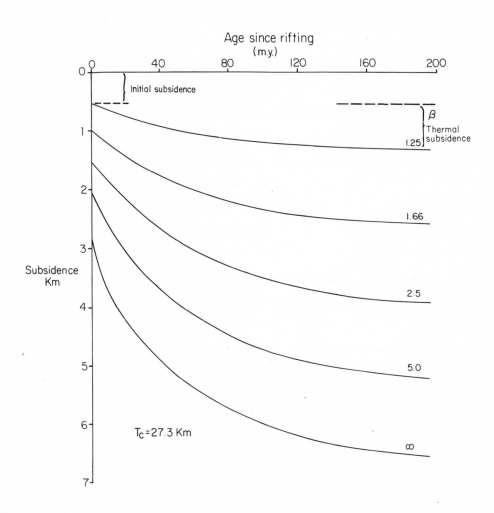

Figure 16. Subsidence as a function of time since rifting. The curves have been obtained from equations (1) and (13) of McKenzie (1978) using the parameters in Table 4, different values of the stretching factor β and an assumed initial crustal thickness T_c of 27.3 km. This value of T_c was chosen since $\beta = \infty$ corresponds to an initial subsidence equal to mid-ocean ridge crest depths (2.5 km).

(1976) have mapped steep normal faults in the margin off Brazil which do not extend above the Albian/Aptian "break-up" unconformity at the margin separating pre- and syn-rift sediments from post-rift sediments.

The stretching model of McKenzie (1978) was first compared to tectonic subsidence data at continental margins by Steckler and Watts (1980) and Royden and Keen (1980). They compared the predictions of the model to biostratigraphic data from deep wells in the eastern North America and western Mediterranean margins.

Steckler and Watts (1980) showed that the tectonic subsidence of the relatively young (Miocene) Gulf of Lyon margin in the western Mediterranean could be generally explained by the stretching model of McKenzie (1978), although large amounts of extension were required. They showed that the largest amounts of extension ($\beta \tilde{>} 10$) were required at the well nearest to the hinge zone while the smallest amount of extension were required for the well furthest seaward of the hinge zone. The more rapid subsidence at the well nearest the hinge zone suggests that cooling occurs both vertically and laterally at a margin. They showed that a modified stretching model, in which β varied as a function of position across the margin, better explained the subsidence data and required smaller values of extension at the margin (β in the range 2 to 6). The main difficulty with the model was that there is no geological evidence in the region of large thicknesses of Oligocene pre- and syn-rift sediments implied by these amounts of extension. The initial subsidence that corresponds to these estimates of β is 2 to 3 km which if infilled to sea-level with sediment* would produce a pre- and syn-rift basin 4 to 7 km thick. Such large thicknesses of pre- and syn-rift sediments have not been observed in the region. Thus geological evidence suggests a small amount of subsidence associated with rifting while the tectonic subsidence requires extensive heating during rifting. Steckler and Watts (1980) suggested that either the initial crustal thickness was unusually high and/or a high thermal gradient already existed in the crust or, some form of active heating occurred at the margin.

Royden and Keen (1980) showed that the McKenzie (1978) model could satis-

*The first post-rift sediments in the Gulf of Lyon are beach conglomerates so it seems likely that the pre- and syn-rift sediments did infill to sea-level.

factorily explain the tectonic subsidence of the relatively old (Early Jurassic) Nova Scotia margin, although it could not explain the tectonic subsidence at the younger (Late Cretaceous) Labrador margin. Royden and Keen (1980) therefore modified the uniform extension model of McKenzie (1978) to include an upper and lower layer which deforms in response to the extension by different amounts so that the upper layer extends by an amount δ while the lower layer deforms independently by an amount β. They argued that a non-uniform extension model better approximated the actual rheological properties of the lithosphere (for example, Goetze and Evans, 1980) since the upper part of the lithosphere probably deforms by brittle failure while the lower part deforms by ductile flow. The initial subsidence in this model depends on the initial crustal thickness as well as on the relative magnitude of δ and β. Thus it is possible, by a suitable choice of parameters, to obtain relatively small values of the initial subsidence together with relatively high values of β. Royden and Keen (1980) showed that the tectonic subsidence of the Labrador margin could be explained by this model with values of δ in the range 1.3 to 1.7 and β in the range 2 to 10. These parameters produced a syn- and pre-rift elevation near sea-level and uplift for about 10 to 20 m.y. after rifting. Stratigraphic data in the Labrador sea wells (Royden and Keen, 1980), all of which either terminated in Precambrian basement or syn- and pre-rift sediments, are consistent with erosional events (due to uplift) occurring soon after rifting.

More recently, Le Pichon and Sibuet (1981) and Cochran (1981) have compared the predictions of the uniform stretching model of McKenzie (1978) to geological and geophysical data at the American margin in the northeast Atlantic and the Gulf of Aden margin. The uniform stretching model implies that the upper and lower crust would extend by equal amounts during rifting. Thus extension inferred from faults in the cooler upper parts of the crust should approximately correspond to extension inferred from the overall change in crustal thickness across a margin. Le Pichon and Sibuet (1981) argued that the estimates of the amount of extension from listric faults in the Bay of Biscay margin were consistent with seismic refraction evidence of the crustal structure at the margin. The stretching model also implies that estimates of extension inferred from different geological and geophysical data should be consistent with each other. Cochran (1981) suggested that the amount of extension inferred using the model from heat flow measurements and present basement depths in the Gulf of Aden were consistent with the amount of extension across the region deduced from present tectonic motions between the African and Arabian plates.   These studies therefore generally support the application of the uniform stretching model, although a number of questions still remain.   These include the reliability of estimates of the amount of extension from fault geometry and the effects of a finite time for the extension.

The simple model of stretching that has been applied to continental margins assumes instantaneous stretching in order to simplify the boundary conditions in the model.   The rifting phase at a margin may, however, extend for a considerable time.   The effects of a finite extension time is to transfer some of the post-rift subsidence to the pre- and syn-rift subsidence.   Jarvis and McKenzie (1979) have shown, based on different assumptions for the strain rate developed during extension, that the stretching model satisfactorily predicts subsidence and heat flow for a period of stretching of 20 m.y. or shorter.   For longer periods a more complete thermal model is required.

The continental margin south of Australia, for example, appears to be characterized by a stretching or rifting phase that is significantly longer in duration than 20 m.y.   Based on the age of the oldest magnetic anomaly in the adjacent ocean floor Falvey (1974) identified a "break-up unconformity" in the margin which spanned the initiation of rifting between the Upper Cretaceous and Paleocene, 55-70 m.y.B.P.   This age for "break-up" implies a substantial thickness of pre- and syn-rift sediments, compared to the thickness of post-rift sediments, at the margin*.   Falvey and Middleton (1981), on the basis of deep well data, have shown that the subsidence of the pre- and syn-rift sediments exponentially decreases with time.   They correctly point out that it would be difficult to invoke two periods of thermal contraction to explain the subsidence since the time of rifting ("break-up") does not represent significant uplift or erosion.   Falvey (1974) and Middleton (1981) therefore considered a different thermal model which includes the effects of

---

*The terminology used in this paper differs from that of Falvey (1974).   The syn- and pre-rift subsidence corresponds to the "infra-rift" and "rift" subsidence of Falvey (1974) and the post-rift subsidence corresponds to the "post-breakup" subsidence of Falvey (1974).

phase changes. In this model, metamorphic reactions during the heating phase cause an increase in density of lower crustal rocks and a tectonic subsidence during the pre- and syn-rift period that overcomes uplift due to heating. They showed that the model subsidence was exponential in form and satisfactorily explained the well data. Recent studies, however, suggest (Cande et al., 1981; Cande and Mutter, in preparation) that the length of the pre-rift and syn-rift period may not have been as long as implied by Falvey (1974). They re-identified the oldest magnetic anomaly between Australia and Antarctica and suggested that the "break-up unconformity" could be as old as 85-110 m.y.B.P., attributing the unconformity identified by Falvey (1974) to sea-level changes. The new age for the margin suggests the most rapid subsidence is restricted to the pre-rift and syn-rift sediments so that it should now be possible to compare the subsidence to predictions based on the stretching model for different values of β. Preliminary comparisons, using the curves in Fig. 17 and the tectonic subsidence inferred from the corrected sediment thicknesses at the Platypus-1, Flaxmans and Pecten wells (Falvey and Middleton, 1981), suggest that β values in the range 1.2 to 1.5 could satisfactorily explain well data at this margin.

The substantial thicknesses of post-rift sediments that occur at the U.S. Atlantic continental margin makes it difficult to distinguish between the different thermal models at this margin. Watts and Steckler (1981) have pointed out, for example, that the tectonic subsidence at the COST B-2 well can be equally well explained by a cooling plate model (Parsons and Sclater, 1977) and the stretching model of McKenzie (1978) with $\beta = 6$. Thermal models mainly differ in the first 60 m.y. following rifting. The COST B-2 well only penetrated the upper 5 km of the post-rift sequence so that the early tectonic subsidence at the well is poorly known. Furthermore, there is no seismic reflection or refraction data available to satisfactorily constrain the form of the early subsidence at the margin.

Figure 17 compares the tectonic subsidence at the COST B-2 and B-3 wells to computed curves based on the stretching model for β in the range 2 to 6. The best fitting curves are for β in the range 3 to 4, corresponding to 200 to 300% extension. The overall fit of the data to the model curves is generally good although the observed tectonic subsidence increases more rapidly with time than do the model curves. There are two possible explanations for

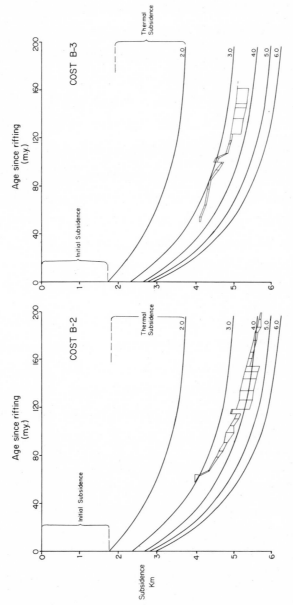

Figure 17. Plot of tectonic subsidence at the COST B-2 and B-3 wells (Fig. 13) compared to theoretical curves based on the stretching model of McKenzie (1978). The calculated curves are based on similar parameters as in Fig. 16. The main difference is that a value of T_c = 31.2 km has been assumed since this value (Steckler, 1981) is in isostatic balance with a crust approximately 6 km thick at a mid-ocean ridge crest. Note that the tectonic subsidence at the wells can be best explained by β in the range 3 to 4, which corresponds to 200 to 300% extension of the continental crust beneath each well.

this. First, the age of rifting of 195 m.y.B.P. (Trias-Lias boundary, Van Houten, 1977) assumed in the "backstripping" calculations may be too old. Second, the flexural rigidity used in "backstripping" the oldest sediments in the well may have been too small. Both these effects could explain the relatively steep tectonic subsidence compared to the model curves.

A useful test of the "backstripping" procedures is to load the U.S. continental margin using the estimated value of β at the wells and compare the resulting stratigraphy to observed geological cross-sections. A complete calculation of the stratigraphy off New Jersey, however, is difficult since we only have an estimate of β at the COST B-2 and B-3 wells. We will therefore assume a simple model in which the flexural rigidity of the basement increases with time, sediments spread rapidly from the shelf to the slope and rise regions of the margin and, the effects of compaction and lateral heat flow and flexure are neglected. The results of the calculations are summarized in Fig. 18 which shows the proportion of pre- and syn-rift sediments to post-rift sediments expected for the simple stretching model. At the COST B-2 well, approximately 8 km of post-rift sediments overlie 7 km of pre- and syn-rift sediments in the vicinity of the COST B-2 and B-3 wells.

The proportions of syn- and pre-rift and post-rift sediments predicted by the thermal and mechanical model (Fig. 18) can be compared to the stratigraphy of the margin inferred from seismic reflection profile data. MCS Line 69 (Fig. 5a) in the vicinity of the COST B-2 well (Fig. 19) shows a number of moderate to strong acoustic reflectors beneath the well. A prominent reflector occurs at about 6 secs on Line 69 in the region of the well and there appears to be little evidence on this profile for fault-controlled pre- and syn-rift sediments beneath the well. Line 69 trends sub-parallel to the local trend of the hinge zone, however, (Fig. 4a) and therefore may parallel the rift features. Schlee (1981) identified a similar prominent acoustic reflector on MCS profiles of other parts of the shelf off New Jersey. The sedimentary units overlying this reflector were classified as Unit A and B, based mainly on the character and intensity of acoustic reflectors. Schlee (1981) suggested Unit A is Triassic to Early Jurassic in age and that it is characterized by interval velocities in the range from 4.0 to 6.4 km/sec. He suggested that Unit A was up to 7 km in thickness beneath the shelf off New Jersey, locally reaching 5 to 6 km in the vicinity of the COST B-2. If Unit A

Table 4

Thermal and Flexural Model Parameters

Initial thickness of lithosphere $\quad a = 125$ km

Crustal density (0°C) $\qquad \rho_c = 2.8$ g cm^{-3}

Mantle density (0°C) $\qquad \rho_m = 3.33$ g cm^{-3}

Water density (0°C) $\qquad \rho_w = 1.03$ g cm^{-3}

Coefficient of thermal expansion $\quad \alpha = 3.4 \times 10^{-5}$ °C^{-1}

Asthenosphere temperature $\qquad T_1 = 1333$°C

Thermal diffusivity $\qquad K = 8 \times 10^{-3}$ cm^2/sec

Average gravity $\qquad g = 981$ cm/sec^2

Young's Modulus $\qquad E = 10^{12}$ dyne/cm^2

Poisson's ratio $\qquad \sigma = 0.25$

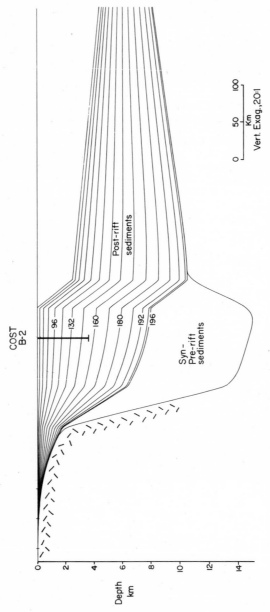

Figure 18. Simple thermal and mechanical model for the development of the continental margin off New Jersey. The model has been calculated assuming a loading history similar to the present day so that sediments infill shelf, slope and rise regions. The model is based on a flexural rigidity of the basement increasing with age and a tectonic subsidence at the COST B-2 well described by a stretching model with $\beta = 3.7$. The simple model does not include the effects of lateral changes in heat flow and flexural rigidity across a margin or corrections for sediment compaction.

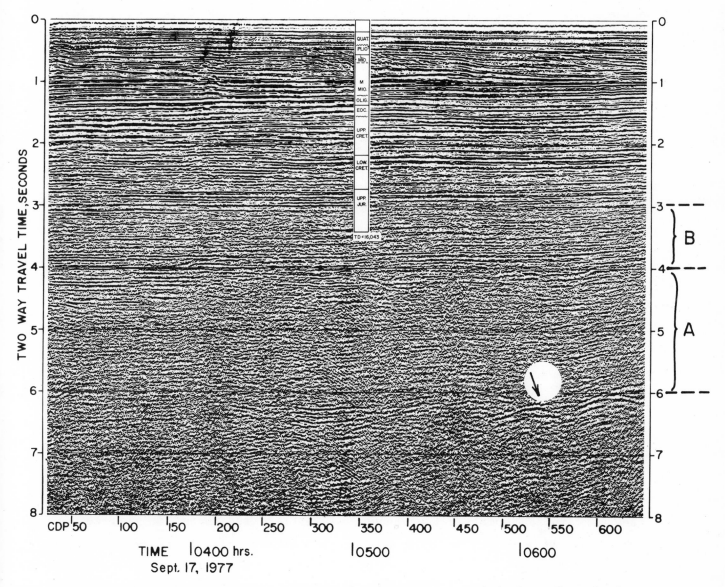

COST B-2
WELL

Figure 19. Lamont-Doherty Geological Observatory multi-channel seismic
Line 69 over the continental shelf off New Jersey in the vicinity of the
COST B-2 well. The MCS data has been processed in a similar manner as
described in Fig. 6. The seismic units of Schlee (1981) where they can be
identified on Line 69 are shown to the right of the profile. Note the
strong reflector at about 6 seconds which is interpreted as acoustic
basement. Schlee (1981) has recognized a similar reflector beneath other
regions of the shelf off New Jersey.

is Triassic to Early Jurassic in age, it is therefore contemporaneous in age to the sediments infilling the Newark basin (Fig. 2). Thus up to 6 km of pre- and syn-rift sediments could occur beneath the COST B-2 well, in agreement with the predictions of the stretching model with β = 3.7 km (Fig. 18). There is little evidence, however, for a "break-up" unconformity at the margin so that these estimates of the proportion of pre- and syn-rift sediments to post-rift sediments cannot be considered as well constrained.

An important feature predicted by the model in Fig. 18 is the progressive onlap of younger sediment onto basement at the edge of the continental margin. Fig. 20, which is an enlarged portion the edge of the margin, shows that the rate of sediment onlap is initially rapid and then slows significantly. The arrows in Fig. 20 show the position of the onlap of the 192, 160 and 52 m.y. horizons. We have assumed in the model calculation that the region of sedimentary infill (shelf, slope and rise) remains constant during margin evolution. The sediment onlap is therefore a consequence of the assumption of the increase of flexural strength of the basement with age. The earliest sediments at the margin load a relatively weak plate forming a relatively narrow basin while sediments formed later in margin evolution load a relatively strong plate forming a relatively wide basin.

The overall shape of the edge of the continental margin predicted in Fig. 20 is similar to observations in the U.S. coastal plain. Fig. 21 summarizes the stratigraphy of the coastal plain in North Carolina, based on a compilation of well data in the region. This figure shows a progressive onlap of sediments onto basement rocks, at least for Latest Jurassic to Upper Cretaceous time. The Latest Cretaceous and Tertiary sediments, in contrast, do not onlap the basement but form an outcrop pattern which decreases in age in a seaward direction. However, individual formations in the Tertiary, such as the Claiborne, show facies evidence for a widening of the sea as sandstones and siltstones in the lower part of the formation are replaced by marine limestones in the upper part (Colquhoun and Johnson, 1968). Thus the present outcrop pattern of the Claiborne may have been modified by later tilting and sub-aerial erosion erosion of the margin.

The cause of the progressive onlapping of sediments observed in the coastal plain of the U.S. continental margin is an important question to address. We have shown that sediment loading on a basement with a flexural

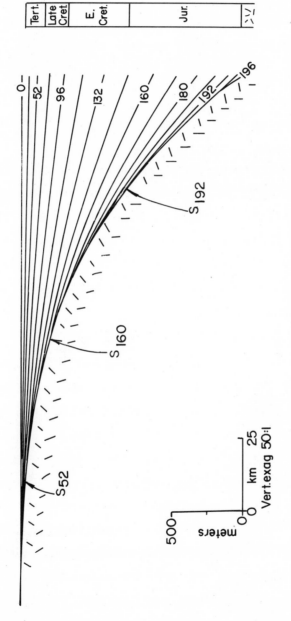

Figure 20. Simple thermal and mechanical model for the coastal plain off New Jersey. The diagram is an enlargement of the coastal plain of Fig. 17. Note the progressive onlap of younger sediments onto the basement. The onlap is initially rapid (about 1 km/my) and then slows (about $\frac{1}{2}$ km/my).

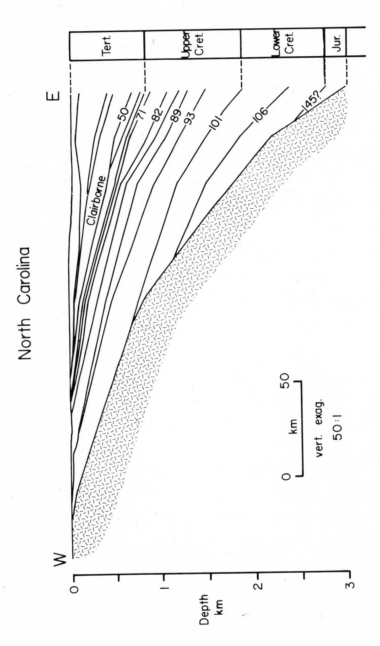

Figure 21. Observed stratigraphy of the U.S. Atlantic coastal plain based on a compilation of data in North Carolina by Sleep and Snell (1976). The vertical exaggeration is similar to Fig. 20. Note the progressive onlap of Lower Cretaceous and Early Upper Cretaceous strata onto continental basement. The Tertiary and Late Upper Cretaceous strata appear regressive but individual formations, such as the Claiborne are transgressive (see text for explanation).

rigidity that increases with time produces onlap of sediments in the region of the coastal plain. Vail et al. (1977), in contrast, interprets coastal onlap as due to changes in sea-level through time (Fig. 22). The results in Fig. 20 therefore suggest that the sea-level changes inferred by Vail et al. (1977) may have a tectonic rather than a eustatic control. This possibility, of course, may only apply to the long-term (20 to 100 m.y.) changes of sea-level, referred to by Vail et al. (1977) as supercycles. The apparent widespread distribution of these supercycles may be due, in part, to tectonic synchroneity rather than to eustasy. The cause of the short-term (<1 m.y.) changes of sea-level of Vail et al (1977), in contrast, are unlikely to be due to flexure and must be caused by other factors.

We have not included in the simple model in Fig. 18 the effects of the lateral conduction of heat or in Fig. 18 a flexural strength of the basement that varies across a margin. The model assumes only vertical conduction of heat and a constant value of elastic thickness across the margin. Since it is important to establish the amount of extension or stretching at a margin these effects should be included.

When a continent rifts, a mid-ocean ridge is created as a culmination of the rifting process so that a margin is extensively heated during rifting. The heat will flow out of the margin into cooler surroundings both vertically into the upper parts of the crust and laterally into the continental crust. Zielinski (1980), Steckler and Watts (1980) and Steckler (1981) have modelled the effects of both lateral and vertical flow of heat at a margin. These studies show that the margin subsides more rapidly since heat can escape both vertically and horizontally. The lateral flow of heat does not cool the lithosphere any faster since heat also flows from out of the margin into the continent which will expand and cause uplift. The effects are largest soon after initial rifting when the greatest temperature contrasts exists across a margin. Zielinski (1980) included the effects of lateral heat flow in a time-dependent thermal model whereas Steckler and Watts (1980) and Steckler (1981) included the effects by modifying the stretching model of McKenzie (1978).

The calculation of the effects of lateral heat flow in the stretching model requires a knowledge of how β varies across a margin. Fig. 23 shows a possible model for the variation of β across the margin off New Jersey. The

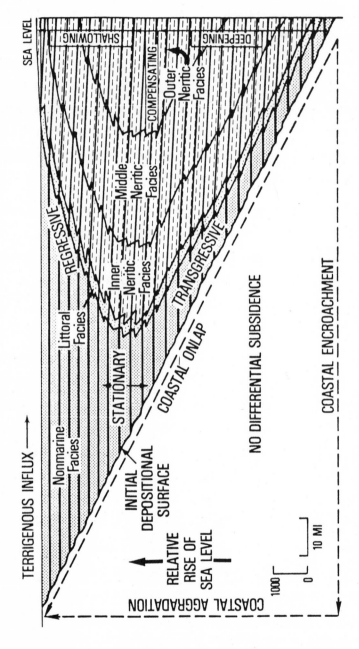

Figure 22. Schematic diagram of coastal onlap based on Vail et al. (1977). The vertical component of coastal onlap, the "coastal aggradation" was used by Vail et al. (1977) to estimate the relative rise in sea level. Note that the vertical exaggeration is similar to Figs. 21 and 20.

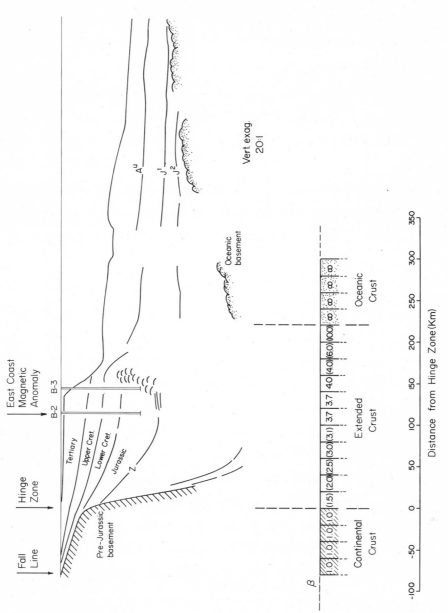

Figure 23. Simple model for the variation of the amount of extension β across the margin off New Jersey. The continental crust landward of the hinge zone is assumed to have undergone no extension (β = 1) while the oceanic crust is assumed to have undergone infinite extension (β = ∞). The estimates of β between the continental and oceanic crust are poorly constrained at present, except in the vicinity of the COST B-2 and B-3 wells (Fig. 17).

values of β assumed at the COST B-2 and B-3 wells are based on the backstripping calculations of Fig. 17. The region of continental crust landward of the hinge zone was assumed to have undergone no extension (β = 1)* while the oceanic crust was assumed to have undergone complete extension (β = ∞). The values of β in intermediate regions are not known but have been interpolated based on the backstripping calculations and the inferred extent of continental and oceanic crust at the margin.

The effect of lateral heat flow is to cause a <u>thermal bulge</u> across a broad region of the margin, landward of the hinge zone. Fig. 24 shows the uplift for different times following rifting. The maximum uplift is about 500 meters and occurs about 16 m.y. after rifting. By about 64 m.y. the amplitude of the uplift is significantly reduced. Thus lateral heat flow affects could modify the stratigraphy of the margin soon after rifting. In particular, lateral heat flow could produce uplift and erosional surfaces in coastal plain regions.

The thermal model in Fig. 23 suggests the flexural strength of the lithosphere will vary as both a function of time and position across a margin. Studies of the flexure of oceanic lithosphere caused by surface loads, such as oceanic islands and seamounts, show that the elastic thickness T_e corresponds closely to the depth of the 450°C oceanic isotherm. Thus T_e is a function of the temperature gradient in the lithosphere. The thermal model in Fig. 23 has been used to compute the depth to the 450°C isotherm across the margin as a function of time. The results are shown in Fig. 25. This figure shows that the flexural strength increases from a relatively weak plate seaward of the hinge zone to a relatively rigid plate landward of the hinge zone. The largest variations (up top 35 km) occur early in margin evolution but they decrease with time as the margin cools and becomes more rigid.

The effect of the variation in flexural strength across a margin is to cause a <u>flexural bulge</u> that migrates over a broad region of the margin, landward of the hinge zone. The width of the coastal plain region in Fig. 20

*The existance of Late Triassic to Early Jurassic rift grabens landward of the hinge zone (see earlier sections) suggest this assumption is not strictly true. However, the relative roles of strike-slip faulting, compression and extension in the formation of these grabens is not understood at present.

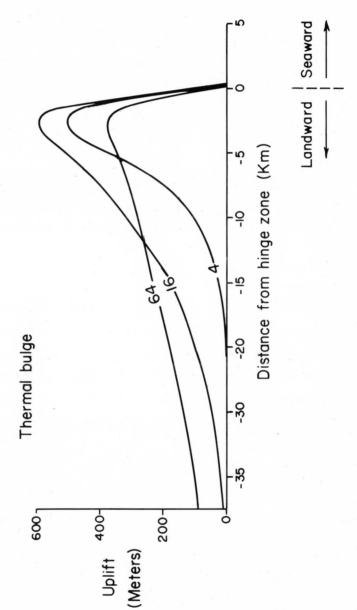

Figure 24. Uplift of the margin due to effects of lateral heat flow. The calculations are based on the thermal model in Fig. 23 for different times after rifting.

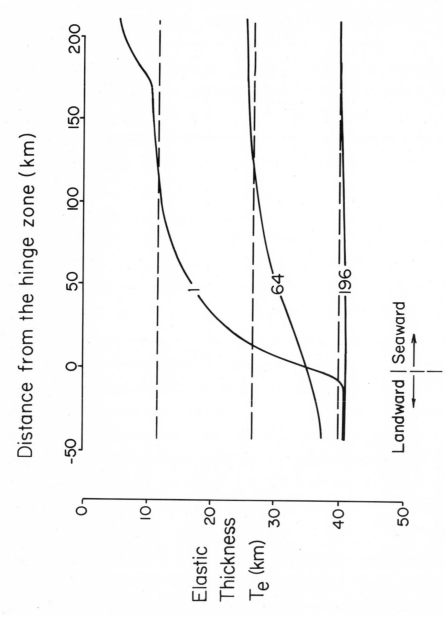

Figure 25. Variation in effective elastic thickness T_e across the margin off New Jersey as a function of time and position. The calculations assume the stretching model for the margin in Fig. 23 and a value of T_e given by the depth to the 450°C isotherm (Fig. 11). The dashed lines indicate the values of T_e assumed in the simple calculations in Figs. 18 and 20. Note the largest variations in T_e occur early in margin evolution. After about 64 m.y. T_e does not vary by more than 10 km across the margin.

therefore increases as the flexural bulge migrates landward although the pattern of onlap of younger sediments onto the basement (Fig. 20) is not significantly altered since T_e still increases with age since rifting.

The effects of lateral heat conduction and variations in flexural strength will not act separately but will interact with each other during the evolution of the margin (Steckler, 1981). Lateral heat conduction causes a thermal bulge of a few hundred meters landward of the hinge zone but the flexural bulge migrates landward of the hinge zone, due to the increase in flexural strength of the basement. Therefore as sediments load the margin the thermal bulge is gradually overcome by flexure, as the flexural depression* migrates inland.

The effects of lateral heat conduction and variations in flexural strength are small at the COST B-2 well. Fig. 26 shows that these effects do not contribute significantly to either the subsidence or heat flow at the well. We can therefore use the heat flow to predict the thermal history of sediments in the vicinity of the well.

A number of studies have previously used the tectonic subsidence at a margin to estimate the heat flow and palaeotemperatures in the sediments (Keen, 1979; Royden et al.,1980; Royden and Keen, 1980; Angevine and Turcotte, 1981). Thermal models predict that as the margin subsides and cools, heat is lost vertically from the basement through the sediments to the sea-floor. Palaeotemperatures in the sediments can be calculated from the heat flow as a function of time provided assumptions are made for the temperature of the sediment surface and the thermal properties of basement rocks and sediments as a function of time.

The thermal gradient in the sediments is a particularly important quantity to estimate since it is widely believed to be one of the major factors that controls the generation of mature hydrocarbons. Margins are characterized by relatively high thermal gradients soon after rifting, which decrease with time as the margin cools. For example, Figure 26 illustrates the temperature gradient in the sediments in the vicinity of the COST B-2 well based on the stretching model with β = 3.6. The highest temperatures (>350°C)

---

*The flexural depression refers to the region in front of (seaward) of the flexural bulge.

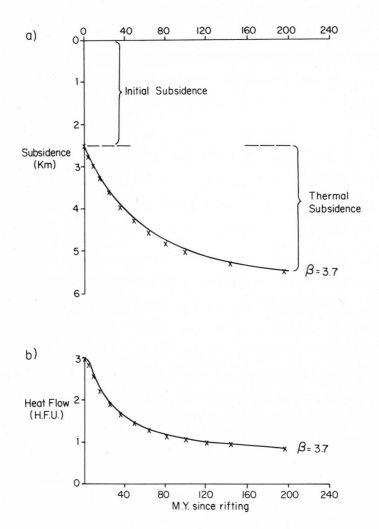

Figure 26. Comparison of calculated curves of subsidence and heat flow based on a) simple stretching model of McKenzie (1978) (solid curves) and b) modified stretching model of Fig. 23 (crosses) at the COST B-2 well. The close agreement between these models suggest the effects of lateral heat flow only slightly modify the subsidence and heat flow at the COST B-2 well.

are reached early in margin evolution. Pusey (1973) has discussed the generation of <u>petroleum</u> in terms of a <u>liquid window concept</u> in which a progression occurs from gas to oil as the temperature increases. Empirical studies of some of the world's largest oil producing basins suggest the liquid or oil phase occurs between 75 to 150°C at depths between about 1 and 5 km, depending on the thermal gradient. The dashed lines in Fig. 26 illustrate the time-depth history of sediments in the vicinity of the well that were subject to temperatures in the range 100 to 150°C. Thus, according to the liquid window concept of Pusey (1973), sediments that formed within a few m.y. after rifting were subject to temperatures too high for the generation of oil while sediments formed 40 m.y. after rifting (Late Jurassic to Recent) were subject to too low temperatures. Sediments formed a few m.y. to 40 m.y. after rifting (Early Jurassic) appear to have been subject to the most suitable temperatures for generation of oil, although they are now buried at depths of 4.5 to 6.5 km beneath the COST B-2 well.

The factors required for the generation of liquid oil are complex and a number of different methods of estimating the optimal conditions for oil production have been suggested. For example, Tissot and Welte (1978) proposed that the rate of production of petroleum from <u>Kerogen</u>* can be described by the mass fraction of the i-th Kerogen X_i, its activation energy E_i, its pre-exponential term A_i, and the ambient temperature. Angevine and Turcotte (1981) used values of X_i, E_i and A_i tabulated by Tissot and Welte (1978) to estimate the potential for generation of petroleum as a function of depth in the vicinity of the COST B-2 well. They showed that a depth of 4.5 km represented the optimal depth for petroleum generation. Lopatin (1971) and Wapples (1980), on the other hand, have proposed the use of a <u>time temperature index</u> (TTI). Experimental studies have shown that the reaction rate for thermal alteration of organic sediments doubles for each 10°C increase in the temperature. Based on these studies a parameter C has been defined which increases as the degree of thermal alteration of organic material increases. Comparisons of the parameter C to other estimates of the thermal alteration suggests that oil generation begins at $C \cong 10$ and is essentially complete at $C \cong 16$. Figure 27 shows that C = 10 closely follows the 100°C isotherm suggesting optimal

*Kerogen is an insoluble polymer resulting from the chemical breakdown of organic material.

conditions for oil generation at depths $\tilde{>}$ 4 km in the vicinity of the COST B-2 well.

There are, unfortunately, few tests that can be made of the validity of the paleotemperatures estimated in Fig. 27. Temperatures measured in the COST B-2 well, as well as heat flow measurements in the shelf, only constrain the present day thermal gradient. One possibility is the use of the vitrinite reflectance R_o which can be measured in the laboratory. The vitrinite reflectance is known to depend on the maximum temperature reached as well as the length of time sediments are heated. Peak oil generation is thought to occur at R_o = 0.07%. Angevine and Turcotte (1981), for example, have shown that the vitrinite reflectance reaches this value at a depth 3.7 km in the COST B-2 well, in general agreement with other indicators of the optimal depth for oil generation (Fig. 27).

We have not considered in these discussions any effects the sediments themselves may have on the tectonic subsidence at a continental margin. In particular, there may be a feedback following the sedimentation that modifies the thermal and density structure of the margin. We have assumed in "backstripping" sediment and water loads through geologic time that there is no irreversible modification of the margin due to loading. There are two effects which may significantly alter the tectonic subsidence. First, the addition of sediments through time causes a thermal blanketing that slows the loss of heat from the cooling basement. Langseth et al. (1980) have shown that thermal blanketing has significantly modified measured heat flow values in the Bering Sea basins. Model calculations, however, show that these affects are most significant for rapid sedimentation rates and small sediment loading times. Second, the addition of sediments on the basement modifies the pressure/temperature conditions in the crust which may cause an increase in crustal density due to phase changes (Falvey, 1974; Middleton, 1980). There is presently too little data to satisfactorily test the effects of phase changes at a margin. The actual extent of metamorphism depends on a number of factors including crustal rock types and these probably vary substantially between margins.

Crustal Structure

The thermal and mechanical models discussed in the last section have

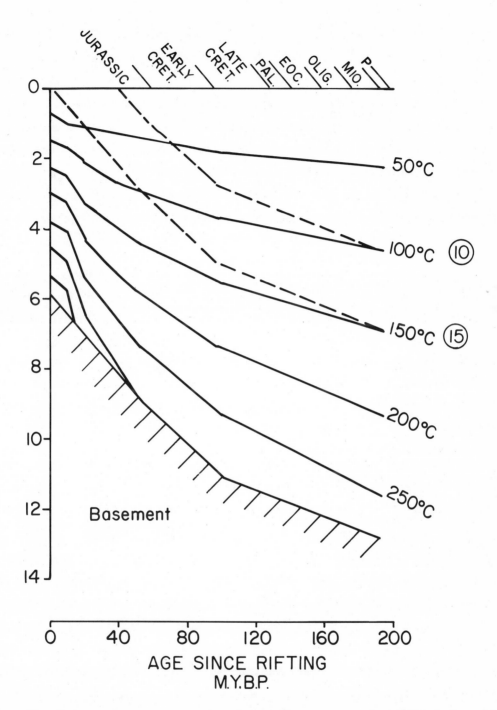

Figure 27. Palaeotemperatures in the sediments at the COST B-2 well as a function of time since rifting. The temperatures are based on a simple stretching model with β = 3.7. The dashed lines trace the history of those sediments, estimated to have experienced temperatures in the range 100 to 150°C. These sediments are of Early Jurassic age in the region of the COST B-2 well. The circled numbers indicate the approximate values of the time-temperature index parameter C.

implications for the crustal structure of the margin. For example, in order to explain the <u>total</u> tectonic subsidence (initial + thermal subsidence) at the COST B-2 well (Fig. 17) a substantial amount of thinning must have occurred at the margin. The total tectonic subsidence at the well is 5.3 km (Fig. 17) which, according to an Airy isostatic model, corresponds to a crustal thinning of more than 20 km at the margin. We do not know, however, whether oceanic crust or thinned/stretched continental crust or some form of "transitional crust" underlies the well. Clearly, further constraints on the crustal structure of the margin are required such as gravity and seismic refraction data.

The first gravity studies of the margin off New Jersey (Worzel, 1965) suggested that, compared to the margin off New England to the north and Carolina to the south, a substantial amount of crustal thinning has occurred beneath the shelf off New Jersey. Worzel (1965) suggested the crust thins from a thickness of about 30 to 35 km in the region of the New Jersey shoreline to a thickness of about 14 km beneath the outer part of the shelf. The width of the "transitional crust" was estimated by Worzel (1965) to extend over a distance of about 100 km.

Unfortunately, there is little seismic refraction data that constrains the crustal structure inferred from gravity studies. Fig. 28 summarizes the available seismic refraction measurements across the margin off New Jersey. The crustal thickness for the U.S. coastal plain is based on the regional study by Pakiser and Steinhard (1968) using a number of long-range seismic refraction measurements. The only seismic refraction measurements that may have reached <u>Moho</u> off New Jersey are those by Ewing and Ewing (1959), beneath the slope off Cape May and Sheridan et al. (1979) beneath the slope near the COST B-2 well (Fig. 5a). There is no deep seismic refraction data available at present which satisfactorily constrains the nature of the crust between the New Jersey shoreline and the continental slope.

We summarize in Fig. 29 a crustal model for the margin off New Jersey which is consistent with present knowledge of seismic refraction, gravity, geoid, and well data. This model, differs from the previous model of Worzel (1965) in that the transition occurs over a smaller distance, but is similar to recent models by Watts and Steckler (1979) and Hutchinson and Grow (personal comm.). The crustal model suggests that the greatest change in

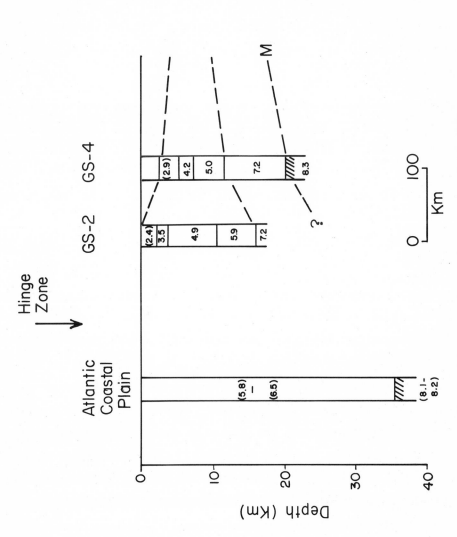

Figure 28. Summary crustal structure of the margin off New Jersey. The Atlantic coastal plain section is based on Pakiser and Steinhard (1968) and GS-2 and GS-4 on the continental shelf are based on Sheridan et al. (1979),

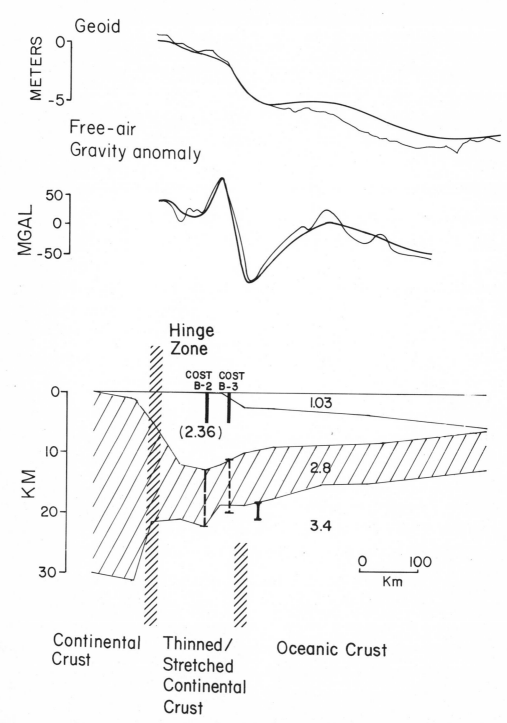

Figure 29. Computed gravity and geoid effect of a simple model for the crustal structure off New Jersey compared to observed free-air gravity anomaly and GEOS-3 satellite altimeter data (Watts and Steckler, 1979). The dashed lines indicate the estimate of crustal thickness at the COST wells, based on the thermal models in Fig. 17. The density in brackets is an average value for the sediments and the computations are based on a density that increases with depth.

crustal thickness at the margin occurs in the vicinity of the hinge zone. The hinge zone therefore represents the major thermal and mechanical boundary at the margin. The sediments at the margin off New Jersey have apparently prograded at least 150 km seaward of the hinge zone. The present day shelf break does not, therefore, appear to correspond to a major crustal boundary and is probably a consequence of sedimentary processes at the margin such as sediment supply and near bottom processes.

Summary and Conclusions

This review has shown that our knowledge of the U.S. Atlantic continental margin has increased rapidly during the past decade. There have been two main reasons for this. First, technological advances based on seismic reflection profiling techniques and the dynamic positioning of drilling ships at sea have led to an improved understanding of the shallow structure of the margin. Second, model studies based on better constraints of the thermal and mechanical properties of the Earth's lithospheric plates have increased our understanding of the origin and evolution of the margin.

We have shown in this study that a number of sedimentary and tectonic factors have contributed to the post-rift subsidence history of the U.S. Atlantic continental margin. The most important factors are thermal contraction of the lithosphere and sedimentary loading. Most studies now consider that thermal contraction is caused by heating and thinning of the margin at the time of rifting, although the actual form of the heating is still not clear. The effects of thermal contraction are greatly amplified by sedimentary loading on a lithosphere that increases its flexural strength with age. Sedimentary loading is now believed to be an important factor controlling the development of a hinge zone, outer stratigraphic highs and coastal plain sequences in which younger sediments progressively onlap older basement rocks. The stratigraphy of the coastal plain is modified by thermal and flexural bulges during margin evolution. Other factors affecting the subsidence history of the margin are compaction, sea-level changes and paleobathymetry, although these effects are generally small compared to the effects of thermal contraction and sedimentary loading.

These concepts for the origin and evolution of the U.S. Atlantic contin-ental margin have important implications for the understanding of the development of continental margins in the geological record. The hinge zone, which is the major thermal and mechanical boundary at a margin separating relatively unstretched continental crust from extensively thinned and heated crust, should be recognizable in stratigraphic reconstructions of ancient margins. For example, Stewart and Poole (1974) have recognized a hinge "line" in reconstructions of the Cambrian-Devonian central Great Basin of Nevada. The sediments that formed "seaward" of the hinge probably formed on thinned, heated crust and may therefore be of interest to the petroleum industry. Furthermore, the subsidence history of these sediments may provide information on the thermal properties of the lithosphere in Paleozoic times. The hinge zone may also be important in the subsequent deformation of an ancient margin. For example, depending on the thickness, width and porosity of the sedimentary wedge in front of it the hinge zone may act as a "ramp" during deformation. The shape of the sedimentary wedge varies significantly along strike of the U.S. Atlantic margin suggesting that significant along strike variations may occur in the resulting deformed zone. The progressive onlap of younger sediments onto basement rocks in coastal plain regions should also be recognizable in the geological record. For example, Kay (1947) has recognized progressive onlap of Cambrian to Ordovician sediments onto the Precambrian margin of the North American craton. This onlap may be due to sediment loading of a basement that increases its flexural strength with age. Thus studies of the subsidence history of these sediments may also provide information on the mechanical properties of the lithosphere in Paleozoic times.

Future work at the U.S. Atlantic continental margin should emphasize both field and laboratory geological and geophysical studies. Field studies should be oriented at obtaining better observational constraints on the extent of crustal thinning that has occurred at the margin. Multichannel seismic reflection profiling, using long seismic arrays and repetitive high energy sound sources, should be used to determine the deep structure in critical areas of the margin, such as between the hinge zone and shelf break off New Jersey. Deep drilling should be carried out in the region of the hinge zone since the progressive onlap of sediments due to flexure makes an excellent stratigraphic trap for migrating fluids from the deeper parts of the basin and, better constraints are needed on the tectonic subsidence of the margin in the region of the hinge zone. Laboratory studies should be aimed at using biostratigraphic data from deep wells and interval velocity data from multichannel seismic reflection profiles to estimate how the stretching factor β varies across the margin. These field studies, in conjunction with the development of more refined thermal and mechanical models, offer the most promise of determining the origin and evolution of the U.S. continental margin during the next decade.

Acknowledgments

This paper is the outcome of many fruitful discussions with my colleagues at Lamont-Doherty Geological Observatory. I would particularly like to thank J. Bodine, J. Cochran, W. Haxby, G. Karner, M. Steckler, and J. Thorne. The multichannel seismic reflection profiles in Fig. 6 and 19 were processed by M. Truchan and P. Stoffa. Technical help in preparing the manuscript was provided by G. Grace, J. Hastings, L. Hurban and P. Roach. The manuscript has been critically reviewed by A. Bally, G. Karner and C. Schreiber. Many of the ideas in this paper originated following the New York State Geological Association meeting on "Rift basins on trailing Atlantic margins" held at Rutgers University, Newark, New Jersey on October 10-12th, 1980. This work has been supported at Lamont-Doherty Geological Observatory by National Science Foundation grant OCE 79-26308 and Office of Naval Research contract N0000-14-80-C-0098, Scope I.

REFERENCES

Amato, R.V. and J.W. Bebout, 1978. Geographical and operational summary COST No. GE-1 well, Southeast Georgia embayment area, South Atlantic OCS, U.S.G.S. Open File Report 78-668, 122pp.

Angevine, C.L. and D.L. Turcotte, 1981. Thermal subsidence and compaction in sedimentary basins: Application to Baltimore Canyon Trough, Amer. Assoc. Petr. Geol. Bull. 65, 219-225.

Artemjev, M.E. and E.V. Artyushkov, 1971. Structure and isostasy of the Baikal rift and the mechanism of rifting, J. Geophys. Res., 76, 1197-1211.

Austin, J.A., E. Uchupi, D.R. Shaugnessy, and R.D. Ballard, 1980. Geology of New England Passive margin, Am. Assoc. Pet. Geol. Bull., 64, 501-526.

Biju-Duval, B., J. Letourzey, L. Montadert, P. Courrier, J.F. Mugniot, and J. Sancho, 1974. Geology of the Mediterranean Sea Basins, in C.A. Burk and C.L. Drake, (Eds.), The Geology of continental margins, Springer Verlag, New York, 695-721.

Boeuf, M.G., and H. Doust, 1975. Structure and development of the southern margin of Australia. Aust. Pet. Expl. Assoc. J., 15, 33-34.

Bond, G., 1978. Speculations on real sea-level changes and vertical motions of continents at selected times in the Cretaceous and Tertiary periods, Geology, 6, 247-250.

Bott, M.H.P., 1973. Shelf subsidence in relation to the Evolution of Young Continental Margins, in Implications of Continental drift to the Sciences. 2, Editors, Tarling, D.M. and Runcorn, S.K., Academic Press.

Brown, P.M., J.A. Miller and F.M. Swain, 1972. Structural and stratigraphic framework and spatial distribution of permeability of the Atlantic coastal plain, North Carolina to New York, Geological Survey Prof. Paper 796, U.S. Govt. Printing Office, Washington, D.C.

Buffler, R.T., J.S. Watkins and W.P. Dillon, 1979. Geology of the offshore southeast Georgia embayment, U.S. Atlantic continental margin, based on multichannel seismic reflection profiles, in J.S. Watkins, L. Montadert, P.W. Dickerson (Eds.), Geological and Geophysical Investigations of Continental Margins, Amer. Assoc. Petr. Geol. Bull. Memoir 29, 11-16.

Caldwell, J.C., 1978. The mechanical behavior of the ocean lithosphere near subduction zones, Ph.D Thesis, Cornell University.

Cande, S., J. Mutter, and J.K. Weissel, 1981. A revised model for the break-up of Australia and Antarctica, EOS (Abstract), 62,384.

Cande, S. and J. Mutter, A revised identification of the oldest sea floor spreading anomalies between Australia and Antarctica, in preparation.

Christie, P.A.F. and J.C. Sclater, 1980. An extensional origin for the Buchan and Witchground Graben in the North Sea, Nature, 283, 729-732.

Cochran, J.R., 1973. Gravity and magnetic investigations in the Guiana Basin, western Equatorial Atlantic, Geol. Soc. Am. Bull., 84, 3244-3268.

Cochran, J.R., 1980. Some remarks on Isostasy and the long-term behavior of the continental lithosphere, Earth Planet. Sci. Lett., 46, 266-274.

Cochran, J.R., 1981. Simple models of diffuse extension and the pre-seafloor spreading development of the continental margin of the northeastern Gulf of Aden, Oceanologica Acta, in press.

Colquhoun, D.J. and J.S. Johnson, Jr. 1968. Tertiary sea-level fluctuation in South Carolina, Palaeogeog., Palaeoclimatol, Palaeocol., 5, 105-126.

de Charpal, D., P. Guennoc, L. Montadert, D.G. Roberts, 1978. Rifting, crustal attenuation, and subsidence in the Bay of Biscay, Nature, 275, 706-711.

Dietz, R.W.,1963. Collapsing continental rises: An actualistic concept of Geosynclines and mountain building, Jour. of Geology, v. 71, p. 314-333.

Dillon, W.P., C.K. Paull, R.T. Buffler, and J-P Fail, 1979. Structure and development of the southeast Georgia embayment and northern Blake Plateau: Preliminary analysis, in J.S. Watkins, L. Montadert and P.W. Dickerson, (Eds.), Geological and geophysical investigations of continental margins, Amer. Assoc. Petr. Geol. Bull., Memoir 29, 27-42.

Drake, C.L., M. Ewing and G.H. Sutton, 1959. Continental margins and geosynclines: The east coast of North America north of Cape Hatteras, Phys. and Chem. of the Earth, 3, p. 110-198.

Emery, K.O., E. Uchupi, J.D. Phillips, C.O. Bowin, E.T. Bunce and S.T. Knott, 1970. Continental rise off eastern North America, Amer. Assoc. Petr. Geol. Bull., 54, 44-108.

Ewing, J. and M. Ewing, 1959. Seismic-refraction measurements in the Atlantic Ocean basins, in the Mediterranean Sea, on the Mid-Atlantic Ridge, and in the Norwegian Sea, Bull. Geol. Soc. America, 70, 291-318.

Falvey, D.A., 1974. The development of continental margins in plate tectonic theory, J. Aust. Pet. Expl. Assoc., 14, 95-106.

Falvey, D.A. and M.F. Middleton, 1981. Passive continental margins: Evidence for a prebreakup deep crustal metamorphic subsidence mechanism, Oceanologica Acta, in press.

Falvey, D.A. and J.C. Mutter, 1981. Regional plate tectonics and evolution of Australia's passive continental margin, BMR J. of Austr. Geol. and Geophys., 6, 1-29.

Foucher, J.P. and X. Le Pichon, 1972. Comments on "Thermal effects of the formation of Atlantic continental magins by continental breakup" by N.H. Sleep, Geophys. J. R. astr. Soc., 29, 43-46.

Given, M.M., 1977. Mesozoic and early Cenozoic geology, Bull. Can. Petr. Geol., 25, 63-91.

Goetze, C. and B. Evans, 1979. Stress and temperature in the bending lithosphere as constrained by experimental rock mechanics, Geophys. J. R. astr. Soc., 59, 463-478.

Gradstein, F.M., G.L. Williams, W.A.M. Jenkins, and P. Ascoli, 1975. Mesozoic and Cenozoic stratigraphy of the American continental margin, eastern Canada, in Canada's continental margin and offshore petroleum exploration, C.J. Yorath, E.R. Parker, and D.J. Glass (Eds.), Can. Soc. Petr. Geol. Memoir 4, 103-130.

Grow, J.A., 1980. Deep structure and evolution of the Baltimore Canyon trough in the vicinity of the Cost No. B-3 Well, in P.A. Scholle (Ed.), Geological Studies of the COST No. B-3 Well, U.S. Mid Atlantic Continental Slope Area, Geo. Survey Circular 833, 117-132.

Grow, J.A. and K. Klitgord, 1980. Structural framework, in Mattick, R.E. and Hennesy, J.L. (Ed.), Structural Framework, Stratigraphy, and Petroleum Geology of the Area of Oil and Gas Lease Sale No. 49 on the U.S. Atlantic Continental Shelf and Slope, Geological Survey Circular 812, 8-35.

Grow, J.A. and R.G. Markl, 1977. IPOD-USGS multichannel seismic reflection profile from Cape Hatteras to the Mid-Atlantic Ridge, Geology, 5, 625-630.

Grow, J.A., R.E. Mattick and J.S. Schlee, 1979. Multichannel seismic depth sections and interval velocities over outer continental shelf and upper slope between Cape Hatteras and Cape Cod, in Geological investigations of continental margins, J.S. Watkins, L. Montadert, and P.W. Dickerson (Eds.), Amer. Assoc. Petr. Geol. Bull., Memoir 29, 65-83.

Gunn, R., 1943. A quantitative evaluation of the influence of the lithosphere on the anomalies of gravity, J. Franklin Inst., 236, 373-396.

Haxby, W.F., D.L. Turcotte and J.M. Bird, 1976. Thermal and mechanical evolution of the Michigan basin, Tectonophysics, 36, 57-75.

Hays, J.D., and W.C. Pitman, III, 1973. Lithospheric plate motion, sea-level changes and climatic and ecological consequences: Nature, 246,18-22.

Hutchinson, D.R. and J.A. Grow, 1981. Personal communication.

Hutchinson, D.R., J.A. Grow, K.D. Klitgord and B.A. Swift, Deep structure and evolution of the Carolina Trough, Amer. Assoc. Petr. Geol. Bull. Memoir, in press.

Jansa, L.F. and J.A. Wade, 1975. Geology of the continental margin off Nova Scotia and Newfoundland, in Offshore geology of estern Canada, Geological Surv. of Canada paper 74-30, 2, 51-105.

Jarvis, J.G., and D.P. McKenzie, 1980. Sedimentary basin formation with finite extension rates. Earth Planet. Sci. Lett., 48, 42-52.

Karner, G. and A.B. Watts, 1981. On Isostasy at Atlantic-type continental margins, J. Geophys. Res, in press.

Kay, Marshall, 1947. Geosynclinal Nomenclature and the Craton, Amer. Assoc. Petroleum Geol. Bull., 31, 1289-1293.

Keen, C.E. and B.D. Loncarevic, 1966. Crustal structure on the eastern seabord of Canada: Studies of the continental margin, Can. J. Earth Sci., 3, 65-76.

Keen, C.E., 1979. Thermal history and subsidence of rifted continental margins. Evidence from wells on the Nova Scotia and Labrador shelves, Can. J. Earth Sci., 16, 505-522.

Kent, P.E., 1973. Geology and geophysics in the discovery of giant oil fields, J. Aust. Petr. Expl. Assoc., 13, 3-8.

Kent, P.E., 1976. Major synchronous events in continental shelves, Tectono-physics, 36, 87-92.

King, L., 1969. Tectonic map of North America, U.S. Geological Survey.

Kinsman, D.J.J., 1975. Rift Valley Basins and Sedimentary History of Training Continental Margins, in Petroleum and Global Tectonics, (ed.) - Alfred G. Fischer and Sheldon Judson, Princeton University Press, p. 83-126.

Klemme, H.D., 1975. Geothermal gradients, heat flow and hydrocarbon recovery, in A.G. Fisher and S. Judson (Eds.), Petroleum and Global Tectonics, Princeton University Press, 251-305, 1975.

Klitgord, K.D. and J.C. Behrendt, 1979. Basin structure of the U.S. Atlantic margin, in J.S. Watkins et al. (eds). Geological and geophysical investigations of continental margins: Amer. Ass. Petr. Geol. Memoir 29, 85-112.

Langseth, M.G., M.A. Hobart and K. Horai, 1980. Heat flow in the Bering Sea, J. Geophys. Res., 85, 3740-3750.

Le Pichon, X., J. Bonin and J. Francheteau, 1973. Plate tectonics, Elsevier, Amsterdam, 300pp.

Le Pichon, X. and J-C. Sibuet, 1981. Passive Margins: A Model of Formation, J. Geophys. Res. 86, 3708-3720.

Lopatin, N.V., 1971. Temperature and geologic time as factors in coalification (in Russian): Akad. Nauk SSSR Izv. Ser. Geol., no. 3, 95-106.

Maher, J.C. and R.R. Applin, 1971. Geologic framework and petroleum potential of Atlantic coastal plain and continental shelf, U.S. Geol. Survey Prof. Paper 659, 98pp.

Manspeizer, Warren, 1980. Rift tectonics inferred from volcanic and clastic structures, in W. Manspeizer, (Ed.), Field Studies of New Jersey Geology and Guide to Field Trips: 52nd Annual Meeting of the New York State Geological Association, 314-350.

Mattick, R.E. and K.C. Bayer, 1980. Geologic setting and hydrocarbon exploration activity, in Scholle, P.A., (Ed.), Geological Studies of the COST No. B-3 Well, U.S. Mid-Atlantic Continental Slope Area, 4-12.

Mattick, R.E. and J.L. Hennesy (Eds.), 1980. Structural framework, stratigraphy, and petroleum geology of the area of oil and gas lease sale no. 49 on the U.S. Atlantic continental shelf and slope, Geological Survey Circular 812.

Mayhew, M.A., 1974. "Basement" to East Coast continental margin of North America, American Association of Petroleum Geologists Bulletin, v. 58, 1069-1088.

McKenzie, D.P., 1978. Some remarks on the development of sedimentary basins, Earth Planet. Sci. Lett., 40, 25-32.

McKenzie, D.P. and C. Bowin, 1976. The relationship between gravity and bathymetry in the Atlantic ocean, J. Geophys. Res., 81, 1903-1915.

McNutt, M. K. and R.L. Parker, 1978. Isostasy in Australia and the Evolution of the compensation mechanism, Science 199, 773-775.

McNutt, M.K. and H.W. Menard, 1978. Lithospheric flexure and uplifted atolls, J. Geophys. Res., 83, 1206-1212.

McNutt, M.K., 1980. Implications of regional gravity for state of stress in the earth's crust and upper mantle, J. Geophys. Res., 85, 6311-6396.

Middleton, M.F., 1980. A model of intracratonic basin formation entailing deep crustal metamorphism, Geophys. J.R. Astr. Soc., 62, 1-14.

Pakiser, L.C. and J.S. Steinhard, 1968. Explosion seismology in the western hemisphere in H. Odishaw (ed.), Research in Geophysics, Vol. 2, Solid Earth and Interface Phenomena, M.I.T. Press, Cambridge, p.123-147.

Parsons, B. and J.G. Sclater, 1977. An analysis of the variation of ocean floor bathymetry and heat flow with age, J. Geophys, Res., 82, 803-827.

Pitman, W.C. III, 1978. Relationship between eustacy and stratigraphic sequences of passive margins, Geol. Soc. Amer. Bull., v. 89, 1389-1403.

Poag, C.W., 1980. Foraminiferal stratigraphy, paleoenvironments, and depositional cyches in the outer Baltimore Canyon trough, in P.A. Scholle, (Ed.) Geological study of the COST No. B-3 Well; U.S. Mid-Atlantic Continental slope area - Geological Survey Circular 833, 44-65.

Ponte, F.C. and H.E. Asmus, 1976. The Brasilian marginal basins: Current state of knowledge, Almeida, F.F.M. de Symposium on Continental Margins of Atlantic-type, Sao Paulo, Brazil.

Pusey, W.C., 1973. How to evaluate potential gas and oil source rocks, World Oil, v. 176, no. 5, 71-75.

Rabinowitz, P.D., 1974. The boundary between oceanic and continental crust in the western North Atlantic. in The Geology of continental margins, C.A. Burk and C.L. Drake, (Eds.), Springer-Verlag, New York 67-84.

Rhodehamel, E.C., 1977. Lithological descriptions, in P.A. Scholle (Ed.), Geological Studies on the COST No. B-2 Well, U.S. Mid-Atlantic Outer Continental Shelf Area - Geological Survey Circular 750, 15-22.

Royden, L. and C.E. Keen, 1980. Rifting processes and thermal evolution of the continental margin of eastern Canada determined from subsidence curves, Earth Planet. Sci. Lett., 51, 343-361.

Royden, L., J.G. Sclater, and R.P. von Herzen, 1980. Continental margin subsidence and heat flow: important parameters in formatin of petroleum hydrocarbons, Amer. Assoc. Petr. Geol. Bull., 64, 173-187.

Sawyer, D.S., A. Swift, J.G. Sclater and M.N. Toksoz, Extensional model for the subsidence of the northern United States continental margin, Geology, in press.

Schlee, J.S., 1981. Seismic stratigraphy of Baltimore Canyon Trough, Amer. Assoc. Petr. Geol. Bull., 65, 26-53.

Schlee, J., J.C. Behrendt, J.A. Grow, J.M. Robb, R.E. Mattick, P.T. Taylor and B.A. Lawson, 1976. Regional geologic framework off northeastern United States, Amer. Assoc. Petr. Geol. Bull., 60, 926-951, 1976.

Scholle, P.A., 1977. Geological studies of the COST B-2 well, U.S. Mid-Atlantic outer continental shelf, U.S. Geol. Surv. Circ. 750, 23, 1977.

Scholle, P.A., 1980. Geological studies of the COST No. B-3 well, United States Mid-Atlantic continental slope area, Geological Survey Circular 833.

Schouten, H. and K.D. Klitgord, 1977. Map showing Mesozoic magnetic anomalies; western North Atlantic, U.S. Geol. Survey Misc. Field Studies Map MF-915, scale 1:2,000,000.

Scientific Party, 1976. Deep Sea Drilling Project, Leg 11, Geotimes, 21, 23-26.

Sclater, J.G. and P.A. Christie, 1980. Continental stretching: An explanation of the post Mid-Cretaceous subsidence of the Central North Sea basin, J. Geophys. Res., 85, 3711-3739.

Sheridan, R.E., 1976. Sedimentary basins of the Atlantic margin of North America, Tectonophysics, 36, 113-132.

Sheridan, R.E., J.A. Grow, J.C. Behrendt, and K.C. Bayer, 1979. Seismic refraction study of the continental edge off the Eastern United States, Tectonophysics, 59, 1-26.

Sleep, N.H., 1971. Thermal effects of the formation of Atlantic continental margins by continental break up, Geophys. J. Roy. Astr. Soc., v. 24, p. 325-350.

Sleep, N.H., 1976. Platform subsidence mechanisms and eustatic sea-level changes: Tectonophysics, 36, 45-56.

Sleep, N.H. and N.S. Snell, 1976. Thermal contraction and flexure of mid-continent and Atlantic marginal basins, Geophys. J. R. Astr. Soc., 45, 125-154.

Smith, M.A., R.V. Amato, M.A. Furbush, D.M. Pert, M.E. Nelson, J.S. Hendrix, L.C. Tamm, G. Wood, Jr., and D.R. Shaw, 1976. Geological and operational summary, COST no. B-2 well, Baltimore Canyon Trough area, Mid-Atlantic outer continental shelf (OBS), U.S. Geol. Surv., open-file rept. 76-744, 79pp.

Spohn, T. and H.J. Neugebauer, 1978. Metastable phase transition models and their bearing on the development of Atlantic-type geosynclines, Tectonophysics, 50, 387-412.

Steckler, M.S., 1981. The thermal and mechanical evolution of Atlantic-type continental margins, Ph.D. Thesis, Columbia University, in press.

Steckler, M.S. and A.B. Watts, 1978. Subsidence of the Atlantic-type continental margin off New York. Earth Planet. Sci. Lett., 41, 1-13.

Steckler, M.S. and A.B. Watts, 1980. The Gulf of Lion: Subsidence of a Young Continental Margin, Nature 287, 425-429.

Stewart, J.H. and F.G. Poole, 1974. Lower Paleozoic and uppermost Precambrian cordilleran miogeocline, great basin, western United States, in W.R. Dickinson (ed), Tectonics and Sedimentation, Soc. of Econ. Paleon. and Min. Special Publ. No. 22, 28-57.

Taylor, P.T., I. Zietz, and L.S. Dennis, 1968. Geologic implications of aeromagnetic data for the eastern continental margin of the United States, Geophysics, 33,755-780.

Tissot, B. and D. Welte, 1978. Petroleum formation and occurrence, Springer Verlag, New York, 538pp.

Turcotte, D.L., J.L. Ahern and J.M. Bird, 1977. The state of stress at continental margins, Tectonophysics, 42, 1-28.

Vail, P.R., R.M. Mitchum and S. Thompson, 1977. Seismic stratigraphy and global changes of sea-level, Part 4: Global cycles of relative changes of sea-level, Am. Assoc. Pet. Geol. Bull., Memoir 26, 83-97.

Valentine, P.C., 1980. Calcareous nonnofossil biostratigraphy, paleoenvironments, and post-Jurassic continental margin development, in P.A. Scholle (ed.), Geological studies of the COST No. B-3 wells, U.S. Mid-Atlantic continental slope area, Geological Survey Circular 833, 67-85.

Van Houten, F.B., 1977. Triassic-Liassic deposits of Morocco and eastern North America: Comparison, Bull. Amer. Assoc. Petr. Geol., 61, 79-99.

Veevers, J.J., D.A. Falvey, L.V. Hawkins, and W.J. Ludwig, 1974. Seismic refraction measurements of northwest Australian margin and adjacent deeps, Amer. Assoc. Petr. Geol. Bull., 58,1731-1750.

Walcott, R.I., 1970. Flexural rigidity, thickness, and viscosity of the lithosphere, J. Geophys. Res., 75,3941-3954.

Walcott, R.I., 1972. Gravity, flexure, and the growth of sedimentary basins at a continental edge, Geol Soc. Am. Bull., 83, 1845-1848.

Waples, D.W., 1980. Time and temperature in petroleum formation: Application of Lopatin's method to petroleum exploration, Amer. Assoc. Petr. Geol., Bull. 64, 916-926.

Watts, A.B., 1978. An analysis of isostasy in the world's oceans, 1. Hawaiian-Emperor seamount chain, J. Geophys. Res., 83, 5989-6004.

Watts, A.B., J.H. Bodine and N.M. Ribe, 1980. Observations of flexure and the geological evolution of the Pacific ocean basin, Nature, 283, 532-537.

Watts, A.B. and J.R. Cochran, 1974. Gravity anomalies and flexure of the lithosphere along the Hawaiian-Emperor seamount chain, Geophys. J. R. astr. Soc., 38, 119-141.

Watts, A.B., J.R.Cochran and G. Selzer, 1975. Gravity anomalies and flexure of the lithosphere: A three-dimensional study of the Great Meteor Seamount, Northeast Atlantic, J. Geophys. Res., 80, 1391-1398.

Watts, A.B. and W.B.F. Ryan, 1976. Flexure of the lithosphere and continental margin basins, Tectonophysics, 36, 24-44.

Watts, A.B. and M.S. Steckler, 1979. Subsidence and eustasy at the continental margin of eastern North America, Maurice Ewing Symp. Series 3, Washington, D.C., 218-234.

Watts, A.B. and M.S. Steckler, 1981. Subsidence and tectonics of Atlantic-type continental margins, Oceanologica Acta, in press.

Williams, G.L., 1975. Dinoflagellate and spore stratigraphy of the Mesozoic-Cenozoic, offshore eastern Canada, in Offshore geology of Eastern Canada, Geological Survey of Canada paper 74-30, 107-161.

Wise, D.U., 1974. Continental margins, freeboard and the volumes of continents and oceans through time, in C.A. Burke and C.L. Drake (eds.), The geology of continental margins, 45-58.

Woods, R., 1981. The subsidence history of Conoco well 15/30-1, Central North Sea, Submitted to Earth Planet. Sci. Lett.

Worzel, J. L., 1965. Deep structure of coastal margins and mid-oceanic ridges, Seventeenth Symp. Colston Res. Soc., Univ. Bristol, Colston papers, 17, 335-361.

Wu, C.H. and R.R. Nichols, 1980. Computer well log analysis, in P.A. Scholle (ed.), Geological studies of the COST No. B-3 well, U.S. Mid-Atlantic continental slope area, 26-43.

Zielinski, G.W., 1977. Thermal history of the Norwegian-Greenland Sea and its rifted continental margin, Ph.D. Thesis, Columbia University, 169p.

Lecture Notes
for
American Association of Petroleum Geologists "Short Course"
Atlantic City, New Jersey – 4 October 1981

Structure of the Atlantic Margin of the United States
by
John A. Grow
U.S. Geological Survey
Woods Hole, Mass., 02543

Abstract

Continental rifting and crustal thinning took place between North America and Africa during the Triassic and Early Jurassic, and sea floor spreading began in the Early to Middle Jurassic. Very rapid and variable subsidence along the continental margin off the eastern United States during the Jurassic was controlled by transverse fracture zones, which segmented the margin into four major sedimentary basins -- the Georges Bank Basin, the Baltimore Canyon Trough, the Carolina Trough and the Blake Plateau Basin. Upper Triassic to Lower Jurassic evaporite deposits (including salt) have been drilled in Georges Bank Basin, and linear chains of salt (?) diapirs have been found along the East Coast Magnetic Anomaly in the Carolina and Baltimore Canyon Troughs. The maximum thicknesses of undeformed postrift sedimentary units in these basins are 7,13,11, and 12 km, respectively. The thickness of deformed synrift sedimentary units (sediments deposited during active rifting) within faulted Triassic grabens beneath these basins probably exceeds 5 km in some places. Gravity models across the three northern basins indicate that 8 to 15 km of transitional crust underlie the basins. The transitional crust probably was formed by extension and thinning of the pre-existing continental crust. Thicker transitional crust (15 to 25 km) that underlies the 350-km-wide Blake Plateau Basin may include mixed continental fragments and extensive volcanics. An eastward jump of the spreading center from beneath the western Blake Plateau to the Blake Escarpment 10 to 15 m.y. after initial continental separation appears to have caused this anomalously wide basin. (Abstract from Grow and Sheridan, 1981).

INTRODUCTION

The earliest marine geophysical measurements along the U.S. Atlantic continental margin were marine refraction studies (e.g. Ewing et al, 1950; Drake et al, 1959; Hersey et al, 1959; Sheridan et al, 1966) and pendulum gravity measurements made from submarines (e.g. Worzel and Shurbet, 1955). The refraction studies observed that high velocity rocks ($V_p \gtrsim 4.5$ km/sec), which were inferred to be "basement", were 3 to 5 km deep beneath the middle shelf, 2 to 3 km deep beneath the outer shelf and slope, and 7 to 8 km deep beneath the upper continental rise. The high velocity ridge was interpreted as a Paleozoic volcanic arc which separated a miogeosynclinal basin beneath the shelf from a eugeosynclinal basin beneath the continental rise (Drake et al, 1959). Two dimensional gravity models by Worzel and Shubert (1955) showed that the crust changed from continental (more than 30 km in thickness) to oceanic (5 to 10 km in thickness) over a 100 to 200 km wide transition zone.

Single-channel seismic reflection, marine magnetic, aeromagnetic, and continuous surface ship gravity measurements became available during the 1960's (e.g. Ewing et al, 1966; Taylor et al, 1968; Emery et a,. 1970). When these techniques were applied to the entire North Atlantic Ocean, the evidence indicated that Africa and North American separated during the Triassic or Early Jurassic, and that the ocean basin formed by sea floor spreading during Jurassic to present time (Heirtzler et al, 1968; Emery et al, 1970; Emery and Uchupi, 1972; Pitman and Talwani, 1972). Keen (1969) suggested that a prominent magnetic anomaly along the continental slope, known as the "East Coast Magnetic Anomaly" (ECMA), was caused by an "edge effect" between highly magnetized oceanic crust on the southeast and continental or transitional crust on the northwest.

During the last 10 years, multichannel seismic reflection profiling and oil exploration drilling along the U.S. Atlantic margin have begun to resolve many aspects of its deep structure and how it evolved during the rifting and early sea floor-spreading stages of this region's separation from Africa. Interpretations of the margin based on proprietary oil company multichannel data began to appear in the early 1970's, and these interpretations suggested that basins containing as much as 12 km of sedimentary rocks underlie the Continental Shelves (Emery and Uchupi, 1972; Mattick et al, 1974; Sheridan, 1974). In 1973, the U.S. Geological Survey contracted the first publicly available multichannel seismic profiles (Schlee et al, 1976). The first exploration leases for the Outer Continental Shelf off New Jersey were granted in 1976, and drilling of the first exploration wells began in 1978.

Between 1973 and 1978, the Geological Survey (USGS) collected or contracted approximately 20,000 km of multichannel seismic reflection data (fig. 1; from Folger et al, 1979), 185,000 km of aeromagnetic data (Klitgord and Behrendt, 1979), 39,000 km of marine gravity profiles (Grow et al, 1979A), and three deep-refractions profiles (Sheridan et al, 1979). Drill hole information from five Continental Offshore Stratigraphic Test (COST) wells has been released since 1978 (fig. 1), and more than 25 commercial exploration wells have been drilled. Although many interpretations of individual basins and segments of the margin have been published (Schlee et al, 1976, 1977; Grow and Markl, 1977; Dillon et al, 1979; Grow et al, 1979B; Grow, 1980; Schlee and Grow, 1980), syntheses of the entire margin's structure and evolution are just beginning to be possible (Klitgord and Behrendt, 1979; Folger

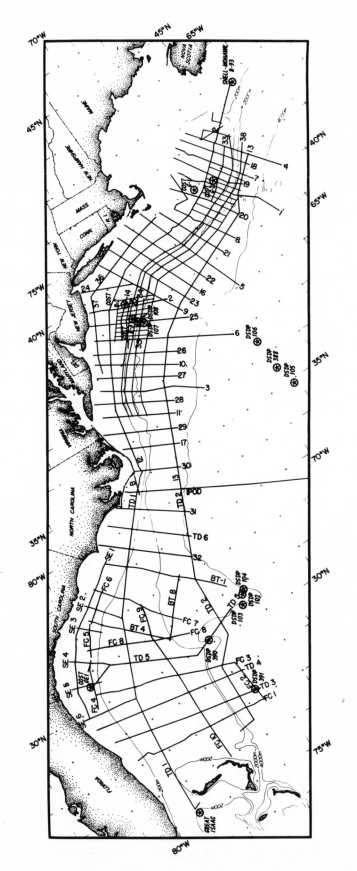

Figure 1: Multichannel seismic reflection profiles collected for the U.S. Geological Survey between 1973 and 1978 (from Folger et al, 1979). Drill sites from DSDP and COST wells are also shown.

et al, 1979; Schlee et al, 1979; Grow et al, 1979A; Grow and Sheridan, 1981).

A preliminary synthesis of these data has delineated four major troughs or basins (Klitgord and Behrendt, 1979; Grow and Sheridan, 1981). From north to south, these basins are the Georges Bank Basin, the Baltimore Canyon Trough, the Carolina Trough, and the Blake Plateau Basin (fig. 2). This lecture is a brief summary of information on each of these basins (primarily from Sheridan and Grow, 1981), incorporating some of the most recently available seismic and drill hole data (Klitgord and Grow, 1980; Schlee, 1981; Schlee, in press; Klitgord and Schlee, in press; Hutchinson et al, in press; Dillon et al, in press; Grow et al, in prep.). Representative profiles through the center of each of the four major basins are given in order to demonstrate how the deep crustal and sedimentary structures across the ocean-continent transition zone evolved.

THE CAROLINA TROUGH (CT)

The CT is approximately 80 km wide and 400 km long and contains as much as 12 km of Jurassic to recent sediment (fig. 3). It lies north of the Blake Spur fracture zone between the East Coast Magnetic Anomaly (ECMA) on the southeast and the Brunswick Magnetic Anomaly (BMA) on the northwest (fig. 4) (Klitgord and Behrendt, 1979; Dillon et al, 1979 and in press; Hutchinson et al, in press). We will start our discussion of the U.S. Atlantic margin with the CT because (1) it has the narrowest and simplest transition zone from continental to oceanic crust, (2) the separation of North American and Africa here appears to have been a simple pulling apart of the continents without oblique or translational complications, (3) the Mesozoic lineations here are parallel to the

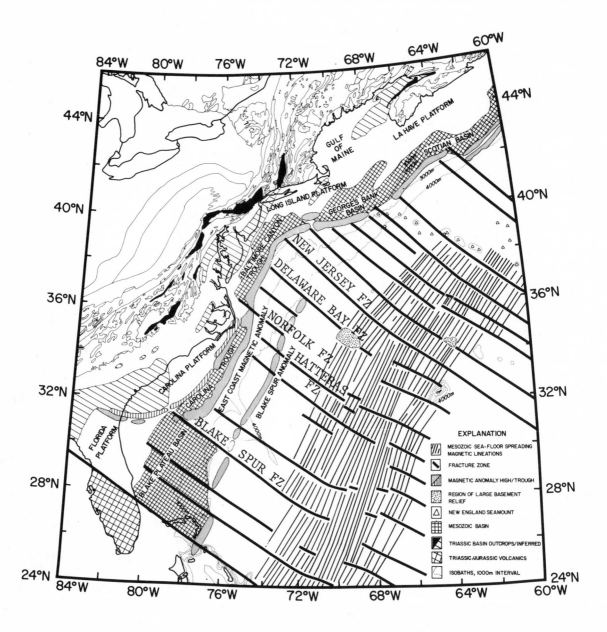

Figure 2: Location of Georges Bank Basin, Baltimore Canyon Trough, Carolina Trough, and the Blake Plateau Basin along the continental margin off the Eastern United States. Information based on multichannel seismic and aeromagnetic results (from Klitgord and Behrendt, 1979). Note correlation of basin boundaries with fracture zones. Major fracture zones also show abrupt changes in the Free-air gravity anomalies along the length of the margin (Grow et al, 1979A).

3-6

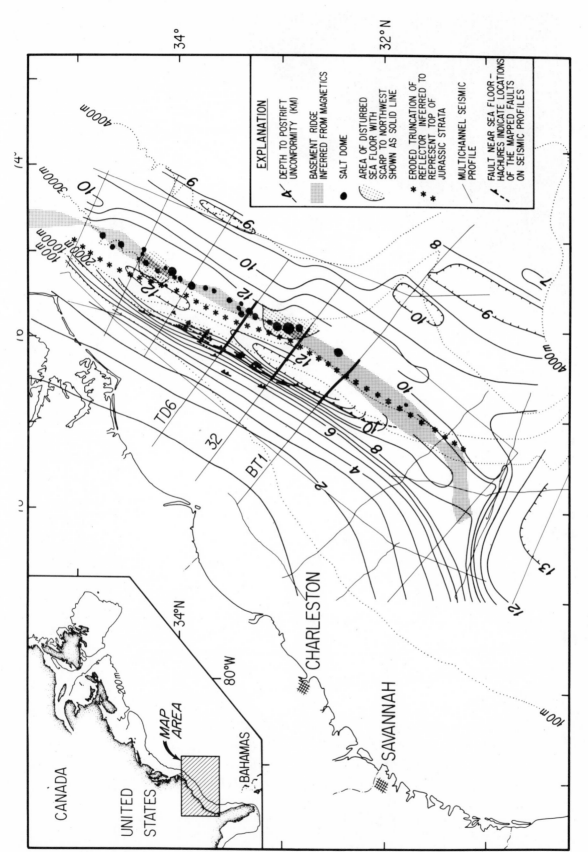

Figure 3: Structure contour map to "breakup" or "postrift" unconformity in Carolina Trough from Dillon et al, (in press). Alternate interpretations have picked a strong reflector at 11 km depth in the center of the trough as the "breakup unconformity" (Hutchinson et al, in press; see fig. 5 and 8).

MAGNETIC ANOMALIES

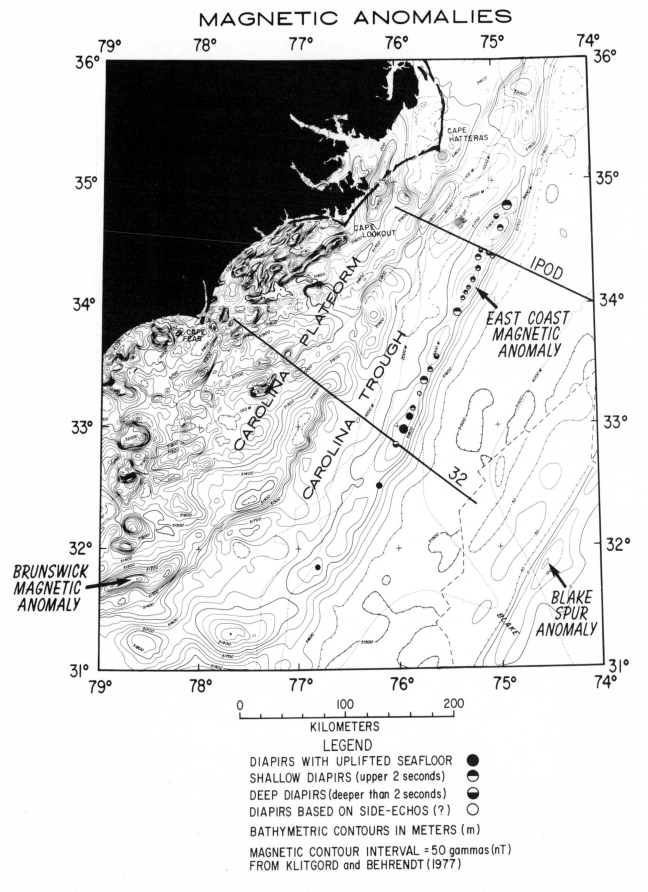

Figure 4: Magnetic contour map of Carolina Trough showing 23 diapir structures along axis of East Coast Magnetic Anomaly (ECMA) (from Grow et al, in prep).

pre-existing Paleozoic tectonic lineations, and (4) there is no evidence of any secondary volcanism or tectonism that has affected the trough itself.

Multichannel seismic line 32 (fig. 5: from Hutchinson et al, in press) crosses the Carolina Platform and Trough revealing a wedge of postrift sediments which thicken seaward and overlie a well defined "breakup unconformity" (Falvey, 1974). The wedge thickens gradually over the Carolina Platform until a "hinge zone" marks a transition into the rapidly deepening CT. A prerift or synrift Triassic graben underlies the breakup unconformity immediately landward of the "hinge zone" and beneath the Brunswick Magnetic Anomaly (fig. 5). A very large growth fault occurs near the landward side of the CT. A diapir is present at the ECMA and the Jurassic shelf edge is about 15 km landward of the axis of the ECMA (fig. 5). Thick continental rise sediments overlying oceanic basement occur seaward of the ECMA (fig. 5).

Gravity models along line 32 (fig. 6) and the IPOD line have been computed by Hutchinson et al (in press) which indicate abrupt changes in crustal thickness beneath the "hinge zone" and ECMA. The depth-to-Moho landward of the "hinge zone" is greater than 35 km and indicates relatively normal continental crust (fig. 6). The depth-to-Moho seaward of the ECMA is approximately 15 km or less and indicates relatively normal oceanic crust underlying a continental rise sedimentary prism (fig. 6). The depth-to-Moho between the "hinge zone" (or Brunswick Magnetic Anomaly) and the ECMA is 20 to 25 km deep (fig. 6) and has been referred to a "rift stage crust" by Hutchinson et al (in press). The rift stage crust is inferred to have formed by a combination of extensional rifting and igneous intrusion during Triassic and Early Jurassic, immediately preceding initiation of sea floor-spreading

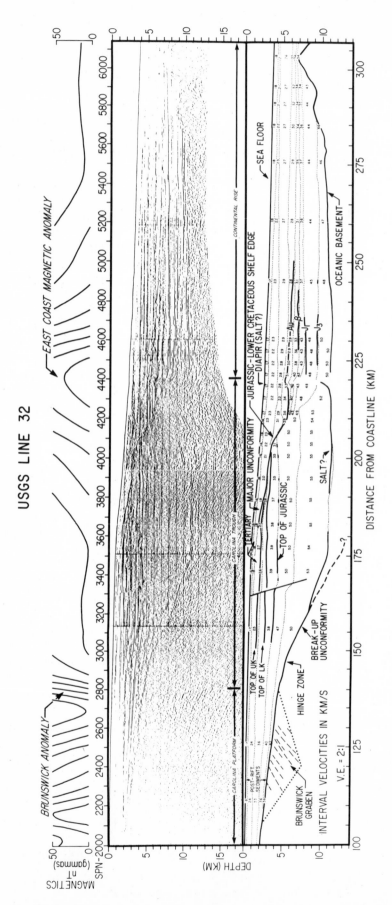

Figure 5: USGS line 32 multichannel seismic profile across Carolina Trough (from Hutchinson et al, in press). The strong reflector at 11 km depth in the center of the trough is inferred to be the "breakup" or "postrift" unconformity and the top of a salt horizon. Dillon et al, (in press) present a different interpretation (fig. 3) with the "breakup" unconformity at 13 km depth on line 32. Discriminating the breakup unconformity between the postrift and synrift sediments is usually difficult and interpretations vary.

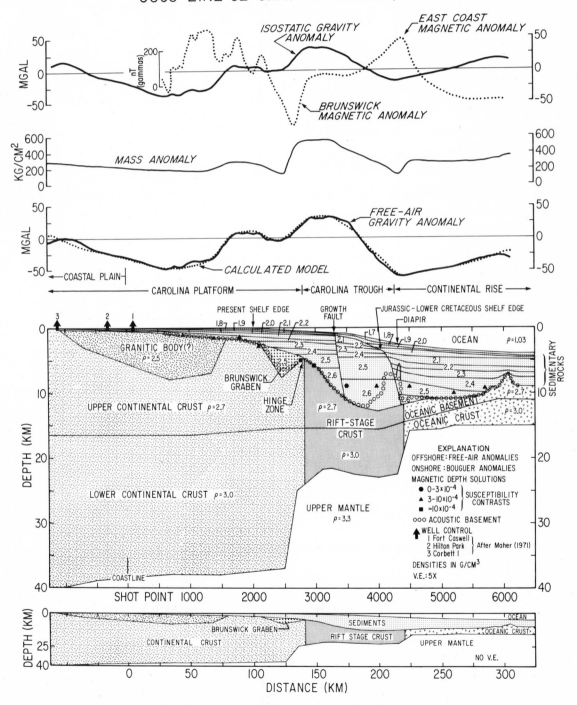

Figure 6: Gravity model across Carolina Trough along USGS line 32 (from Hutchinson et al, in press). Note the abrupt change in depth to Moho beneath the "hinge zone" and ECMA.

between Africa and North America.

A magnetic model along line 32 (fig. 7) indicates that the ECMA can be explained as a simple "edge effect" between negatively magnetized oceanic crust and weakly induced positive magnetization landward of the ECMA (Hutchinson et al, in press). This is agreement an earlier hypothesis by Keen (1969). The magnetic model shows that the Brunswick Magnetic Anomaly (BMA) can be explained by a variation in depth to basement within the Triassic graben and over the hinge zone assuming that the basement is all due to weakly induced magnetization. The first publicly available multichannel profile across the trough was the IPOD (International Phase of Ocean Drilling) line which crossed the northern part of the trough (Grow and Markl, 1977). The IPOD line showed three diapiric structures near the ECMA; approximately 20 other diapirs have since been found along the ECMA (fig. 4) in the CT (Grow et al, in prep.). The diapirs are inferred to be salt on the basis of a small salinity anomaly detected over one diapir and the presence of salt along the margin from the Grand Banks to Nova Scotia (Jansa & Wade, 1975) and to Georges Bank (Amato & Simonis, 1980). Three additional diapiric structures have been found along the ECMA in the Baltimore Canyon Trough, and salt has been drilled in one exploration well near these structures (Grow, 1980).

An interpretive crustal section along line 32 summarizes the structure of the CT (fig. 8). The source zone of the salt diapirs is inferred to lie beneath the breakup unconformity and within the synrift sediments at 11 to 12 km depth between the growth fault and the ECMA (Grow et al, in prep.). Dillon et al (in press) have described the growth fault in detail and hypothesize that it formed in response to salt withdrawal during formation of the diapirs along the ECMA.

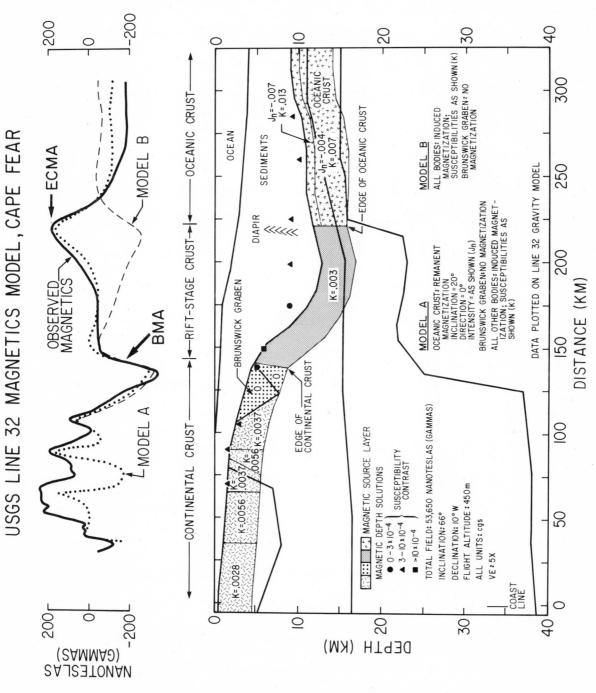

Figure 7: Magnetic model across Carolina Trough along USGS line 32 (from Hutchinson et al, in press). Note that the ECMA can be explained as a simple "edge effect" between negatively magnetized oceanic crust and weakly induced positive magnetization in the "rift stage" crust under the Carolina Trough.

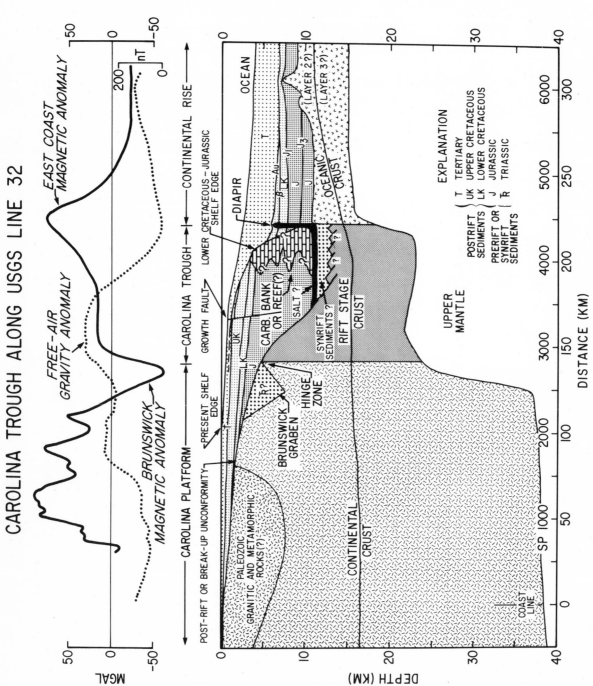

Figure 8: Crustal interpretation across the Carolina Trough along USGS line 32 (from Hutchinson et al, in press). The salt is inferred to have been deposited in late synrift sediments in the bottom of the Carolina Trough and then to have been squeezed laterally to the southeast until encountering the landward edge of oceanic crust.

The CT and the "rift stage crust" underlying it are unique in that the transition zones at the ECMA and BMA are very narrow, while broader zones of transitional thickness crust have been observed beneath the Baltimore Canyon Trough and Georges Bank Basin (Grow et al, 1979A).

BALTIMORE CANYON TROUGH (BCT)

The BCT lies beneath the Outer Continental Shelf between Virginia and New Jersey. It varies in width from 50 km off Virginia to 150 km wide off New Jersey, and in depth from 10 km off Virginia to more than 16 km deep off New Jersey (fig. 9: from Schlee, 1981) with an abrupt increase in width and depth north of Delaware Bay (Klitgord and Behrendt, 1979). The southern BCT is similar to the CT in that the separation from Africa was a direct pulling apart, but the similarities decrease northward where the trough and zone of transitional crust are wider.

Multichannel seismic profile 25 (fig. 10 and 11) crosses the B CT at its widest and simplest region. In this area, a 40-km progradation of the shelf edge took place during the Jurassic and was followed by a 20 km retreat of the shelf edge during the Tertiary. The 4823 m deep COST B-3 well was drilled 10 km north of line 25 and penetrated Late Jurassic horizons near the bottom (Amato & Simonis, 1979; Scholle, 1980). Subhorizontal reflectors, presumed to represent undeformed postrift deposits are present down to 13 km depth (fig. 11), and synrift (Triassic and Early Jurassic?) deformed sedimentary rocks are interpreted between 13 and 18 km depth (Grow, 1980).

A gravity model along USGS line 25 (fig. 12) (Hutchinson and Grow, unpubl. data) displays a thicker and wider sedimentary basin than line 32 over the CT (fig. 6), while their underlying crustal structures have

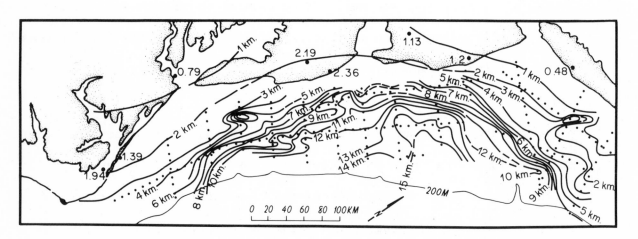

Figure 9: Depth to basement map of Baltimore Canyon Trough (BCT) from
Schlee (1981). Mapped units include both synrift and postrift
sediments. The maximum thickness of postrift sediments in BCT
is 13 km on USGS line 25 (Grow, 1980; Schlee, 1981). Synrift
sediments on USGS line 25 appear to continue down to a depth of
18 km near the ECMA on USGS line 25 (Grow, 1980; Schlee, 1981;
see figures 10 and 11).

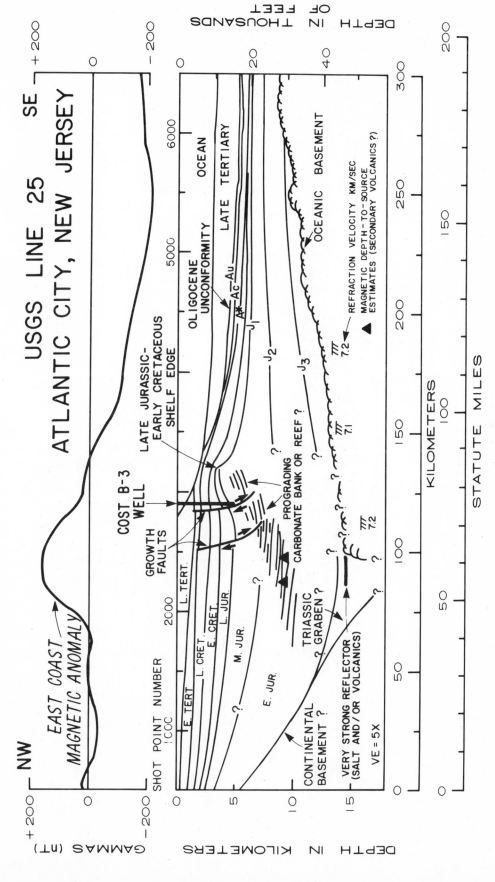

Figure 10: Line drawing interpretation of USGS line 25 across Baltimore Cnayon trough (from Grow, 1980).

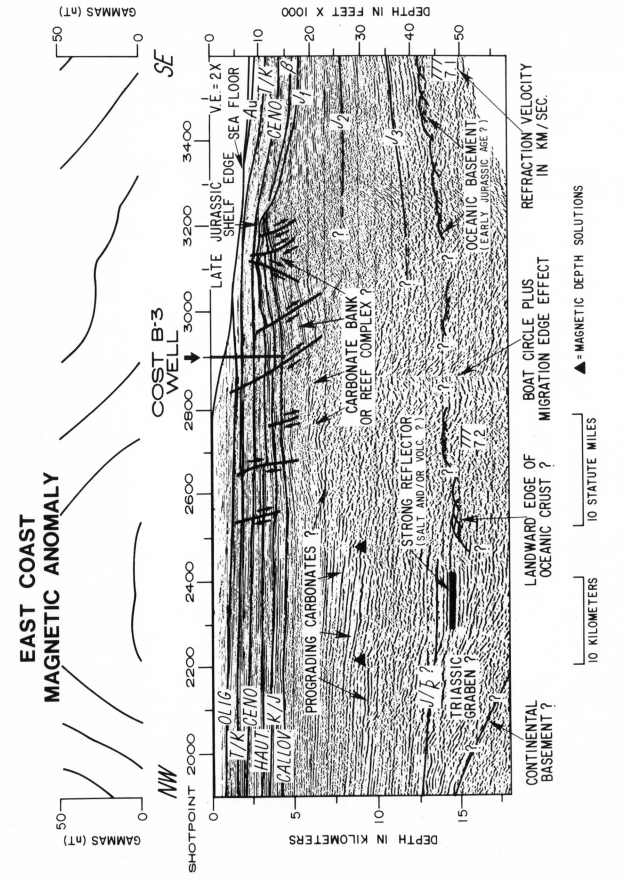

Figure 11: Multichannel depth section of USGS line 25 between ECMA and Jurassic paleoshelf edge complex (from Grow, 1980).

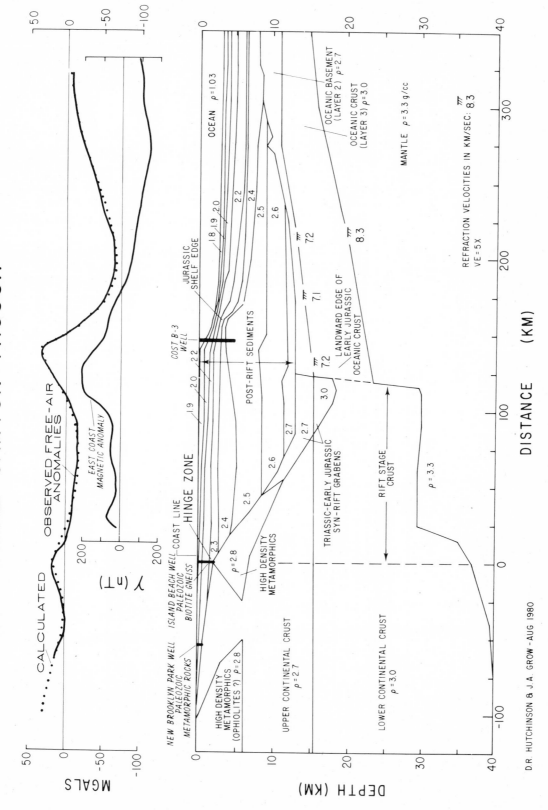

Figure 12: Gravity model along USGS line 25 (from D. R. Hutchinson and J. A. Grow, unpubl. data). Note abrupt change in depth to Moho at "hinge zone" and ECMA, which is similar to Carolina Trough (fig. 6).

similar abrupt changes in depth-to-Moho beneath the "hinge zone" and ECMA. A similar zone of intermediate thickness crust or "rift stage crust" underlies the BCT in a manner nearly identical to that of the CT. The postrift sedimentary wedge in BCT is much thicker, and the Jurassic paleoshelf edge has prograded on to the oceanic crust. Off New Jersey, several high density metamorphic complexes occur in the continental crust near the "hinge zone" (i.e. coast line in this area), which are probably due to Paleozoic suture zones within the Appalachians (Williams, 1978). The major similarities in the gravity models between CT and BCT are that (1) thick continental crust lies landward of the hinge zones, (2) intermediate thickness crust lies between the hinge zone and the ECMA, and (3) thin oceanic crust lies seaward of the ECMA.

A geologic section (Fig. 13) across BCT summarizes the line 25 and COST B-3 data. Some salt structures and a mafic intrusion slightly northeast of line 25 have been projected to illustrate the types of structures in BCT (Grow, 1980). The hinge zone seen clearly in the CT (Fig. 5 and 6) is just landward of the northwest end of line 25 (Fig. 10 and 12), near the coastline. Refraction profiles have established that a 7.1 to 7.2 km/s refractor lies at 13 to 15 km depth beneath the upper Continental rise and Continentl slope; this reflector is interpreted to indicate the top of oceanic-crust (layer 3) (Sheridan et al, 1979). Note that the 7.1 to 7.2 km/s refractor continues northwestward to the ECMA (Fig. 10), which marks the landward edge of oceanic crust (Keen, 1969; Klitgord and Behrendt, 1979; Sheridan et al, 1979; Grow et al, 1979A).

The BCT off New Jersey is the only area along the U.S. Atlantic margin where the Jurassic or younger shelf edge appears to have prograded seaward of the ECMA onto the Lower Jurassic oceanic crust.

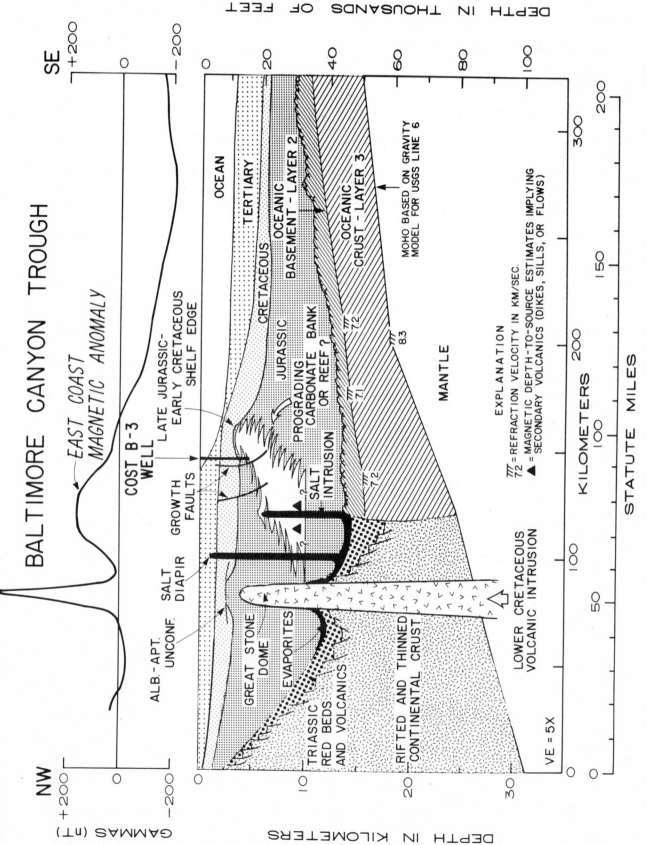

Figure 13: Interpretive crustal section across Baltimore Canyon Trough in vicinity of USGS line 25 with mafic intrustion and diapirs projected from north of line 25 (modified from Grow, 1980).

GEORGES BANK BASIN

Georges Bank Basin formed as a result of an oblique separation from Africa; the ocean-continent boundary marked by the ECMA is at a 30 to 40 degree angle with respect to Paleozoic and Triassic tectonic lineations (Fig. 2). The basin is elongate along its southern border, and its width ranges from 60 km to 140 km because of several Triassic synrift grabens that splay off the main trough at various angles. Although the postrift sedimentary units reach a maximum thickness of about 7 km, synrift troughs at least 16 km deep underlie parts of the basin (Fig. 14) (Schlee, in press; Schlee et al, 1976, 1977; Klitgord and Schlee, in press; Klitgord and Behrendt, 1979; Uchupi and Austin, 1979). The COST G-1 well penetrated to 4900 m, passed through Middle and probably Lower Jurassic dolomitic sandstones and entered lower Paleozoic metamorphic basement rocks (Amato and Bebout, 1980; Schlee, in press). The COST G-2 well penetrated to 6669 m, passed through Upper and Middle Jurassic carbonate deposits and ended up in Upper Triassic or Lower Jurassic dolomites and evaporites including salt (Amato and Simonis, 1980). Georges Bank Basin is also complicated by the New England Seamounts that disturbed the adjacent oceanic crust and nearby parts of the continental margin because of local secondary volcanism and secondary tectonic movements in Jurassic through Late Cretaceous time.

Seismic interpretations across Georges Bank Basin USGS seismic lines 4, 18, 19, and 1 are summarized in figure 15 (from Klitgord and Schlee, in press). Because the postrift sediments in Georges Bank Basin are relatively thin (7 km), seismic evidence for prerift and/or synrift grabens (down to depths of 11 to 16 km?) is generally better than in either the BCT or CT. Austin et al (1980) have pointed out that a hinge

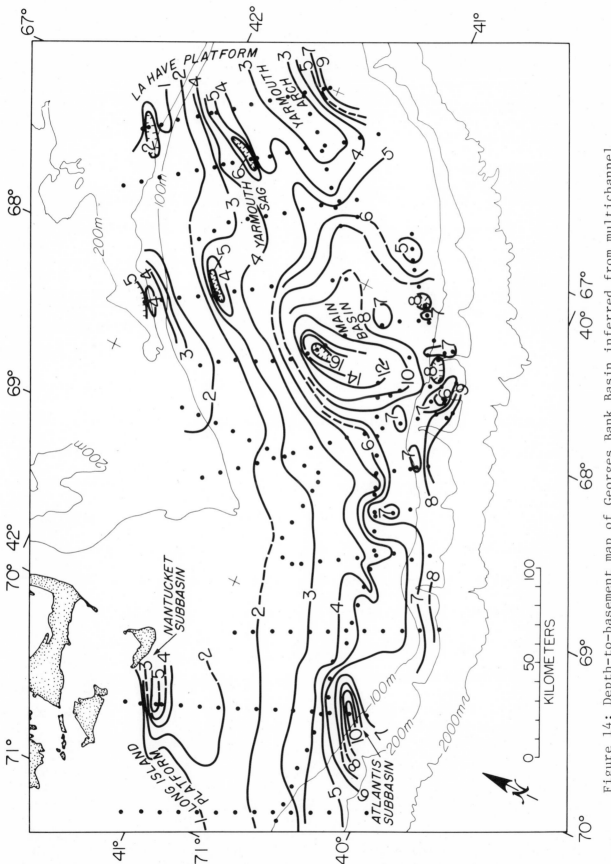

Figure 14: Depth-to-basement map of Georges Bank Basin inferred from multichannel seismic reflection (from Schlee, in press). Map includes both synrift and postrift sediments. The maximum thickness of postrift sediments in Georges Bank Basin is approximately 7 km (Schlee, in press).

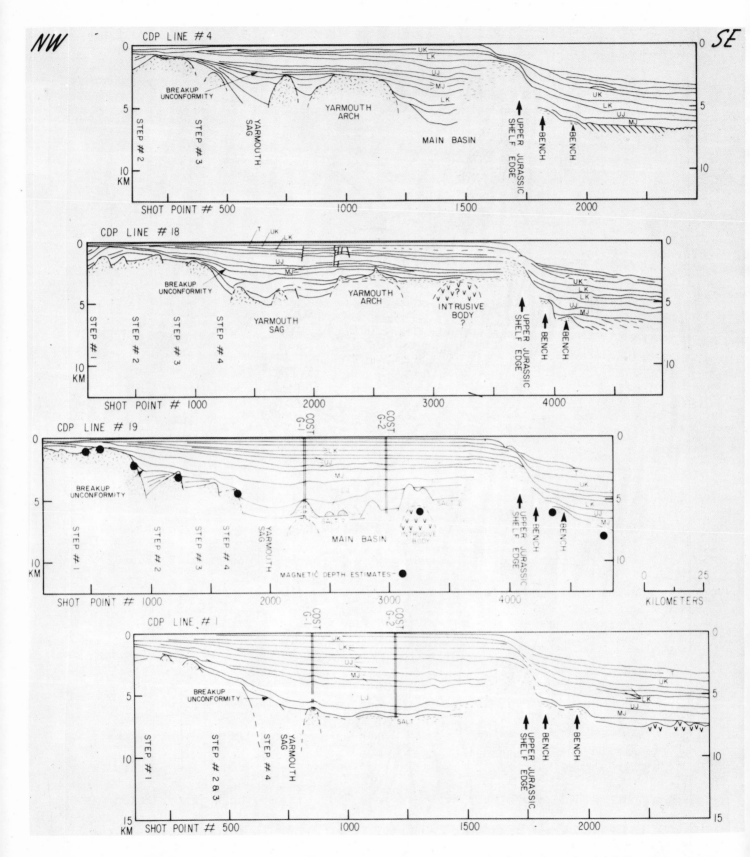

Figure 15: Line drawing summary of USGS lines 4, 18, 19, and 1 across Georges Bank Basin (from Klitgord and Schlee, in press).

zone lies along the northwest margin of Georges Bank Basin which is similar to a hinge zone reported beneath the Nova Scotian Shelf by Jansa and Wade (1975). However, Klitgord and Schlee (in press) have shown that the hinge zone in Georges Bank may be broken into 3 or 4 steps in some areas. While the pattern of hinge zones in Georges Bank is somewhat more complex than is the CT or BCT the general pattern still exists.

A gravity model along USGS line 5 (fig. 16) across the southwest end of Georges Bank shows again that thick continental crust lies landward of the hinge zone and thin oceanic crust lies seaward of the ECMA. The depth-to-Moho line 5 does not change as abruptly beneath the hinge zone and ECMA as it did on lines 32 and 25 (fig. 6 and 12), and a more gradual or tapered transition into and out of the rift stage crust is seen here. The Early Cretaceous and Jurassic shelf edge on line 5 (Fig. 17) is directly over the boundary between thin continental and oceanic crust and about 20 km seaward of the present shelf edge. This position suggests that the shelf edge did not migrate significantly either landward or seaward of the initial ocean-continental boundary during the Jurassic and Cretaceous but that it did retreat during the Tertiary.

BLAKE PLATEAU BASIN

The Blake Plateau, a 350-km-wide marginal plateau between water depths of 500 and 1500 m, is underlain by postrift sedimentary units that are as much as 12 km thick (Dillon et al, 1979). The plateau is south of the Blake Spur fracture zone and the southern termination of the East Coast Magnetic Anomaly (fig. 2). The thickest part of the basin is beneath the western plateau, and the sedimentary horizons

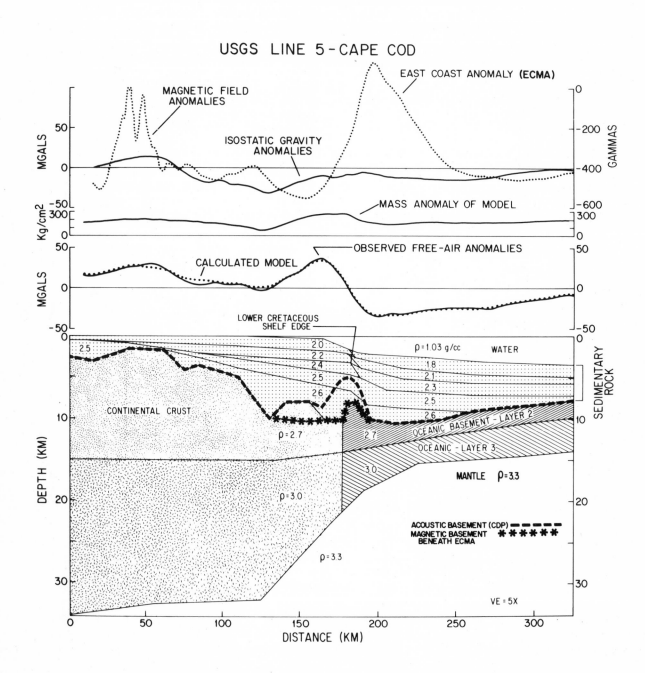

Figure 16: Gravity model along USGS line 5 across southwest end of Georges Bank Basin (from Grow et al, 1979A).

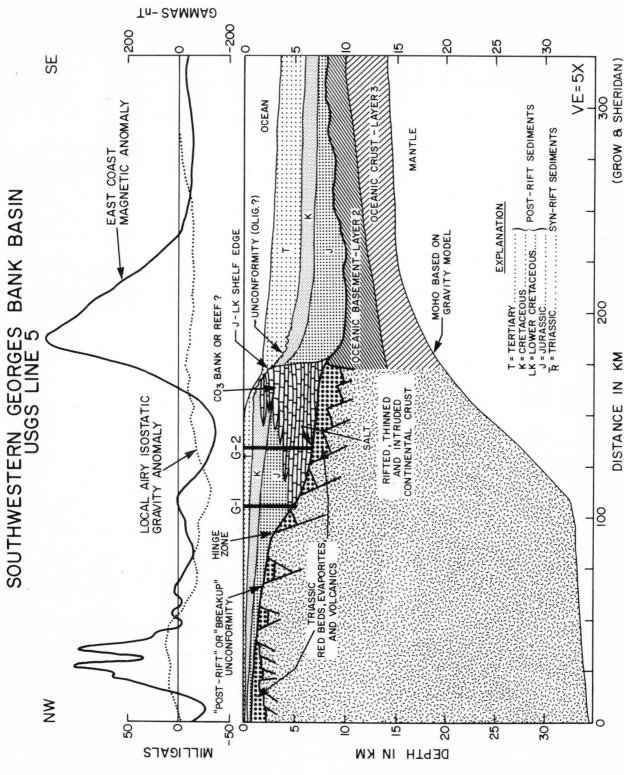

Figure 17: Composite geologic section across southwest end of Georges Bank Basin along multichannel seismic line 5 with recently available drill hole data projected from the COST G-1 and G-2 wells (Amato and Bebout 1980; Amato and Simonis, 1980). Moho structure based on gravity model along line 5 (Grow et al, 1979A). Note hinge zone and underlying change in depth to the Moho; the structure is similar to the gravity models across the Carolina Trough (fig. 3 and 5).

beneath the middle and outer part of the plateau dip gently toward the west (fig. 18).

Gravity modeling across the plateau indicates that a transitional crust 15-20 km thick underlies the western Blake Plateau Basin and that a transitional crust nearly 25 km thick underlies the eastern Blake Plateau Basin (fig. 18, modified from Kent, 1979). A very abrupt transition takes place beneath the Blake Escarpment and a thin oceanic crust underlies the Blake Basin.

The configuration of the sedimentary and crustal units, combined with the absence of the ECMA south of the Blake Spur fracture zone, indicates a broad zone of extensional rifting and volcanism between Africa and North America in this area (Kent, 1979). Although the processes of Triassic rifting and crustal thinning beneath the western plateau probably were similar to those beneath the CT and other basins to the north, the Early Jurassic history of the Blake Plateau Basin was different. Normal sea floor spreading between the ECMA and the Blake Spur Magnetic Anomaly began in the earliest Jurassic north of the Blake Spur fracture zone, but volcanic intrusions appear to have penetrated the thinned continental crust over a broad zone beneath the middle and western Blake Plateau for the first 10 to 15 million years. After an eastward jump of the extension and volcanic axis from the western plateau to the Blake Escarpment, normal sea floor-spreading began in the Blake Basin with the formation of typical thin oceanic crust (fig. 18). The above mentioned conclusions of Kent (1979) are consistent with earlier interpretations for sea floor-spreading or extension-center jumps beneath the Blake Plateau (Sheridan, 1978; Dillon et al, 1979; Klitgord and Behrendt, 1979).

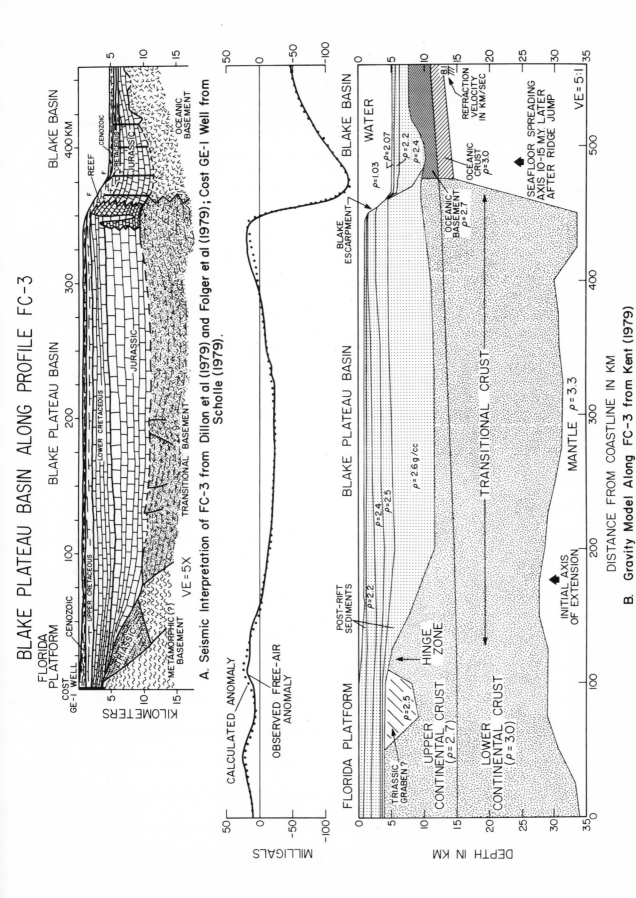

BLAKE PLATEAU BASIN ALONG PROFILE FC-3

A. Seismic Interpretation of FC-3 from Dillon et al (1979) and Folger et al (1979); Cost GE-1 Well from Scholle (1979).

B. Gravity Model Along FC-3 from Kent (1979)

Figure 18: Composite geologic section across the Blake Plateau Basin along multichannel seismic line FC-3, modified from Dillon et al, (1979) and Folger et al, (1979): Moho configuration is based on gravity model of Kent (1979). The COST GE-1 well data are from Scholle Blake Plateau, where initial rifting probably began. A seaward jump in the extension axis from the western plateau to the Blake Escarpment probably took place 10 to 15 m.y. after initial continental separation.

CONCLUSIONS

1. Four major sedimentary basins formed along the U.S. Atlantic continental margin in response to Triassic-Early Jurassic continental rifting and Early to Middle Jurassic sea floor spreading between Africa and North America: Georges Bank Basin, BCT, CT, and the Blake Plateau Basin.

2. Postrift sedimentary units in the four basins range are as much as 7, 13, 11, and 12 km in thickness from north to south, respectively. The postrift units are typically separated from basement or synrift sedimentary rocks by a breakup or postrift unconformity underlain by synrift grabens, which may contain as much as 5 km of sedimentary rocks.

3. Upper Triassic and/or Lower Jurassic salt has been drilled at 6.7 km in the COST G-2 well within Georges Bank Basin in what appears to be late synrift or earliest postrift sedimentary units (Plate 4, Amato and Simonis, 1980). Three diapirs along the ECMA in the BCT and 23 diapirs along the ECMA in the CT also appear to rise from near the top of the synrift sedimentary units. Therefore, conditions favorable for evaporite deposits appear to have existed during the late rift stage and/or into the earliest postrift stage.

4. The Jurassic sedimentary units that have been drilled to date in the BCT (COST B-2 and B-3 wells: Scholle, 1977, 1980, respectively) and Georges Bank Basin"(COST G-1: Amato and Bebout, 1980; COST G-2: Amato and Simonis, 1980) were primarily of shallow-marine and non-marine origin. This fact supports an inference that these basins subsided during the postrift stage in response to sediment loading and lithospheric cooling, as suggested by Watts and Steckler (1979).

5. Gravity models across the three northern basins indicate that the deepest parts of these basins are underlain by transitional crust 8 to 15 km thick, which appears to have formed primarily by extension and thinning of the pre-existing continental crust. The initial subsidence probably was controlled by this extensional mechanism (MacKenzie, 1978; LePichon and Sibuet, 1981).

6. Beneath the Blake Plateau, the 15 to 25 km thick transitional crust probably formed via a complicated mixing of continental fragments and volcanic intrusion over a zone 350 km wide zone during the first 10 to 15 m. y. of continental drift. Formation of this crust was followed by an abrupt eastward jump of the spreading center to the Blake Escarpment and the beginning of normal sea floor spreading, which formed thin oceanic crust beneath the Blake Bahama Basin.

POSTSCRIPTS

This lecture has concerned itself primarily with geophysical and structural aspects of the margin and has only dealt with sedimentalogy and stratigraphy in the most general terms. For a more thorough discussion of the latter subjects, the reader is referred to Schlee (1981B) who has summarized the stratigraphy of the COST G-1 and G-2 wells on Georges Bank and their relationship to Baltimore Canyon Trough (B-3 well) and wells on the Scotian margin (see my figure 19 which is from Schlee, 1981B).

A great deal of high frequency seismic reflection data, side-scan sonar images of the continental slope, and shallow coring data have been collected during the last five years which relate to geologic and environmental hazards on the Outer Continental Shelf and Slope. These are also beyond the scope of this paper, and the reader is referred to Popenoe (1981) and Robb et al (1981) for further discussions of these aspects.

The reader is referred to individual COST well reports for discussion of the petroleum potential and to Mattick et al (1981) for a recent summary paper. Hard minerals such as phosphorite (Pilkey and Luternauer, 1967; Manheim et al, 1980) and manganese modules (Pratt and McFarlin, 1966) have been found in offshore areas of the Atlantic margin. These may become commercially prospective in the not too distant future.

Shallow drilling (300 meters) along the continental shelf has also demonstrated the existence of fresh ground water extending nearly to the edge of the continental shelf (Hathaway et al, 1979), and this may become an important fresh water resource in the future.

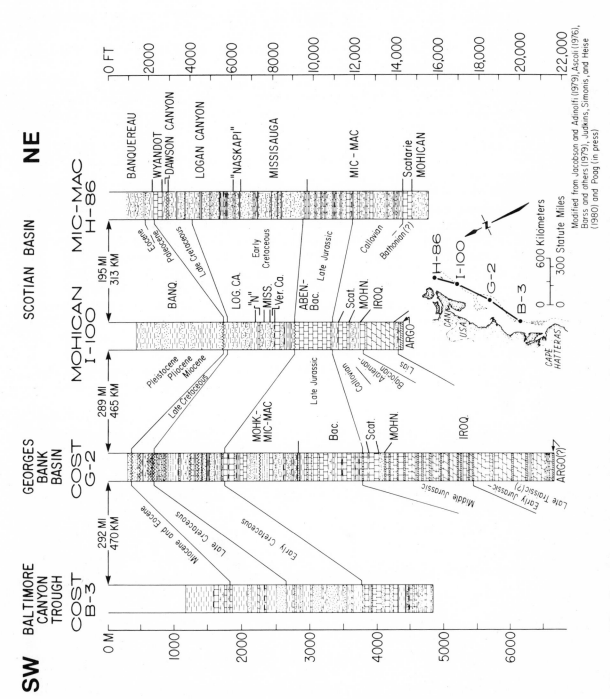

Figure 19: Stratigraphy and lithology of COST B-2, COST G-2, and Nova Scotian wells (from Schlee, 1981B).

U.S.G.S. multichannel seismic reflection profiles discussed in this paper may be purchased from the "National Geophysical, Solar, and Terr'strial Data Center" (NGSDC) at the following address:

NGSDC (Code D-621)

325 Broadway

Boulder, Colo. 80303

Phone No. 303-497-6338

ACKNOWLEDGEMENTS

Much of the material presented in this lecture has been taken from Grow and Sheridan (1981). I thank Robert E. Sheridan, Kim D. Klitgord, John S. Schlee, William P. Dillon, and Deborah R. Hutchinson for many valuable discussions and assistance in addition to preprints of their current manuscripts. I also thank Albert W. Bally for critically reviewing the lecture material.

REFERENCES

Amato, R.W., and J. W., Bebout (editors), 1980, Geologic and Operational Summary, COST No. G-1 Well, Georges Bank Area, North Atlantic Outer Continental Shelf: U.S. Geological Survey Open-File Report No. 80-268, 111 p.

Amato, R. W., and E. K. Simonis (editors), 1979, Geological and Operational Summary, COST No. B-3 Well, Baltimore Canyon Trough Area, Mid-Atlantic Outer Continental Shelf: U.S. Geological Survey Open-File Report No. 79-1159, 118 p.

Amato, R W., and E. K. Simonis (editors), 1980, Geological and Operational Summary, COST NO. G-2 Well, Georges Bank Area, North Atlantic Outer Continental Shelf: U.S. Geological Survey Open-File Report No. 80-269, 116 p.

Austin, J. W., Jr., E. Uchupi, D. R. Shaughnessy, III, and R. D. Ballard, 1980, Geology of New England Passive Margin: AAPG Bull., v. 64, p. 501-526.

Dillon, W P., C. K. Paull, R. T. Buffler, and J. P. Fail, 1979, Structure and Development of the southeast George Embayment and Northern Blake Plateau -- Preliminary Analysis: in J. S. Watkins, L. Montedert, and P. W. Dickerson (editors), Geological and Geophysical Investigations of Continental Margins, AAPG Memoir 29, p. 27-41.

Dillon, W. P., P. Popenoe, J. A. Grow, K. D. Klitgord, B. A. Swift, C. K. Paull, and K. V. Cashman, in press, Growth faulting and salt diapirism - their relation and control in the Carolina Trough, eastern North America: in J. S. Watkins (editor), AAPG Hedberg Symposium Memoir volume.

Drake, C. L., M. Ewing, and G. H. Sutton, 1959, Continental margins and geosynclines - the east coast of North America north of Cape Hatteras: in L. H. Ahrens, et al, Physics and Chemistry of the Earth, v. 3, London, Program Press, p. 110-198.

Emery, K. O., E. Uchupi, J. D. Phillips, C. O. Bowin, E. T. Bunce, and S. T. Knott, 1970, Continental rise off eastern North America: AAPG Bull., v. 54, p. 44-108.

Emery, K. O., and E. Uchupi, 1972, Western North Atlantic Ocean - Topography, rocks, structure, water life and sediments: AAPG Memoir 17, 532 p.

Ewing, M., and R. Leyden, 1966, Seismic profiler survey of Blake Plateau: AAPG Bull., v. 50, p. 1948-1971.

Ewing, M., J. L. Worzel, N. C. Steenland, and F. Press, 1950, Geophysical investigations in the emerged and submerged Atlantic Coastal plain: Part V, Woods Hole, New York, and Cape May sections: Geol. Soc. Amer. Bull., v. 61, p. 877-892.

Falvey, D. A., 1974, The development of continental margins in plate tectonic theory: Australian Petroleum Exploration Assoc. Journal, v. 14, p. 95-106.

Folger, D. W., W. P. Dillon, J. A. Grow, K. D. Klitgord, and J. S. Schlee, 1979, Evolution of the Atlantic continental margin of the United States: in Talwani, M., W. Hay, W. B. F. Ryan, (editors), Deep drilling results in the Atlantic Ocean--Continental margins and Paleoenvironments, American Geophysical Union, Maurice Ewing Series 3, Stroudburg, PA., Dowden-Hutchinson and Ross, p. 87-108.

Grow, J. A., 1980, Deep structure and evolution of the Baltimore Canyon Trough in the vicinity of the COST B-3 Well: in Scholle, P. A., (editor), Geologic studies of the COST B-3 Well: U.S. Geological Survey Circular No. 833, p. 117-125.

Grow, J. A., C. O. Bowin, and D. R. Hutchinson, 1979A, The gravity field of the U.S. Atlantic continental margin: Tectonophysics, v. 59, p. 27-52.

Grow, J. A., W. P. Dillon, and R. E. Sheridan, 1977, Diapirs along the Continental Slope off Cape Hatteras (abs): Society of Exploration Geophysics Annual Meeting, 47th, Calgary, p. 51.

Grow, J. A., and R. G. Markl, 1977, IPOD-USGS multichannel seismic reflection profile from Cape Hatteras to the Mid-Atlantic Ridge: Geology, v. 5, p. 625-630.

Grow, J. A., R. E. Mattick, and J. S. Schlee, 1979B, Multichannel seismic depth section and interval velocities over Outer Continental Shelf and Upper Continental Slope between Cape Hatteras and Cape Cod: in Watkins, J. S., L. Montadert, and P. W. Dickerson, (editors), Geological and Geophysical Investigations of Continental Margins, AAPG Memoir 29, p. 65-83.

Grow, J. A., P. Popenoe, W. P. Dillon, and F. T. Manheim, in prep., Diapirs along th East Coast Magnetic Anomaly off North Carolina: in J.S. Watkins (editor), AAPG Hedberg Symposium, Memoir volume.

Grow, J. A. and R. E. Sheridan, 1981, Deep Structure and Evolution of Continental Margin off the Eastern United States: Proceedings of the International Geologic Congress (1981), in Oceanologica Acta, in press.

Hathaway, J. C., et al., 1979, U.S. Geological Survey core drilling on the Atlantic Shelf: Science, v. 206, p. 525-527.

Heirztler, J. R. et al., 1968, Marine magnetic anomalies, geomagnetic field reversals and motions of the ocean floor and continents: Jour. Geophys. Research, v. 73, p. 2119-2136.

Hersey, J. B., E. T. Bunce, R. F. Wyrick, and F. T. Dietz, 1959, Geophysical investigation of the continental margin between Cape Henry, Virginia, and Jacksonville, Florida: Geol. Soc. Amer. Bull., v. 70, p. 437-466.

Hutchinson, D. R., J. A. Grow, K. D. Klitgord, and B. A. Swift, in press, The deep structure and evolution of the Carolina Trough: in J. S. Watkins (editor), AAPG Hedberg Symposium Memoir volume.

Jansa, L. F., and J. A. Wade, 1975, Geology of the continental margin off Nova Scotia and Newfoundland: in Van Der Linden, W. J. M., and J. A. Wade (editors), Offshore Geology of Eastern Canada, v. 2, Regional Geology, Geol. Surv. of Canada Paper 74-30, p. 51-150.

Keen, M. J., 1969, Magnetic anomalies off the eastern seaboard of the United States - A possible edge effect: Nature, v. 222, p. 72-74.

Kent, K. M., 1979, Two-diminsional gravity model of the Southeast Georgia Embayment - Blake Plateau: Masters Thesis - University of Delaware, Newark, Delaware, 89 p.

Klitgord, K. D. and J. C. Behrendt, 1979, Basin Structure of the U.S. Atlantic Margin: in Watkins, J. S., L. Mondedert, and P. W. Dickerson (editors), Geological and Geophysical Investigations of continental margins, AAPG Memoir 29, p.85-112.

Klitgord, K. D. and J. A. Grow, 1980, Jurassic seismic stratigraphy and basement structure of the Western Atlantic magnetic quiet zone: AAPG Bull., v. 64, p. 1658-1680.

Klitgord, K. D. and J. S. Schlee, in press, Basement structure, sedimentation and tectonic history of Georges Bank Basin: in P. A. Scholle (editor), Geological studies of the COST No. G-1 and G-2 wells, United States North Atlantic Continental Shelf, U.S. Geological Survey Circular.

LePichon, X., and J. Sibuet, 1981. Passive Margins - A Model of Formation: J. Geophys Research, v. 86, p. 3708-3720.

Manheim, F. T., R. M. Pratt, and P. F. McFarlin, 1980, Composition and origin of phosphorite deposits of the Blake Plateau, in Phosphorite: SEPM Spec. Pub. No. 29, p. 117-137.

Mattick, R. E., et al. 1974, Structural framework of United States Atlantic Outer Continental Shelf north of Cape Hatteras: AAPG Bull., v. 58 , 1179-1190.

Mattick, R. E., J. S.. Schlee, and K. Bayer, 1981, The geology and hydrocarbon potential of the Georges Bank - Baltimore Canyon area: Canadian Society of Petroleum Geologists Memoir 7, in press.

Pilkey, O. H. and J. L. Luternauer, 1967, A North Carolina shelf phosphate deposit of possible commercial interest: Southeastern Geology, v. 8, p. 33-51.

Pitman, W. C. and M. Talwani, 1972, Sea floor spreading in the North Atlantic: Geol. Soc. Amer. Bull., v. 83, p. 619-646.

Popenoe, P. (editor), 1981, Environmental geologic studies on the southeastern Atlantic Outer Continental Shelf, 1977-1978: U.S. Geological Survey Open-File Report No. 81-582A.

Pratt, R. M. and P. F. McFarlin, 1966, Manganese pavements on the Blake Plateau: Science, v. 151, p. 1080-1082.

Robb, J. M., J. C. Hampson, Jr., and D. C. Twitchell, 1981, Geomorphology and sediment stability of a segment of the U.S. Continental Slope off New Jersey: Science, v. 211, p. 935-937.

Schlee, J. S., 1981A, Seismic stratigraph of Baltimore Canyon Trough: AAPG Bull., v. 65, p. 26-53.

Schlee, J. S., 1981B, Seismic stratigraphy of the Georges Bank Basin complex, offshore New England: in P. A. Scholle (editor), Geological studies of the COST No. G-1 and G-2 Wells, United States North Atlantic Continental Shelf, U.S. Geological Survey Circular, in press.

Schlee, J. S., et al, 1976, Regional geologic framework off northeastern United States Amer: AAPG Bull., v. 60, p. 926-951.

Schlee, J. S., et al, 1977, Petroleum geology on the United States Atlantic Gulf of Mexico margins: in V. S. Cameron, ed., Proceedings of the Southwest Legal Foundation - Exploration and economics of the petroleum industry: New York, Matthew Bender and Company, Inc., v. 15, p. 47-93.

Schlee, J. S., W. P. Dillon, J. A. Grow, 1979, Structure of the Continental Slope off the eastern United States: in Doyle, L. J. and others, Geology of Continental Slopes: Society of Economic Paleontologists and Mineralogists Special Publication 27, p. 95-117.

Schlee, J. S., and J. A. Grow, 1980, Buried carbonate shelf edge beneath the Atlantic Continental Slope: Oil and Gas Journal, February 25, 1980, p. 148-156.

Scholle, P. A. (editor), 1977, Geological studies on the COST No. 2 well, U.S. Mid-Atlantic Outer Continental Shelf area: U.S. Geol. Survey Circular 750, 71 p.

Scholle, P. A., (editor), 1979, Geological Studies of the COST GE-1 Well, United States South Atlantic Outer Continental Shelf Area: U.S. Geo. Survey Circular 800, 114 p.

Scholle, P. A. (editor), 1980, Geological Studies of the COST No. B-3 Well, United States Mid-Atlantic Continental Shelf area: U.S. Geological Survey Circular 833, 132 p.

Sheridan, R. E., C. L. Drake, and J. Hennion, 1966, Seismic-refraction study of the continental margin east of Florida: AAPG Bull., v. 50, p. 1972-1991.

Sheridan, R. E., 1974, Atlantic continental margin off North America: in Burk, C. A., and Drake, C. L., (editors), The geology of continental margins: New York, Springer-Verlag, p. 391-407.

Sheridan, R. E., 1978, Structure, stratigraphy, evolution, and petroleum potential of the Blake Plateau: Offshore Techonology Conf. Proceedings, Houston, Texas, p. 363-368.

Sheridan, R. E., J. A. Grow, J. C. Behrendt, and K. C. Bayer, 1979, Seismic refraction study of the continental edge off the eastern United States: Tectonophysics, v. 59, p. 1-26.

Taylor, P. T., I. Zietz and L. S. Dennis, 1968, Geological implications of aeromagnetic data for the eastern continental margin of the United States: Geophysics, v. 33, p. 755-780.

Uchupi, E., and J. A., Austin, 1979, The geologic history of the passive margin off New England and the Canadian maritime provinces: Tectonopysics, v. 59, p. 53-69.

Watts, A. B., and M. S. Steckler, 1979, Subsidence and Eustary at the Continental Margin of Eastern North America: in Talwani, M., Hay, W., and Ryan, W. B. F. (editors), Deep Drilling results in the Atlantic Ocean--Continental margins and paleoenvironment, Maurice Ewing, Series 3, Amer. Geophysical Union, Washington, D. C., p. 218-234.

Williams, Harold, 1978, Tectonic lithofacies map of the Appalachions, MAP No. 1 (2 sheets, scale - 1:1,000,000): Memorial University of Newfoundland, St. Johns, Newfoundland.

Worzel, J. L., and Shurbet, G. L., 1955, Gravity anomalies at continental margins: Proc. Nat. Acad, Sci. (U.S.A.), v. 41, p. 458-469.

EARLY MESOZOIC BASINS OF THE CENTRAL ATLANTIC PASSIVE MARGINS

Warren Manspeizer
Geology Department
Rutgers University
Newark, New Jersey   07102

INTRODUCTION

Inherent in the concept of plate tectonics is the view that strike-slip displacement induces vertical motion, controlling the site and tectonic history of evolving basins. As in the San Andreas and Dead Sea Rifts, many Early Mesozoic basins originated in a strike-slip setting where crustal segments were pulled apart, forming a complex array of basins and source terraines. Sedimentation may have begun in small sag ponds that evolved into pull-apart basins, half-grabens or rhomb-shaped grabens as transform segments passed each other in episodes of crustal extension and compression. Since virtually none of the Mesozoic basins seem to fit the definition of a "rift valley" or "graben", i.e., a fault-bounded trough of tensional origin (A.G.I. Glossary of Geology, 1974; International Tectonic Dictionary, 1967), it would appear to be inappropriate to use these terms when describing these basins or the processes leading to the origin of passive margins.

The Atlantic passive margin seems to have formed in two stages: (1) continental breakup, "rifting"; and (2) drifting. The breakup occurred within a plate interior by wrench tectonics and transform faulting associated with a thinned continental-type "transitional" crust that now lies at the junction of the continental and oceanic crusts. Since the Early Jurassic the continental margin has been dominated by subsidence and drifting so that its early formative and evolutionary history is now buried under a vast prism of sediment. Study of the onshore record of the Triassic-Jurassic basins provides insights into this early history and into some of the fundamental questions surrounding the origin of ocean basins and continental margins, hydrocarbon production in juvenile ocean basins, and the climatic changes associated with these evolving basins.

Since these basins, lying on the continental margin, serve as depocenters for huge quantities of sediment (e.g., in the Baltimore Canyon Trough and the Scotian Shelf), their origin and evolution impacts heavily on petroleum exploration.

The objective of this paper is primarily to examine the rock record of these proto-Atlantic basins in North America and northwest Africa for clues to the early evolution of the passive continental margin. It will also explore wrench tectonics and transform faulting as mechanisms for the evolution of these basins. Finally, these basins will be examined as possible sources of hydrocarbons.

GENERAL OVERVIEW

The Atlantic continental margin has incorrectly been regarded as a passive margin during Triassic-Jurassic. It is in fact the product of profound crustal dynamics, having formed under an extensional phase of crustal deformation during the latter part of the Triassic. Its history contrasts markedly with the compressional deformation of the Hercynian Orogeny (Permo-Carboniferous).

Whereas Triassic basins were once considered as the end-phase of the Appalachian Revolution, they are now assigned to the initial phase of the Atlantic tectonic cycle.

The splitting of North America from Eurasia and Africa was hardly a passive Triassic-Jurassic event. It was accompanied by intracratonic faulting and tilting of the basement, plutonism and vulcanism on a vast scale, transform faulting, folding, transgression of the Tethys Sea into the Atlantic Realm, and strongly contrasting climates with monsoon circulation.

Vast quantities of coarse clastics were deposited adjacent to horsts being eroded by torrential streams, while subaqueous fans and turbidites accumulated in deep-water lakes along the border faults. Subaqueous fissure flows erupted in pull-apart lacustrine basins. Elsewhere platform carbonates and evaporites accumulated in sagged pull-apart basins submerged by the Tethyan transgression. Intrusive and extrusive igneous activity did not cease with the tholeiitic extrusives of the Newark-type rift basins. Continuing into the Cretaceous, in New England and Canada as the North American Plate moved west and north, perhaps over a hot spot, a trail of igneous activity extended from the Monteregian Hills to the New England Seamounts. A similar trail of hot spot activity, extending from Morocco through the Canary Islands to the New England Seamounts, was active as the African Meseta moved northeast past the African Platform.

Many researchers speculate that crustal uplift, attenuation and faulting are all manifestations of hot spot activity. We shall examine this notion and the data upon which the above syntheses is based.

BASINS: SPATIAL AND TEMPORAL DISTRIBUTION

About thirty onshore and offshore proto-Atlantic basins may be identified from North America to northwest Africa (Fig. 1). Their distribution

4-3

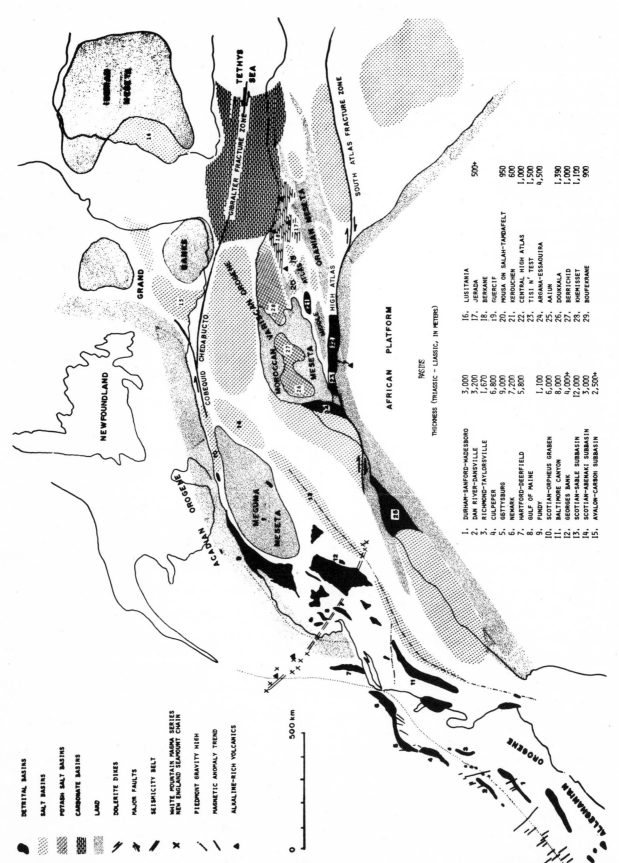

Fig. 1. Early Mesozoic pre-drift reconstruction of eastern North America and northwestern Africa, modified from Van Houten, 1977.

and evolution is strongly related to their setting in the plate, i.e., proximity to a plate margin, type of plate margin, and nature of the substratum (Dickinson, 1974). Many proto-Atlantic basins have very similar characteristics (geometry, size, volcanic and sedimentary facies, tectonic structures, and relation to underlying bedrock) and presumably formed under a similar tectonic setting. However, other basins are markedly different.

Two divergent types of basins are recognized: the more common Newark-type rift basin; and the evaporite-carbonate platform basin (Fig. 1). The Newark-type basins are strongly asymmetric in cross-section, elongate (about 100-200 km long, 30 km wide) in map view, and contain thick (1-10 km) continental clastic and volcanic facies that may be drag folded and faulted along the active border fault. The shelf-type basin, on the other hand, contains a substantially thinner (0.5 to 1.5 km) evaporite, carbonate and mudstone facies. Basins with both clastic and evaporite components are common in Morocco, and probably exist on the continental shelves.

The distribution of these basins, in both time and space, compels us to ask: What factors control their distribution, govern their sedimentary facies, hydrocarbon production, and thermal history? What age are the basins below the coastal plain sediments on the continental shelf? This presentation will explore these questions.

CORRELATION CHART: A CONCEPT FOR TRANS-ATLANTIC CORRELATION

The events leading to the formation of the Atlantic continental margins may be inferred from the Early Mesozoic record of eastern North America and northwest Africa (see Correlation Chart, Fig. 2). While it is not the intention to substantiate the correlation in this paper (see Manspeizer and others, 1978), a brief discussion of the data base is in order. The data (including basalt geochemistry, isotopic dates, palynology and stratigraphic sequence) show that the volcanics form a paragenetic time-sequence on both sides of the spreading center. Proposed reconstructions of the rifting process, based on a Moroccan Mesozoic stratigraphy which presumed that the volcanics form an isochronous horizon throughout the country (as shown on the Geologic Map of Morocco, 1956) are incorrect, as explained below.

The tholeiites of North America fall into four main geochemical types: (1) olivine-normative; (2) high-TiO_2 quartz normative; (3) low-TiO_2 quartz normative; and (4) high-Fe_2O_3 quartz normative (Weigand and Ragland, 1970). Smith

4-5

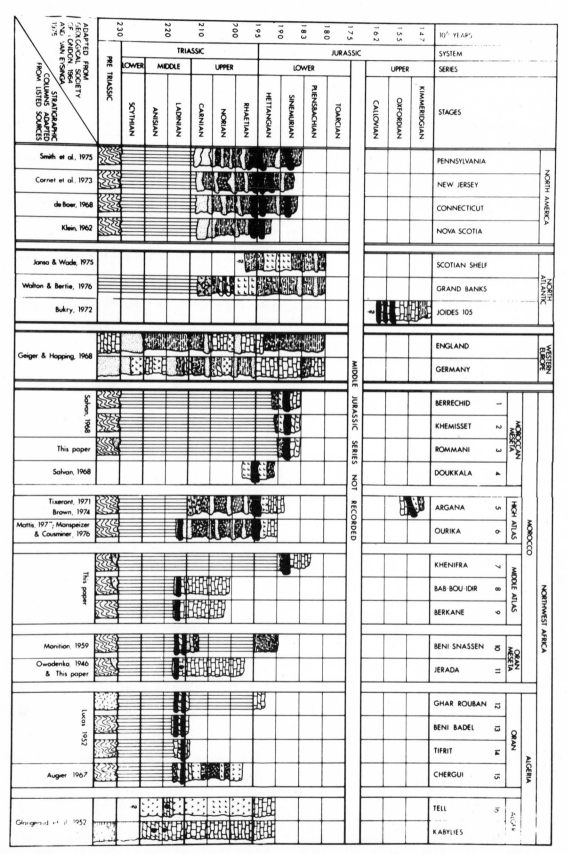

Fig. 2. Intercontinental correlation chart (Manspeizer and others, 1978).

and others (1975) demonstrated that the tholeiites of Pennsylvania comprise a
time-stratigraphic sequence of igneous activity throughout the central Appalachians. On the basis of cross-cutting field relationships, Smith and others
(1975) showed that the Quarryville magma (an olivine-normative type) formed
early in the tectogenetic phase, and was followed by the emplacement first of
the York Haven magma (a quartz normative, high-TiO_2 type), and later by the
intrusion of the Rossville magma (a quartz normative, low-TiO_2 type). Recent
studies by Puffer and Lechler (1979) and Puffer and others (1981) show that the
same paragenetic sequence occurs in the Newark and Hartford Basins and in the
Fundy Basin of the Maritime Provinces.

In Morocco the volcanics occur in three distinct, partially synchronous volcanic-sedimentologic provinces: the Oran Meseta, the High Atlas, and
the Moroccan Meseta. The oldest volcanics, dated at 211 m.y. and immediately
overlain by a Middle Triassic Anoplophora fauna, are alkaline basalts of the
Oran Meseta. Except for one unconfirmed report, this volcanic type has not
been reported in North America. The oldest volcanics are overlain by olivine
and quartz normative tholeiites of the High Atlas Province, which yield dates
of 196 m.y. and are underlain by a thick coarse clastic facies carrying the
Minutosaccus-Patinosporites Assemblage of Middle Carnian age. Low alkaline
quartz tholeiites, dated at 186 m.y. and intercalated with evaporites of the
Moroccan Meseta, are the youngest volcanics in the sequence (Fig. 3).

The chemical and stratigraphic data from Morocco indicate that a
similar paragenetic sequence of magma emplacement occurred on both sides of the
spreading center, and the isotopic age data and palynological data suggest that
these events are approximately (but not precisely) isochronous.

NEWARK-TYPE BASINS

Age

A thick basin facies of continental clastics and igneous rocks rests
unconformably on a crystalline core of older Acadian and Allegheny Orogenies in
about 20 elongate pull-apart basins and half-grabens from Newfoundland to North
Carolina (Fig. 1). The major rock types include reddish-brown mudstone, petro-
mict conglomerate, arkose sandstone and gray-to-black shale along with subordinate
evaporites, and coal lenses (Fig. 4). While tholeiitic lava flows occur extensively throughout the upper part of the section from Nova Scotia to Virginia,
sills and dikes of a similar age commonly occur from the Carolinas through New

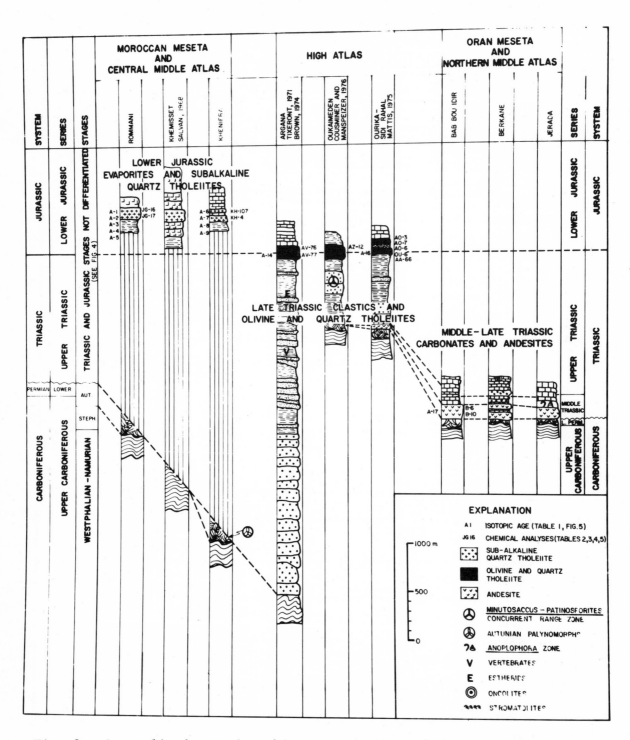

Fig. 3. Generalized stratigraphic cross section of Permian-Triassic and
Liassic strata in Morocco (Manspeizer and others, 1978).

4a

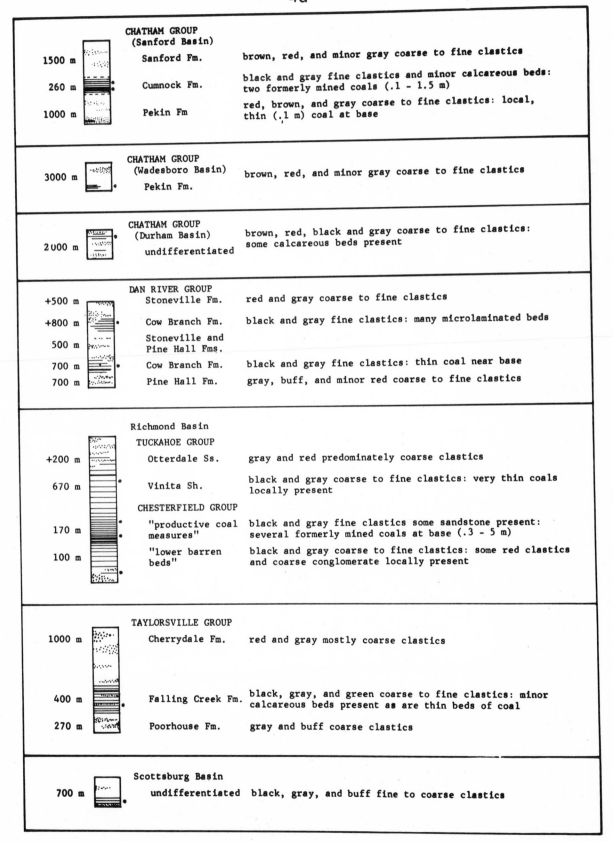

Fig. 4. Formations and divisions of the Newark Supergroup (Olsen and others, in press).

4b

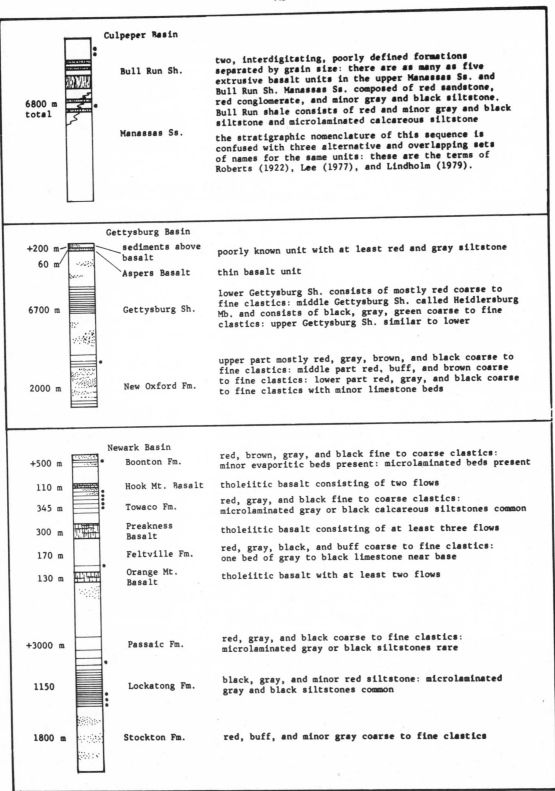

Culpeper Basin

6800 m
total

Bull Run Sh.

Manassas Ss.

two, interdigitating, poorly defined formations separated by grain size: there are as many as five extrusive basalt units in the upper Manassas Ss. and Bull Run Sh. Manassas Ss. composed of red sandstone, red conglomerate, and minor gray and black siltstone. Bull Run shale consists of red and minor gray and black siltstone and microlaminated calcareous siltstone

the stratigraphic nomenclature of this sequence is confused with three alternative and overlapping sets of names for the same units: these are the terms of Roberts (1922), Lee (1977), and Lindholm (1979).

Gettysburg Basin

+200 m
60 m

6700 m

2000 m

sediments above basalt

Aspers Basalt

Gettysburg Sh.

New Oxford Fm.

poorly known unit with at least red and gray siltstone

thin basalt unit

lower Gettysburg Sh. consists of mostly red coarse to fine clastics: middle Gettysburg Sh. called Heidlersburg Mb. and consists of black, gray, green coarse to fine clastics: upper Gettysburg Sh. similar to lower

upper part mostly red, gray, brown, and black coarse to fine clastics: middle part red, buff, and brown coarse to fine clastics: lower part red, gray, and black coarse to fine clastics with minor limestone beds

Newark Basin

+500 m

110 m

345 m

300 m

170 m

130 m

+3000 m

1150

1800 m

Boonton Fm.

Hook Mt. Basalt

Towaco Fm.

Preakness Basalt

Feltville Fm.

Orange Mt. Basalt

Passaic Fm.

Lockatong Fm.

Stockton Fm.

red, brown, gray, and black fine to coarse clastics: minor evaporitic beds present: microlaminated beds present

tholeiitic basalt consisting of two flows

red, gray, and black fine to coarse clastics: microlaminated gray or black calcareous siltstones common

tholeiitic basalt consisting of at least three flows

red, gray, black, and buff coarse to fine clastics: one bed of gray to black limestone near base

tholeiitic basalt with at least two flows

red, gray, and black coarse to fine clastics: microlaminated gray or black siltstones rare

black, gray, and minor red siltstone: microlaminated gray and black siltstones common

red, buff, and minor gray coarse to fine clastics

4-10

4c

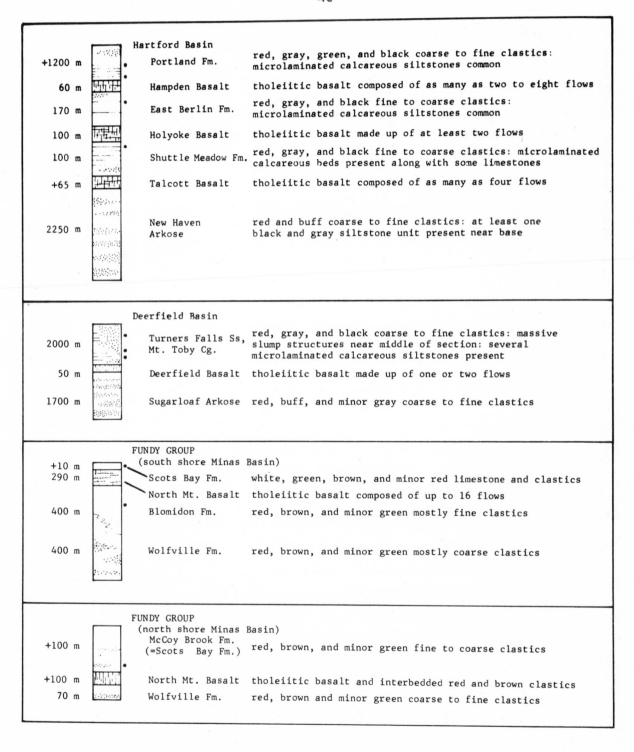

Hartford Basin

+1200 m		Portland Fm.	red, gray, green, and black coarse to fine clastics: microlaminated calcareous siltstones common
60 m		Hampden Basalt	tholeiitic basalt composed of as many as two to eight flows
170 m		East Berlin Fm.	red, gray, and black fine to coarse clastics: microlaminated calcareous siltstones common
100 m		Holyoke Basalt	tholeiitic basalt made up of at least two flows
100 m		Shuttle Meadow Fm.	red, gray, and black fine to coarse clastics: microlaminated calcareous beds present along with some limestones
+65 m		Talcott Basalt	tholeiitic basalt composed of as many as four flows
2250 m		New Haven Arkose	red and buff coarse to fine clastics: at least one black and gray siltstone unit present near base

Deerfield Basin

2000 m		Turners Falls Ss, Mt. Toby Cg.	red, gray, and black coarse to fine clastics: massive slump structures near middle of section: several microlaminated calcareous siltstones present
50 m		Deerfield Basalt	tholeiitic basalt made up of one or two flows
1700 m		Sugarloaf Arkose	red, buff, and minor gray coarse to fine clastics

FUNDY GROUP
(south shore Minas Basin)

+10 m		Scots Bay Fm.	white, green, brown, and minor red limestone and clastics
290 m		North Mt. Basalt	tholeiitic basalt composed of up to 16 flows
400 m		Blomidon Fm.	red, brown, and minor green mostly fine clastics
400 m		Wolfville Fm.	red, brown, and minor green mostly coarse clastics

FUNDY GROUP
(north shore Minas Basin)

+100 m		McCoy Brook Fm. (=Scots Bay Fm.)	red, brown, and minor green fine to coarse clastics
+100 m		North Mt. Basalt	tholeiitic basalt and interbedded red and brown clastics
70 m		Wolfville Fm.	red, brown and minor green coarse to fine clastics

England into southern Newfoundland. With only local exceptions the strata dip towards the border fault, where they become conglomeratic and are broadly warped into anticlines and synclines (Rodgers, 1970). Similar rock sequences with evaporites and salt diapirs (?) occur on the continental margin (Sheridan, 1973; Ballard and Uchupi, 1975; and Grow, 1980).

Throughout this century, until about 1972, these rocks were considered to be Triassic. The pioneering palynological studies of Cornet and others (1973) and Cornet and Traverse (1975) have shown that many of these basins contain Early Jurassic beds. Determining the age of these continental beds and correlating the various basins in North America and around the Atlantic Ocean have posed a problem because they were thought to be nearly barren of fossils and they particularly lacked the marine fossils generally used for Mesozoic biostratigraphy. Isotopic age dating and paleomagnetic data alone are too ambiguous to date this stratigraphic section. It has now been determined that the basin sequence contains a rich and varied fossil assemblage (Thomson, 1979, and Olsen, 1980). The studies of Cornet and his colleagues and the research of Dunay and Fisher (1974) in North America, Geiger and Hopping (1968) in the North Sea Basin, Clarke (1965) and Fisher (1972) in England, Klaus (1960) in Austria, Leschik (1955) and Scheuring (1970), and Cousminer and Manspeizer (1976) in Morocco have demonstrated the importance of using spores and pollen to date and correlate the basin facies (Fig. 5). Similarly, Olsen and Galton (1977) and Olsen and others (in press) have demonstrated respectively the use of terrestrial vertebrates and of fishes for correlating rocks of the Newark Group. While there is still substantial disagreement over the correlation of various stratigraphic horizons within the sequence (see, for example, Puffer and others, 1981), the fundamental age framework established by biostratigraphic criteria seems to have been accepted by most researchers (see Fig. 6). The basins with only Late Triassic (Middle to Late Carnian) rocks are the Richmond, Taylorsville, Scottsburg, Sanford, Durham and Dan River. The basins where sedimentation extended from Late Triassic (Carnian to Norian) to Early Jurassic (Hettangian and even perhaps to Toarcian) are the Culpeper, Gettysburg, Newark, Hartford, Deerfield and Fundy (Fig. 6). Data (from these remnant basins) indicate that while sedimentation may have begun earlier in the southern basins, it lasted longer in the north (Fig. 6).

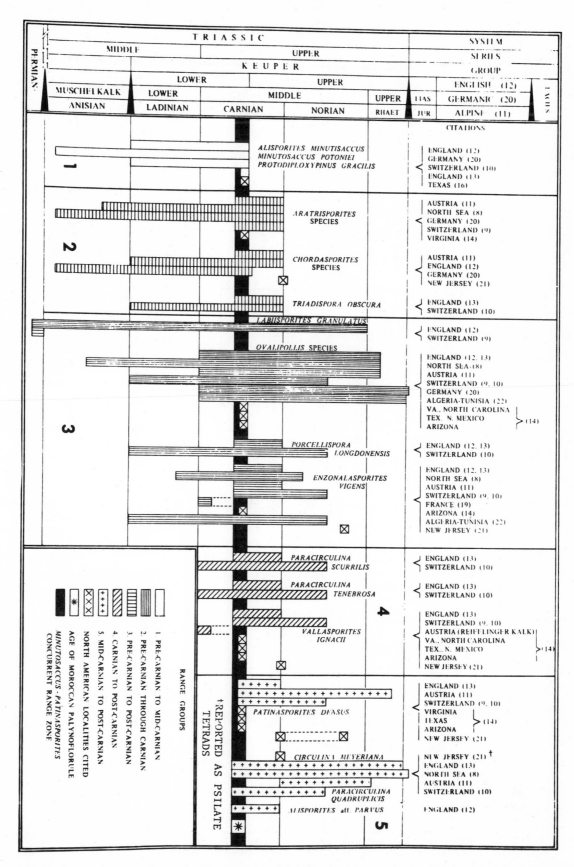

Fig. 5. Cited stratigraphic and geographic occurrences of age-diagnostic palynomorphs from the Central High Atlas of Morocco (Cousminer and Manspeizer, 1976).

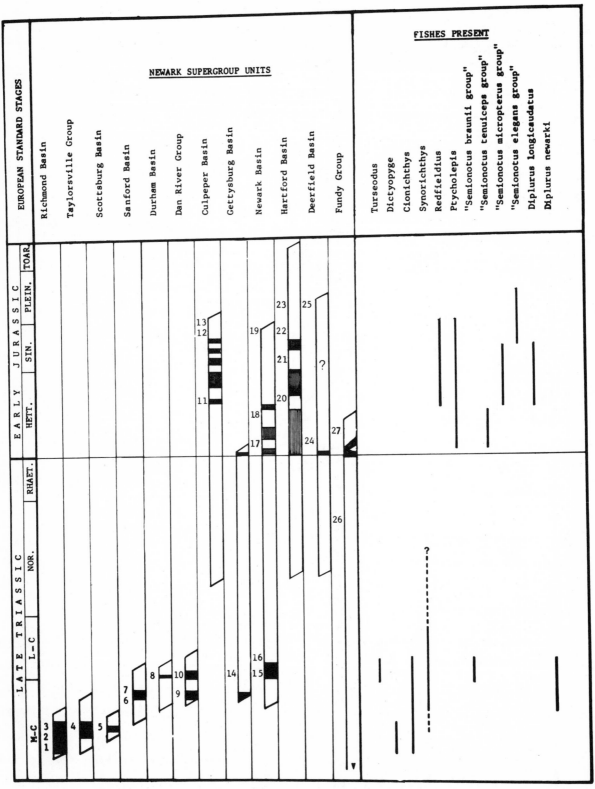

Fig. 6. Summary chart for correlation of the Newark Supergroup by fossil
fish. The numbers refer to fish-producing horizons given in the
text. Vertical ruling indicates extrusive basalt units. The
righthand side of the chart shows the ranges of the fish taxa
used in constructing this correlation. Thickness of units not
to scale. (Olsen and others, in press.)

Igneous Rocks

The tholeiitic lavas and intrusives that characterize the upper part of the rift sequence from the Carolinas to the Avalon Peninsula of southern New-foundland, provide unique information on basin tectonics, mantle dynamics, plate motion and time-stratigraphic correlation.

The lava flows, which occur only in the upper part of the stratigraphic sequence from Virginia to Nova Scotia, were emplaced in the Hettangian-Sinemurian, or about twenty million years after the accumulation of 3 to 5 km of coarse clastics and the onset of wrench faulting (in the Carnian). Their emplacement signals a fundamental change in the stress field. Most of the tholeiitic lava was emplaced as multiple flows through a series of lava tunnels and tubes that occasionally arched and pierced the overlying thin pahoehoe shell, but some flows were emplaced as deep-water (lacustrine), pillow lava, fissure eruptions and volcanic breccias in pull-apart basins (Manspeizer, 1980).

The trend of the sedimentary basins follows the strike of the pre-Triassic rocks, but the dike swarms cut across the basin and are densely concentrated in the Carolinas. Almost none of the intrusives occur along known border faults. May (1971) has also shown that the dikes of North America, South America and Africa form a radial pattern, centered on the Blake Plateau. Their distribution on land coincides with the Appalachian gravity high, and on the shelf with aeromagnetic anomalies. Many of the dikes must be considerably younger than the lava flows, since they cut across the border faults, the marginal highlands and even the folded and faulted rift strata. Since the volcanics are Rhaetic-Liassic or younger, the dikes are mostly Early Jurassic to possibly Malm (DeBoer and Snider, 1979).

Based on the regional distribution of magnetic and chemical properties, DeBoer and Snider (1979) concluded that the basins and the distribution of radial dikes could be explained by a two-phase tectonic model resulting from hot spot (mantle plume) activity located first (Late Triassic-Earliest Jurassic) over the Carolinas and then (Later Jurassic) over the Blake Plateau. The earliest phase, beginning in the south and progressing northward along the Appalachian axis, was characterized by crustal arching and the formation of basins generally concordant with the Appalachian fabric. The second phase involved longitudinal shearing and caused strike-slip motion along pre-existing fractures, folding, regional fracturing, and the injection of dikes discordant to the Appalachian trend. Both the mafic chemistry and Triassic age of dikes throughout New England (McHone, 1978) and into the Avalon Peninsula of Newfoundland (Papezik and Hodych, 1980), however, are clearly not compatible with the "zipper effect" of a simple or single hot spot model.

Geochemical studies by Puffer and others (1981) show that where multiple flows occur in different basins, e.g., the Newark and Hartford Basins, the magma underwent a sequence of distinct chemical changes that are predictable from one basin to the next. The crystallization pattern for the First, Second, and Third Watchung lavas of the Newark Basin is the same for the Talcott, Holyoke and Hampden flows of the Hartford Basin. These researchers also present very cogent stratigraphic arguments that the lavas are both rock- and time-rock units, and that the paleomagnetic and radiometric data are too ambiguous at this level of correlation. These data provide us with powerful support for the uniformity of sub-crustal processes during rifting within a broad area.

Tectonic Framework

The system of basins comprises a long curved string of elongate, northeast trending half-grabens that follows the core of the Acadian-Allegheny Orogenies and the main gravity high of the Appalachians (Fig. 1). In the Southern Appalachians, the gravity high is located in the Piedmont Province and the basins are distributed about its axis. For example, the Durham-Deep River-Wadesboro Basin, which lies southeast of the gravity high, has a west-facing border fault with east-dipping strata, and forms a complementary pair with the Dan River Basin to the northwest, as mirror images across a plane of symmetry. In the Northern Appalachians, one branch of the gravity high extends east of the Newark-Gettysburg-Culpeper Basin and west of the Hartford Basin into the Berkshire-Green Mountain-Sutton Mountain Axis, while another branch extends along the western Gulf of Maine through the Fundy Basin, along the Cobequid-Chedabucto Fault Zone and into the Orpheus Graben (Mayhew, 1975). If the northern end of the Newark Basin or the southern end of the Hartford Basin were extended a few kilometers, they too would constitute paired half-grabens facing each other, giving rise to the notion that these basins evolved from a single graben that was subsequently separated into half-grabens by regional uplift along the axis of the basin (see Sanders, 1963, the broad terrane hypothesis).

The border fault zone of each half-graben is several kilometers wide with high-angle normal faults that appears to "step down" into the basin, and thick fanglomerate sequences that overstep the border. The margins of the basin are marked by fluvial-deltaic conglomerate and sandstones that overlap the basement with no evidence of faulting. Ratcliffe (1980) has shown that in the Newark Basin the location of the Ramapo border fault is controlled by major semi-ductile shear zones of Proterozoic and Ordovician age in the basement, and that these younger and more brittle Triassic and Jurassic border faults truncate the older ductile shear zones (see, also, Lindholm, 1976).

Although horizontal slickensides are common on most fault surfaces in the border zone, indicating strike-slip displacement, vertical displacement (calculated from the thickness of the stratigraphic section) may have been greater and in the order of 7,000 to 9,000 m in the Newark-Gettysburg Basin (Olsen, in press), 4,000 m in the Hartford Basin (Hubert, 1978), 4,000 m in the Durham Basin (Bain and Harvey, 1977), and about 8,000 m in the Baltimore Canyon Trough for a similar stratigraphic interval (see Schlee, 1981). Even the approximate determination of the basin fill is questionable and complicated by two facts: (1) the lack of substantial subsurface data, and (2) the presence of growth faults that step down into the basin. Recurrent vertical movement along the border fault provided the necessary displacement for the accumulation of the section which thickens and coarsens towards the border fault (see Klein, 1962; Wessel, 1969; Van Houten, 1969; Thayer and others, 1970; Hubert, 1978; and Manspeizer, 1980). Geophysical studies (Sumner, 1977; and Bain and Harvey, 1977) also show that faulting was concurrent with episodes of sedimentation, and that the northeast and southwest margins of several basins are terminated by oblique-trending normal faults providing intrabasin grabens for the syntectonic accumulation of vast quantities of sediment (see Cloos and Pettijohn, 1973). However, in the absence of a continuous system of faults along the margin of the basin and the sparsity of evidence for syndepositional faulting, Faill (1973) argues that major faulting occurred after sedimentation had ceased in basins that had been previously thinned by horizontal crustal extension and downwarped. Moreover, some researchers (e.g., Van Houten, 1977, and Ratcliffe, 1980) have reported horizontal displacement along the border fault, while others (e.g., Bain, 1941 and 1957, and Ballard and Uchupi, 1975) have shown that strike-slip faulting was concurrent with both sedimentation and basin evolution.

The strata within the basins dip gently towards the border fault, where they may be warped into broad folds or are compressed into tight en echelon folds with axes that are at acute angles to the border faults. Major oblique-trending faults with substantial throw cut the basin into prominent rhomb-shaped blocks. In the Newark Basin, for example, some of the principal faults show stratigraphic displacements of 3,000 m along a fault trace of twenty miles (Van Houten, 1969). Sanders (1963) speculates that these same faults may have strike-slip displacements in the order of twelve miles. Where these oblique faults intersect the border fault, they cause rhombic offset of the marginal highlands.

Sedimentary Facies

The geometry of the depositional basin, inferred from sedimentary facies and paleocurrent studies, was asymmetric and considerably deeper along the border fault than along the Piedmont gravity high. Subsidence along the border fault was about two to three times greater during the volcanic-lacustrine phase than during the earlier non-volcanic red bed phase, which is estimated (Van Houten, 1969) at about 0.3 m/1,000 years. Within this depositional prism, three sedimentary facies are identified (Fig. 7):

1) A marginal border fault facies, up to 10 km thick in some basins, of coarse pebbly conglomerates of alluvial fan and fan delta complexes that are interbedded with moderately deep-water lacustrine gray-black siltstones and shales. Where fans prograded into the basin, they deposited coarse-grained, angular and fresh detritus from debris flows, sheet floods and high discharge ephemeral streams eroding local horsts and growth folds along the border fault (Manspeizer, 1980).

2) A marginal piedmont facies of proximal fluvial-deltaic sandstones and conglomerates that thin along the piedmont gravity highs, and thicken towards the center of the basin, where they interfinger with lacustrine and playa deposits. Perennial streams of low sinuosity drained these deeply weathered, gently sloping pediments, spreading arkosic sands along the axis of the basin (see Glaeser, 1966; and Hubert and others, 1978).

3) A central basin facies of lacustrine black-gray, finely laminated shale and siltstone with coal, fish and conchostracans that typically inter-fingers with a playa red mudstone facies of evaporites, eolian sands and caliche soils. Although the regional climate became increasingly more arid from south

4-18

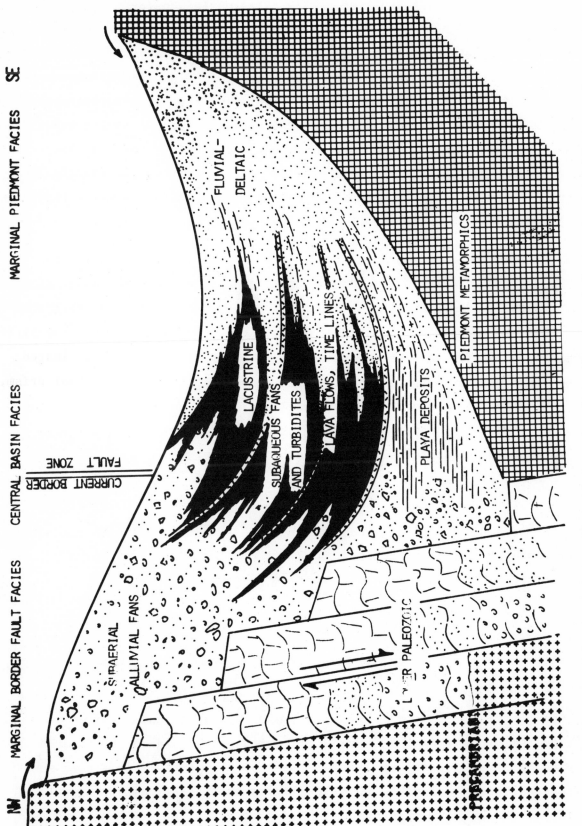

Fig. 7. Fan-delta sequence illustrating the distribution of facies in Newark-type rift basins.

to north at this time (see Robinson, 1973), alternating and/or interfingering sequences of playa and paludal deposits occur in each basin. For example, the occurrence of limestone above a thin coal seam from the lacustrine Cumnock formation in the Sanford Basin (Reinemund, 1958); the interfingering of chemical (analcime- and dolomite-rich) and detrital cycles of the Lockatong formation of the Newark Basin (Van Houten, 1969); and the association of coal and lacustrine gray mudstone with playa red beds of limestone and chert in the Deep River Basin (Wheeler and Textoris, 1978). Noteworthy in this connection are the deep-water lacustrine deposits of Early Jurassic age in the Newark Basin (Olsen, 1980), and the eolian sands (Wolfville formation) and playa red mudstones (Blomidon Formation) of the Fundy Basin (Hubert and Mertz, 1980).

NORTHWEST AFRICA

Variscan Basement

Early Mesozoic rocks of Morocco rest with profound unconformity on the Meseta, a pre-Mesozoic basement consisting primarily of Paleozoic metamorphics that were deformed during the Late Paleozoic (Namurian to Westphalian) Variscan (Hercynian) Orogeny (Michael and Sougy, 1974) and may have been continuous with the Alleghenyan Orogeny of North America (Van Houten, 1976). Late orogenic intramontane basins containing Autunian (Late Carboniferous to Early Permian) clastics (up to 2,000 m thick) with some coal and lignite unconformably overlie the massif in 15 remnant basins that were ultimately destroyed in the final phases of the Late Variscan Orogeny (Van Houten, 1976). On the bases of the palynoflorule zonation, Potonieisporites and Vittatina Assemblage Zone, Cousminer and Manspeizer (1977) correlated the Autunian of Morocco with the type Autunian of France (as described by Daubiner, 1974) and with the Pictou Group of Nova Scotia (as described by Barss and Hacquebard, 1967). Subsequent faulting in the Mesozoic broke up the older Late Paleozoic massif (Alleghenyan-Variscan Orogeny) into the Moroccan, Oranian, Meguma and Iberian Mesetas (Fig. 1; and Van Houten, 1976, Fig. 4). Triassic faulting was accompanied by extensional tectonics (including clastic sedimentation and vulcanism) and occurred only along the fragmented borders of the mesetas. A contrasting, thinner shelf carbonate-evaporite facies of Liassic age formed on the stable platform in slowly subsiding pull-apart basins of the Moroccan Meseta, as we shall explore in the following sections.

Mesozoic Basins: An Overview

Unlike the very thick Late Triassic-Liassic Newark-type clastic-volcanic facies in North America, the northwest African sequence consists primarily of a thin reddish-brown mudstone and evaporite paralic facies of Lower Jurassic age in isolated basins on the Moroccan Meseta, and a thicker, more extensive carbonate platform facies of Middle to Upper Triassic age along the northern border of the Oranian Meseta.

Only in the High Atlas, where Triassic strike-slip faulting reactivated the Late Paleozoic/South Atlas Fracture Zone, a major east-west, right-lateral lineament, about 3,000 km long, did Newark-type basins develop. Vertical displacement along the boundary of the Variscan Orogeny and the African Platform produced an east-west trough across northwest Africa that was later filled with Mesozoic and Cenozoic sediments and deformed by the Alpine Orogeny (Brown, 1980). Today this zone comprises the Tunisian Atlas of Tunisia, the Saharan Atlas of Algeria, and the High Atlas of Morocco. In general, these basins are not as extensive, deep, or numerous as their North American counterparts. A thin clastic, mudstone and carbonate facies of Triassic and Liassic age also occurs in small basins in the Middle Atlas, where faulting separated the Oranian from the Moroccan Mesetas.

Except for the slight discordance of the Middle Atlas trend, the location, geometry and northeast trend of many individual basins reflect the older fabric and structures established by the Variscan Orogeny.

Oranian Meseta

Autunian and Late Paleozoic rocks of the Oranian Meseta are unconformably overlain by Ladinian (Late Middle Triassic) high-potassic lavas (with an isotopic age of 211 ± 12 m.y.), a pink-to-buff dolomite bearing _Anoplophoa lettica_ of Late Muschelkalk (Ladinian Stage), and several hundred meters of massively bedded micrites without identifiable fossils (Fig. 3). These alkaline-rich basalts also occur in localized zones at the base of the section in the High and Middle Atlas Mountains indicate a significant volcanic event associated with the onset of transform faulting and basin development along the South Atlas Fault Zone, and with the marine transgression of the Tethys Ocean across northern Morocco. Some of these alkaline basalts contain up to ten per cent potassium and are interpreted as mantle-derived plumes, similar to and perhaps continuous with the White Mountain magma series (see discussion under Stratigraphic Synthesis).

High Atlas

Coarse clastic Newark-type sections of Late Triassic to Liassic age, measuring from 1,000 to 5,000 m thick, occur in a series of basins of the High Atlas Mountains along the northern border of the African Platform. The sections are a continental red bed facies consisting of intertonguing alluvial fan, fluvial deltaic and lacustrine deposits that are overlain by olivine- and quartz-normative tholeiites that are in turn overlain and intercalated with a sebkha facies of limestone, dolomite, mudstone and anhydrite (Fig. 8). In the largest of these basins, the West Atlas Basin of Brown (1980), the upper clastics of the Argana Valley section (Fig. 1) grade westward along the basin axis into thick salt deposits on the continental shelf (Beck and Lehner, 1974; and Uchupi and others, 1976), which crop out as salt diapirs at Essaouria and Tidsi (Robb, 1971) and are overlain by extensive Cenozoic deposits on the shelf margin (Societe Cherifienne des Petroles, 1966). Sedimentation within the basin was influenced by a system of west-trending fault blocks that stepped down against the older African craton on the south, creating a half-graben whose east-west axis differed in orientation from the northeast trend of most Mesozoic basins, e.g., the Aauin, Doukkala, and the Berrichid (Brown, 1980). Post-rift regional subsidence on the African margin is represented by a Liassic section of transgressing carbonate lagoons and oolitic shoals that give way landward to intertidal-supratidal algal laminated carbonates and gypsum-depositing sebkhas (Fig. 9; Harding, 1975).

To the east, in the Central High Atlas, the Triassic section thins, becoming finer grained where it occurs in several small east-northeast-trending fault-controlled basins that reflect the underlying Hercynian structure (Mattis, 1976). Whereas the regional paleoslope in the West Atlas Basin was inclined to the west away from the Massif Ancien, the paleoslope in the Central High Atlas was to the northeast, away from the Massif Ancien. The massif, therefore, served as the principal source for both basins. The Hercynian influence is also reflected in the overlying Early Jurassic rocks, which are composed of supratidal deposits (chicken-wire gypsum, cargneules, caliche crusts, vadose pisoliths);

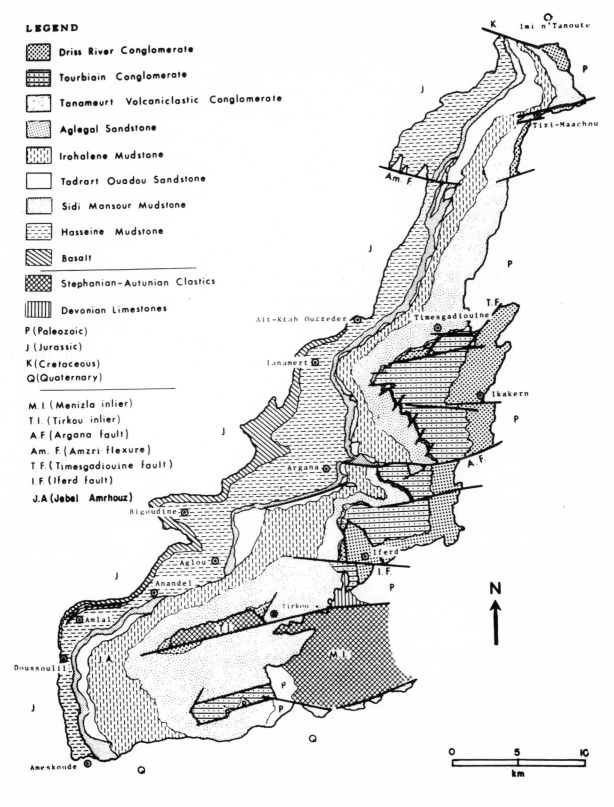

Fig. 8. Geologic map showing the distribution of stratigraphic units in the Argana Valley, Morocco, modified from Tixeront, 1971 and 1973 (Brown, 1980).

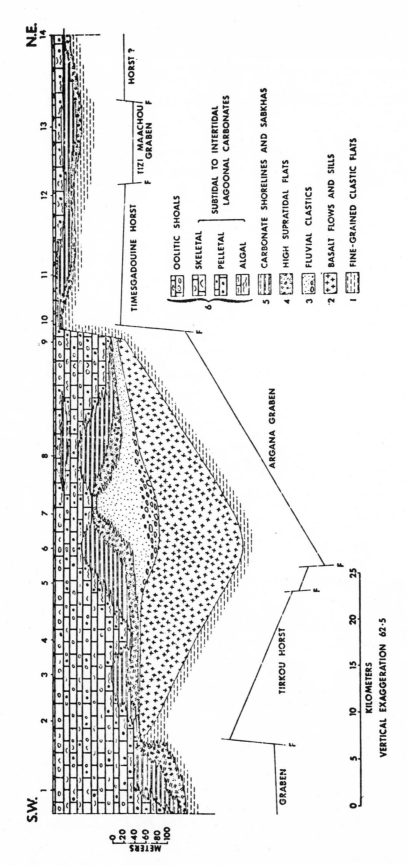

Fig. 9. Vertical and lateral spatial distribution of environments with the positions of structures known to be previously active (Harding, 1975).

intertidal deposits (algal laminated boundstones, bioturbated pelletiferous mudstones, wackestones with disruptive channels and storm sequences); and subtidal deposits (skeletal lime packetstones, oolitic tidal deltas and offshore bars, oncolites, and occasional coral and Opisoma reefs) (Lee and Burgess, 1979). These shallow water and supratidal marine carbonates accumulated in fault-controlled basins at the westernmost end of the High Atlas trough as it was transgressed by an arm of the deep water Tethys Sea from the northeast. These waters terminated against the massif and did not invade the West Atlas Basin, which was receiving marine waters from the proto-Atlantic Ocean.

The tholeiites of the High Atlas have an average isotopic age of 196 m.y., placing them near the Triassic-Jurassic systemic boundary and making them time- and rock-stratigraphic correlatives of the York Haven-Watchung quartz-normative tholeiites and the Quarryville olivine-normative tholeiites of Pennsylvania (Figs. 2 and 3). The lower part of the High Atlas section is dated by the Minutosaccus-Patinosporites Concurrent Range Zone of Middle Carnian Age (Fig. 5), and is, therefore, a time-stratigraphic correlative of the Swiss and English Middle Keuper, the type Carnian of Austria, and the lower portion of the Newark Group in the Taylorsville and Richmond Basins of Virginia and the Deep River Basin of North Carolina, the Dockum Group of Texas and New Mexico, and of the lower and middle New Oxford Formation of the Gettysburg Basin in Pennsylvania (Cousminer and Manspeizer, 1976). The base of the section, dated on the alkaline basalts, is of Ladinian age.

Moroccan Meseta

The Moroccan Meseta contains two distinctive and synchronous sedimentary facies: a thin (about 1,000 m) cratonic clastic facies of sandstone shale, gypsum and dolomitic limestone, and a thicker (about 1,400 m) evaporite facies of salt, gypsum and shale. Unique potash salts occur in the Berrichid, Khemisset, Doukkala, and Boufekrane basins of northwestern Morocco, indicating a time of extreme aridity (Salvan, 1968 and 1972). The general succession from sulphates to thick salt deposits suggests that precipitation occurred at structurally restricted saline lagoons fed by marginal marine incursions (Van Houten, 1977). (See further discussion under Evaporite Basins.) Uniquely, low-alkaline quartz tholeiites, characteristic of this sequence, were extruded as thin (50 m) multiple flows across the stable meseta into the shallow saline basins, where it thickens to about 100 to 200 m. These tholeiites (isotopic age of 186 m.y.) are distinctly different from all other volcanics in Morocco (Fig. 3). They may be correlated to the Rossville basalts of Sinemurian age (Liassic) in Pennsylvania (Manspeizer and others, 1978).

Middle Atlas

Basins of the Middle Atlas Province are similar to the Liassic basins on the Moroccan Meseta. They are shallow (less than 600 m), small, isolated and asymmetric basins filled with fluvial-deltaic red beds, playa mudstones and evaporites, and multiple lava flows of sub-alkaline quartz tholeiites that are interbedded and overlain by massively bedded limestone (see Lorenz, 1976; and Manspeizer, 1978). The province also includes isolated occurrences of potassium-rich basalts similar to those on the Oran Meseta.

EVAPORITE BASINS

A Tethys Transgression

During the Late Triassic as clastic sedimentation was occurring in eastern North America, the western margin of the transgressing Tethys Sea was the site of a complex network of northeast-trending sub-basins that were domi-nated by carbonates and sulphates in proximal basins of the southern Alps and southern Spain, and by halite with minor amounts of anhydrite and dolomite in the distal basins of Algeria, Tunisia and the Aquitaine (Fig. 10; Jansa and Buscow, 1972; and Jansa and others, 1980). Farther west, in the Lusitania Basin and in eastern Grand Banks, over 2,000 m of pure halite (Osprey Evapo-rites) was deposited without any carbonates in broad pull-apart basins on a Variscan basement (Figs. 10 and 11). To the south, extreme evaporation caused the precipitation of more than 1,000 m of halite with potash salts in the Doukkala, Berrichid, Khemisset and Pre-Rif basins on the Moroccan Meseta (Fig. 1). The depletion of calcium ions in the distal basins resulted from the extraction by biological activity and chemical precipitation over carbonate banks to the east (Jansa and others, 1980). A remarkable balance must have been maintained between the influx of calcium-depleted brines from the east and sub-sidence of this vast salt flat. But the basin must have experienced periods of non-precipitation when salt may have been dissolved, since the thickness of the Moroccan salt is less, as pointed out by Van Houten (1977). Evaporite sedimen-tation continued into the Hettangian-Sinemurian, when sea level changes flooded

4-26

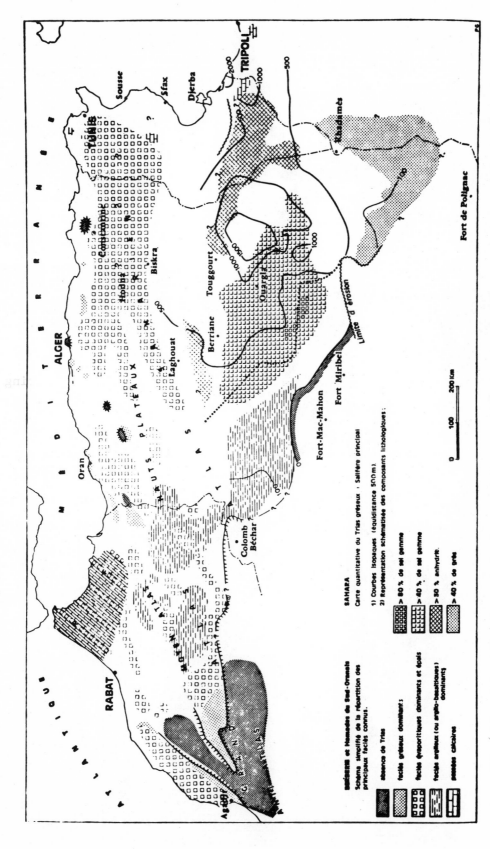

Fig. 10. Distribution of dominant Triassic facies in northwest Africa; the isopachous lines are schematically drawn on the principal Triassic sandstones and salt deposits of the Sahara Platform (Busson, 1972).

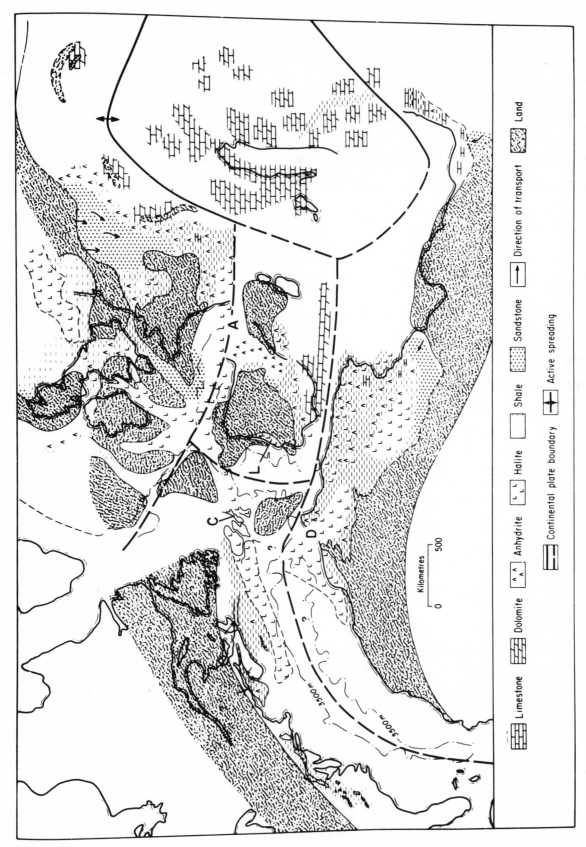

Fig. 11. Late Triassic paleogeography of the western margin of Tethys. The continental plate reconstruction of LePichon et al. (1977) has been modified in the North Atlantic region after Jansa and Wade (1975). A = Aquitaine Basin; C = Carson Sub-basin; D = Doukkala Basin; L = Lusitanian Basin (Jansa and others, 1980).

the continental margins with marine transgressions building up carbonate platforms.

As marine seas transgressed Grand Banks in the Late Triassic (Fig. 12),
continental clastic deposition prevailed on the Scotian Shelf about 1,000 km to
the west. The Shelf, underlain by an Acadian basement, received sediment almost
continuously from the Middle Triassic through the Pliocene. In that regard, its
subsidence (drifting) history differed markedly from Grand Banks, which shows
four major unconformities during the same time interval. On the Scotian Shelf
continental red beds (Eurydice Formation) of Middle and Late Triassic and evaporites (Argo Formation) of Early Jurassic were replaced by normal marine sediments during the remainder of the Jurassic (Fig. 13).

Although the basins of the Scotian Shelf and Grand Banks show substantial similarities to the onshore basins of eastern North America and northwest
Africa, respectively, they differ significantly from those basins, as they lack
volcanics. Papezik and Hodych (1980), however, document the occurrence of
mafic Triassic dikes in the Avalon Peninsula of Grand Banks, thereby extending
the known Triassic igneous activity 800 km east of the Fundy Basin.

STRATIGRAPHIC SYNTHESIS: IN SEARCH OF A MECHANISM

One of the outstanding geodynamic problems of passive margins, according to Bott (1980), concerns the mechanism of continental breakup and regional
subsidence of the newly formed continental margin. Although the stratigraphic
record is somewhat unclear in this area, it helps direct us to reasonable solutions by providing a timetable of sequential tectonic events (Fig. 14):

1) Prolonged and extensive Permo-Triassic supracrustal thinning following Hercynian mountain
   building.

2) Hot spot or mantle plume activity, yielding
   alkaline-rich rocks astride the proto-Atlantic
   Axis.

3) Wrench and transform faulting and sedimentation
   with concomitant leakage of the Tethys waters
   south along the axis of the proto-Atlantic
   Ocean.

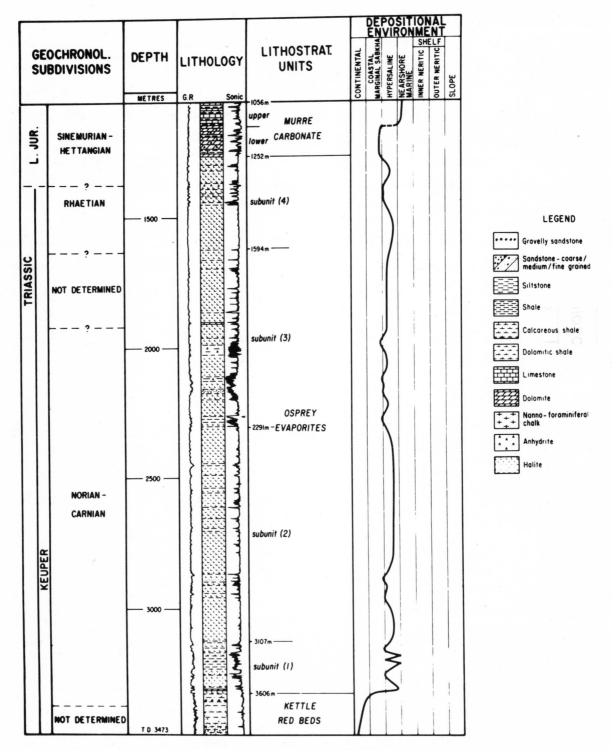

Fig. 12. Stratigraphy and depositional environments of Triassic-
Jurassic deposits in the Amoco-Imp-Skelly Osprey H-84
well, Grand Banks (Jansa and others, 1980).

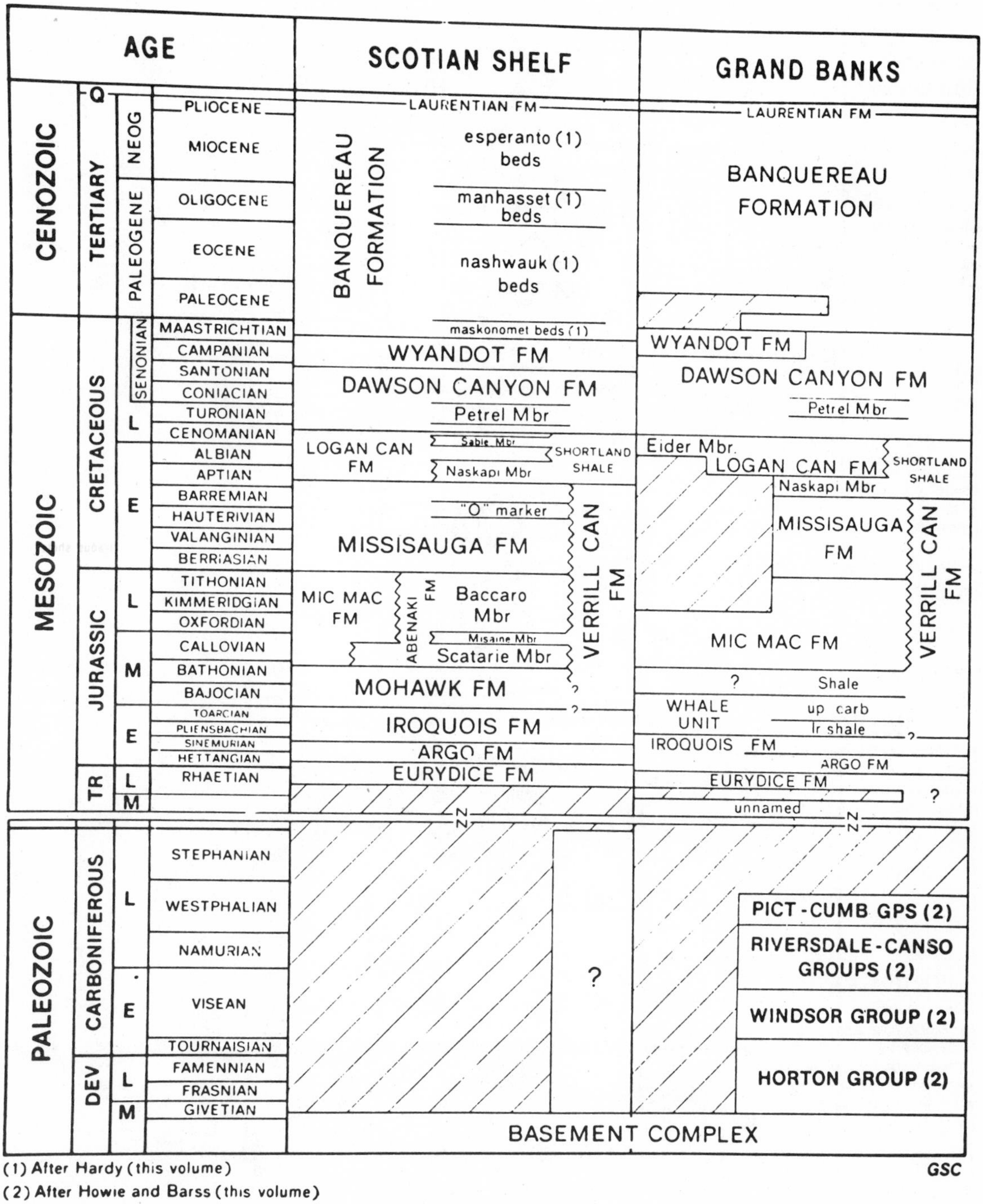

AGE			SCOTIAN SHELF	GRAND BANKS
CENOZOIC	TERTIARY	Q / NEOG: PLIOCENE, MIOCENE / PALEOGENE: OLIGOCENE, EOCENE, PALEOCENE	LAURENTIAN FM — BANQUEREAU FORMATION: esperanto (1) beds, manhasset (1) beds, nashwauk (1) beds, maskonomet beds (1)	LAURENTIAN FM — BANQUEREAU FORMATION
MESOZOIC	CRETACEOUS	Senonian: MAASTRICHTIAN, CAMPANIAN, SANTONIAN, CONIACIAN, TURONIAN, CENOMANIAN / L: ALBIAN, APTIAN / E: BARREMIAN, HAUTERIVIAN, VALANGINIAN, BERRIASIAN	WYANDOT FM; DAWSON CANYON FM; Petrel Mbr; LOGAN CAN FM (Sable Mbr, Naskapi Mbr), SHORTLAND SHALE; "O" marker; MISSISAUGA FM; VERRILL CAN FM	WYANDOT FM; DAWSON CANYON FM; Petrel Mbr; Eider Mbr; LOGAN CAN FM; Naskapi Mbr; SHORTLAND SHALE; MISSISAUGA FM; VERRILL CAN FM
	JURASSIC	L: TITHONIAN, KIMMERIDGIAN, OXFORDIAN / M: CALLOVIAN, BATHONIAN, BAJOCIAN / E: TOARCIAN, PLIENSBACHIAN, SINEMURIAN, HETTANGIAN	MIC MAC FM; ABENAKI FM: Baccaro Mbr, Misaine Mbr, Scatarie Mbr; MOHAWK FM; IROQUOIS FM; ARGO FM	MIC MAC FM; ? Shale; WHALE UNIT: up carb, lr shale; IROQUOIS FM; ARGO FM
	TR	L: RHAETIAN / M	EURYDICE FM	EURYDICE FM; unnamed ?
PALEOZOIC	CARBONIFEROUS	L: STEPHANIAN, WESTPHALIAN, NAMURIAN / E: VISEAN, TOURNAISIAN	?	PICT-CUMB GPS (2); RIVERSDALE-CANSO GROUPS (2); WINDSOR GROUP (2); HORTON GROUP (2)
	DEV	L: FAMENNIAN, FRASNIAN / M: GIVETIAN	BASEMENT COMPLEX	

(1) After Hardy (this volume)
(2) After Howie and Barss (this volume)

GSC

Fig. 13. Generalized stratigraphic table of the Scotian Shelf and Grand Banks (Jansa and Wade, 1975).

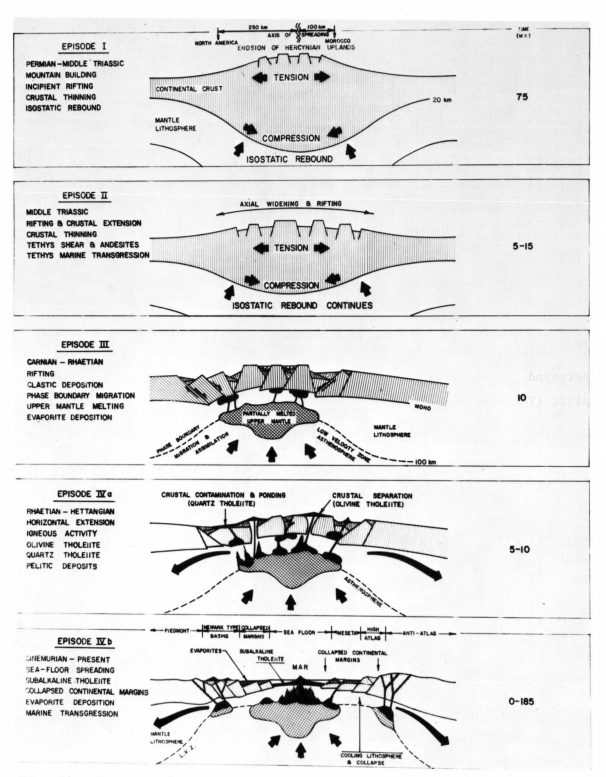

Fig. 14. Conceptual model illustrating tectonic episodes from initial
crustal thinning and rifting to sea-floor spreading (Manspeizer and others, 1980).

   4) Tholeiitic vulcanism and sea-floor spreading
       with the development of the Mid-Atlantic ridge
       basalts.

   5) Lithospheric cooling, plate subsidence and
       marine transgression.

Permo-Triassic Crustal Thinning

        The most outstanding feature of the stratigraphic record is the
profound ubiquitous unconformity in eastern North America and northwest Africa
separating the Triassic-Jurassic sequence from the underlying Lower to Middle
Paleozoic metamorphics and/or Late Carboniferous to Early Permian sediments
(Fig. 2). Extensive supracrustal thinning followed a major episode of Late
Paleozoic (Hercynian) crustal thickening and mountain building through continental collision. Many of the Late Carboniferous basins that had formed in the
Allegheny-Variscan Orogens of North America and North Africa were ultimately
destroyed in the final phase of the Hercynian deformation and the subsequent
uplift (Van Houten, 1976; and Manspeizer and others, 1978).

Early Thermal Events: Hot Spots

        A fundamental premise in most plate tectonic schemes is that plate
activity is primarily controlled by the thermal history of the underlying lithosphere and asthenosphere (Kinsman, 1975). In the context of this stratigraphic
record, however, the initial crustal uplift and subsequent faulting were primarily controlled by Hercynian and older plate collisions. We may infer that
erosion throughout the Permo-Triassic, for perhaps 75 million years, gradually
reduced the lithospheric pressure on the sub-crustal lithosphere causing partial
melting and the upward migration of the asthenosphere-lithosphere boundary.
Further uplift, doming and faulting of the crust may have resulted from thermal
expansion and phase-boundary migration within the lithosphere (Falvey, 1974), or
by mantle plumes (Morgan, 1980).

        Is there any evidence supporting a pre-depositional thermal episode?
Triassic sediments of the onshore basin in North America rest directly on basement rock without any apparent evidence of an earlier thermal event. In fact,
tholeiitic volcanic and intrusive rock, characteristic of ridge-type basalts, are
typically restricted to the youngest part of the stratigraphic sequence, where
they are cut by a younger set of tholeiitic dikes that are discordant with the
basin proper.

Existence of an early thermal event may be inferred from the occurrence of alkaline-rich rocks, which are characteristic of mantle plumes, and occur along a major lineament of transforms that extend from the Monteregian Hills and White Mountain magma series to the New England Seamounts and to Morocco, through the Canary Islands and the South Atlas Fault Zone (see Manspeizer and others, 1978, for details). The New England Seamount chain formed as a transform fault during the early opening of the Atlantic Ocean and corresponds to the landward line of alkaline intrusions dated from about 230 m.y. to about 110 m.y. While Burke and others (1973), Morgan (1971, 1972) and others believe that the White Mountain magma series and the New England Seamounts formed as North America migrated over a line of deep mantle plumes, Ballard and Uchupi (1975) and Foland and Faul (1977) believe they formed along continental extensions of the transform that localized the intrusions (Fig. 15).

What is the stratigraphic and/or structural relationship of this hot spot to the Mesozoic basins? Kay (1965) has speculated that the hot spot gave rise to the Ottawa-Bonnechere Graben, DeBoer and Snyder (1979) suggest on the bases of geochemical data, that a hot spot centered over the Carolinas and along the Appalachian Gravity High caused crustal stretching, faulting and vulcanism.

Unlike the White Mountain magma series and the New England Seamount track or the hypothetical Carolina hot spot, which cannot be related directly in time and space to the basin fill, the alkaline rocks of Morocco and Algeria occur as localized high-potassic flows and intrusives within rift basins from the Oran Meseta to the High Atlas Mountains. Dated at 211 m.y., or Middle Triassic, these alkaline rocks occur at the base of the section, where they are overlain by up to 600 meters of Late Triassic carbonates and/or clastics and Early Jurassic tholeiitic lavas (dated at 195 m.y.) and marine carbonates (Fig. 3). Lower Triassic volcanic sequences, including andesites overlain by evaporites, also have been reported from well sections throughout the Oranian Meseta (Augier, 1966) and in the Northern Saharan Salt Basin (Busson, 1972) in Algeria. Some of these rocks contain as much as ten percent potassium and are, therefore, similar to the Leucite Hills flows of Wyoming, which Carmichael (1967) interpreted as mantle-derived potassic, extreme ultramafic rock. The Eifel Province of western Europe (Rhine/Graben region) and the Birunge and Toro-Ankolo fields of the East African Rift are two examples where similar high potassium volcanics occur in

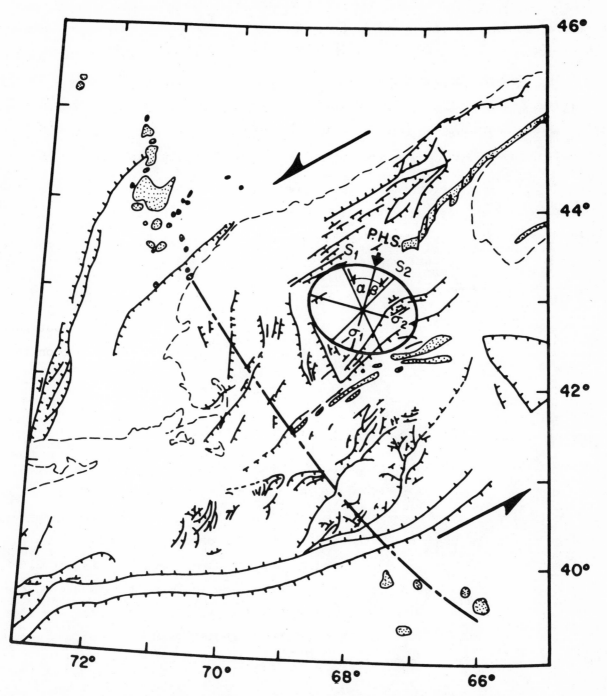

Fig. 15. Proposed orientation of left-lateral shear couple and
associated strain ellipsoid derived from normal fault
pattern in Gulf of Maine and surrounding regions. S_1
and S_2 are probable shear fracture planes; σ_1 and σ_2
are planes of tensional fractures; and P.H.S. = principal horizontal stress. Dotted pattern indicates
intrusives of Late Triassic to Early Cretaceous age.
Dashed line is trend of seismicity belt along which
lies the White Mountain magma series and the New England Seamounts chain (Ballard and Uchupi, 1972).

large alkaline provinces, and are thought to be underlain by mantle plumes (see Duncan and others, 1972; and Baker and others, 1972). It seems likely that the alkaline rocks of Morocco and Algeria are part of the larger plume-derived alkaline intrusive province of the New England Seamount-White Mountain magma series.

A more intriguing notion involves two separate hot spots, one tracking North America northwest over the White Mountain magma plume and the other tracking northwest Africa (from a North American domain) northeast over the Canary plume and along the African platform. This idea is being tested by the writer.

The stratigraphic record, therefore, documents two distinct and genetically different thermal events in the opening of the Atlantic: an early episode of alkaline igneous activity, probably derived from a mantle plume; and a later tholeiitic event, more closely related to oceanic ridge basalts and sea-floor spreading.

The time interval between these events is of the order of 15 m.y. (211 to 194 m.y.). During that time about 800 m to 8,000 m of clastics were deposited in typical Newark-type basins, giving a sedimentation rate of 0.05 to 0.5 km/m.y., or from 50 to 500 Bubnoff's (meter/million years). In contrast, the subsidence of the Los Angeles Basin and the Michigan Basin is 58 to 24 Bubnoff's, respectively (see Fischer,1975, Figs. 8 and 9).

Most importantly, however, it appears that the heat of the hot spot weakened the lithosphere sufficiently to permit the continents to be stretched and pulled apart along older zones of crustal weakness (see Fig. 16). Further cooling of the lithosphere caused additional subsidence of the basin. A. B. Watts (written communication, 1980) estimated that for the Newark Basin up to 2.4 to 2.6 km of subsidence was related to stretching and that was followed by a thermal subsidence of 2.6 to 2.9 km. The sediments which accumulated during the initial subsidence would correspond to the pre- and "syn-rift" sediments of the basin, while the sediments which accumulated during the thermal subsidence would correspond to the "post-rift" sediments. In all Triassic basins known to the writer, faulting occurs along pre-existing planes of structural weakness and/or older plate boundaries (e.g., the South Atlas Fracture Zone separating the combined mesetas from the African Platform, and the Ramapo Fault of New Jersey and New York separating the Precambrian Highlands from the Piedmont metamorphics). Data presented by many researchers show that hot spot activity was accompanied not

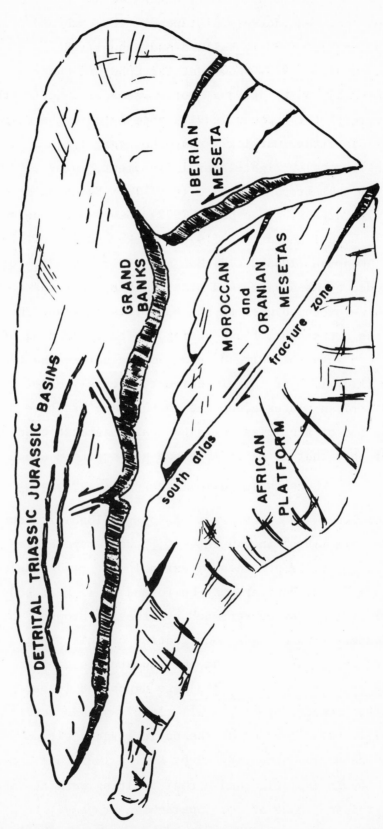

Fig. 16. Hypothetical hot spot bulge over the proto-Atlantic Axis, modified from H. Cloos' (1951) drawing of the rift bulge bordering the Red Sea, in Fischer, 1975, p. 59.

only by igneous activity, but also by extensive strike-slip faulting and intra-plate movement over considerable distances. The combined studies of King and MacLean (1970), Schenk (1971), Ballard and Uchupi (1972), Jansa and Wade (1975) and Uchupi and others (1976) show that the Cobequid-Chedabucto fault (a right-lateral strike-slip fault) of Nova Scotia was active during the Triassic and may be extended through the Orpheus gravity anomaly onto the Grand Banks and into the Strait of Gibraltar, marking a plate boundary (Fig. 1). The South Atlas fracture zone is a major right-lateral lineament, about 2,000 km long, separating the Meseta from the African Platform (Fig. 1). Based on studies of Pitman and Talwani (1972), Mattauer and others (1972), Dewey and others (1973), Evans and others (1974), Uchupi and others (1976), Burke and others (1973), Sbar and Sykes (1973), Chapman (1968), LePichon and others (1977), Foland and Faul (1977), it was concluded by Manspeizer and others (1978) that the South Atlas fracture system should be extended west to the Canary Islands and the New England Seamounts (which acted as a transform fault during the early opening of the Atlantic Ocean), and then into the White Mountain magma series and the Boston-Ottawa seismic zone (Fig. 1). If this is correct, then all major movement between the Variscan and African plates along the South Atlas Fracture Zone must have ceased by the end of the Triassic, since paleomagnetic studies (Sichler and others, 1980) show that no major movement had occurred since Liassic time.

WRENCH TECTONICS AND PULL-APART BASINS

Beginning with the studies of Rogers (1858) in Pennsylvania, and Davis (1886) and Barrell (1915) in Connecticut, Newark-type basins were considered grabens or fault troughs produced by extension at right angles to the basin axis. The same strain field, however, may be formed by a shear couple in the horizontal plane (Fig. 17). The "broad terrane" hypothesis, proposed by Russel (1892) and revived by Sanders (1963) was a modification of this thesis, and it introduced the concept that some or all of the now isolated outcrop belts were formerly connected and that the Newark strata were deposited in one or more great grabens. The occurrence, however, of many small closely spaced basins with sediment derived locally from all sides of the basin largely vitiates the orthodox view of this hypothesis (see Glaesser, 1966; Klein, 1969; and Van Houten, 1973). In this context, basin evolution and normal faulting were thought of as the terminal- or release-phase of the Appalachian Orogeny.

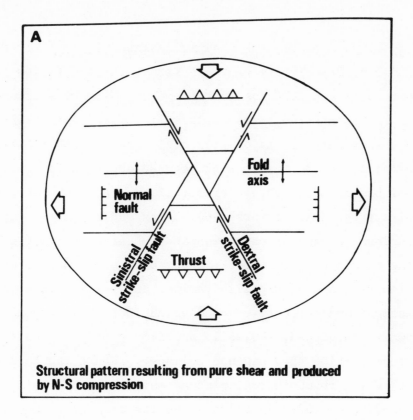

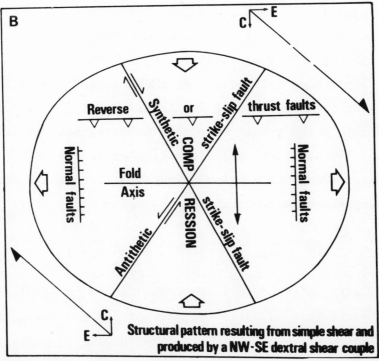

Fig. 17. Apparently similar structural patterns resulting from
(a) pure shear produced from N-S compression, and from
(b) simple shear produced by a NW-SE dextral shear
couple (Reading, 1978).

Today many of these same basins, assigned to the initial phase of the Atlantic tectonic cycle, display tectonic structures and facies characteristic of rhomb-shaped, pull-apart basins that formed within transforms due to horizontal shear. In this sense the terms strike-slip, wrench and transcurrent faults are synonymous; they refer to major high-angle faults with substantial horizontal slip. As crustal plates move past each other along transform boundaries, different types of basins may form especially if the transforms are irregular, with branching faults (Fig. 18). Newark-type basins and high-standing upthrown blocks may form in regions of crustal extension and convergence, respectively. Largely oriented by the fabric of the bedrock, these basins may have steep walls formed by transform faulting and/or dip-slip faults, and tilted basin floors formed on attenuated basement and/or newly erupted volcanic rock. Inasmuch as the crust has been heated and weakened, the walls and floors of pull-apart basins may be stretched so that in time they sag and collapse. Where the basement has been pulled apart creating rhombochasms, plutons may enter the basin floor in the form of dikes and be extruded as flows along its axis (see Crowell, 1974; discussion of the Cenozoic basins of California). Differential horizontal shear along the active fault zone may create an asymmetric basin, consisting of an upthrown leading plate and a subsiding trailing plate that is tilted and broken by a series of step faults, as in the Dead Sea Rift. The asymmetric distribution of facies and the successive sedimentary overlap of the older prism of sediments in the direction of the active border fault reflects this tectonic asymmetry. As shown by Choukroune and others (1978) in the FAMOUS expedition of the Mid-Atlantic Ridge, the main topographic expression of the transform, the transform valley and the rift shoulders are mainly the result of normal faulting and vertical motion. Continuous wrench faulting along the transform creates complex structural patterns of en echelon drag folding, en echelon conjugate fracture systems, and isolated basins with complicated unconformities and sedimentary overlap along the active shear zone.

Newark-Type Basin

What attributes of pull-apart basins can be identified in this Triassic-Jurassic record? Instead of selectively examining certain features from various basins to advance a particular thesis, we shall examine structures only from the Newark Basin, the largest and best known of these basins.

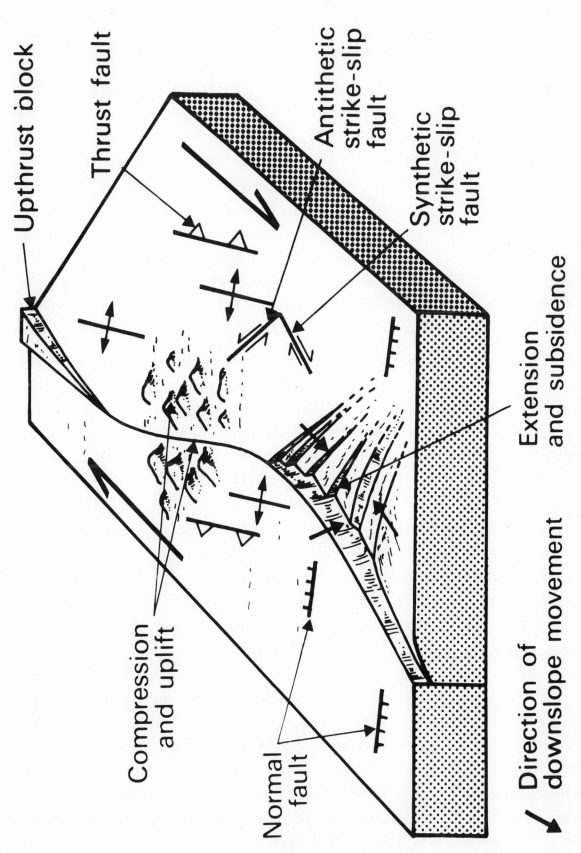

Upthrust block

Thrust fault

Antithetic strike-slip fault

Synthetic strike-slip fault

Compression and uplift

Extension and subsidence

Normal fault

Direction of downslope movement

Fig. 18. Block diagram illustrating how the curvature of a strike-slip fault may produce closely adjacent extensional basins and uplift and erosion, with superimposed tectonic pattern (Reading, 1978).

By inference we will also be saying things about the other basins. Perhaps the least ambiguous arguments and best evidence for this pull-apart interpretation are:

1) The fundamental structures of wrench tectonics include en echelon folds, en echelon conjugate strike-slip faults, the main wrench fault zone, and en echelon normal faults (Moody and Hill, 1956; Wilcox and others, 1973). While no single basin shows all these structures, in the Newark Basin the variety of tectonic structures displayed, when taken together, is suggestive of wrench tectonics. Note (Fig. 19), particularly: (a) the Hopewell and the Flemington Faults, which are en echelon right-lateral faults that may be continuous into the Ramapo Fault and show up to twelve miles of horizontal slip; (b) the Chalfont Fault, which is part of a major en echelon left-lateral fault system, may be continued into the east-west trending narrow neck between the Newark and Gettysburg basins and along the Cornwall-Kelvin displacement (Drake and Woodward, 1963).

Figure 15 shows that these major structural elements define a left-lateral, east-west oriented, shear couple, with the principal horizontal shear and principal tensional strain oriented northeast-southwest (B-B'), the principal compressional strain oriented northwest-southeast (A-A'), and the principal strike-slip faults trending parallel to shear planes S_1 and S_2. This regional strain field is almost identical to the one established by Ballard and Uchupi (1975) for the Gulf of Maine (Fig. 15). Note the sense of motion and orientation of the Flemington-Hopewell faults and the shear plane defining the White Mountain magma series-New England Seamount Lineament (S_1), and the Chalfont fault system with the Cobequid-Chedabucto fracture system (S_2). Since the tectonic activity of the White Mountain magma series encompasses the time (215 to 110 m.y.) prior to and following the breakup of the continent and the opening of the oceans, we can infer that the opening of the basins, the syntectonic and post-tectonic of the Triassic-Jurassic sediment, and the post-basin dike intrusions may be related to the same east-west shear couple. Drake and Woodward (1963), LePichon and others (1976), and Van Houten (1977) have all related the Cornwall-Kelvin displacement with transform faulting just prior to the opening of the Atlantic Ocean. It appears that these basins may have actually grown or opened in a westerly direction (i.e., towards the current border fault and the site of the youngest basin sediments) as growth faulting propagated along diverging antithetic (S_1) and synthetic (S_2) en echelon faults.

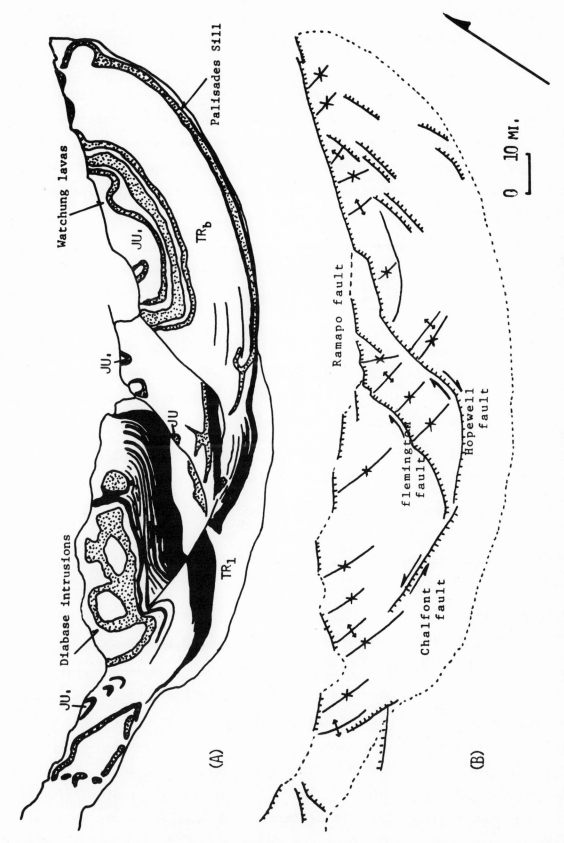

Fig. 19. The Newark Basin: (A) Generalized geologic map; and (B) generalized map of tectonic structures (modified from Olsen, 1980).

2) Syntectonic development of both extension and compressional tectonics along the border fault, leading to zones of drag-folded "syn-rift" sediments with angular unconformities, and zones of evolving depositional basins (Figs. 19 and 20; also, see Ratcliffe, 1980).

3) Moderately deep-water fissure eruptions with pillow lavas, dikes and volcanic flow lobes are restricted to deep volcanic troughs near the structural axis of the basin (Manspeizer, 1980; Fig. 20). In fact, in none of the basins examined, do Triassic and Jurassic feeder dikes and volcanics invade or occur along the border fault, a fact we would have difficulty reconciling with an extensional model.

4) Pronounced asymmetry of sedimentary facies with fan deltas and deep-water lacustrine deposits are restricted to the western border fault, and fluvio-deltaic-lacustrine sediments occur along the eastern tilt block of the Piedmont Province (Fig. 7).

5) The absence of a continuous system of faults along the margins of the basin, indicating that the early phases of sedimentation may have begun (like the Baikal Rift) on a downwarped, sagged and/or otherwise weakened crust prior to faulting (see particularly the cogent observations made by Faill, 1973).

6) Progressive overlap of the Triassic sediment by the younger Jurassic strata in the direction of the western margin of the basin.

7) The prevalence of essentially horizontal slickensides on near vertical fault planes along the western margin of the basin, and the predominance of vertical slickensides on high angle fault planes near the east margin of the basin.

Evaporite Basins

Where strike-slip faulting occurs along a straight non-branching transform, little or no uplift and erosion will occur. Basins forming in this setting will be broad, shallow and characterized by a deficiency of coarse clastics. Evaporite and carbonate sedimentation, on the other hand, may be quite substantial, e.g., in the evaporite basins of Morocco, Grand Banks, and the Scotian Shelf. These basins all lie adjacent to plate boundaries, such as the Chedabucto-Cobequid Transform fault zone or along the divergent margins of the continental shelves (Fig. 11). While local evaporites formed in Newark-type

4-44

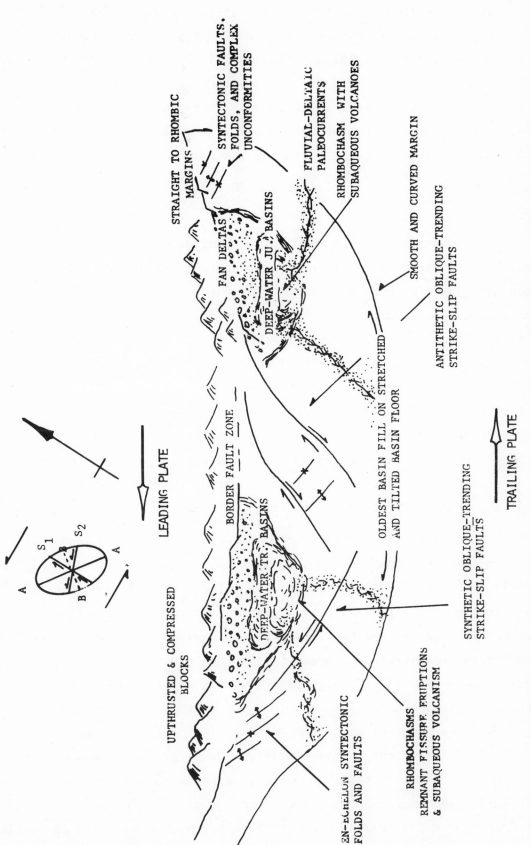

Fig. 20. Schematic diagram of the Newark Basin viewed as a pull-apart basin formed by an east-to-west-trending, left-lateral shear couple. S_1 and S_2 are shear planes.

basins under a continental setting (e.g., in the Central High Atlas), the formation of marine evaporites over a vast expanse of salt flats requires extreme res-
triction of sea water circulation (Kingsman, 1975). Plume-generated oceanic
islands, transform margins and upthrown continental faulted margins all make
effective barriers to oceanic circulation. Where faulted margins restrict
oceanic circulation, thick evaporite deposits may be laid down (e.g., the thick
salt deposits of the Essaouira Basin and the Aaiun Basin of Northwest Africa).

TECTONISM AND CLIMATE

Factors

Sedimentary processes are largely influenced by tectonism and climate.
Tectonism plays the dominant role because it controls the distribution of land
and sea, the location and dynamics of the source region and basin, and the local
relief which influences precipitation, evaporation and, to a lesser extent, temperature. Climate, while influencing the type of detritus laid down in the
depositional basin, plays a prominent role over the chemical and biological processes of the region. Before considering the effects of climate on Triassic-
Jurassic sedimentation, let us briefly examine some important terrestrial-
atmospheric factors controlling climates, namely: general circulation model,
monsoon circulation, rift topography, and the opening of the ocean basins. We
make no attempt to present such extraterrestrial factors as precession of the
earth's axis, solar flares, and so forth.

Using a modified Bullard reconstruction of the continents on which was
plotted the distribution of climatically sensitive rocks (e.g., salt, anhydrite
and coal), Robinson (1973) inferred a general circulation model for the Triassic-
Liassic atmosphere (Fig. 21). The climatic-sedimentologic implications of that
reconstruction are far-reaching, because the dominant factors controlling air
masses, winds and patterns of precipitation and evaporation over the proto-
Atlantic basins are: (1) the high pressure belt of the horse latitudes, and
(2) the low pressure belt (Intertropical Convergence Zone) of the doldrums. As
dry air descends from the upper troposphere of a high pressure cell, it warms
adiabatically (due to the increase of atmospheric pressure) and spreads out laterally near the surface to form the westerlies poleward and the tropical easterlies
equatorward. The convergence of these warm tropical easterlies at the Intertropical Convergence Zone causes the air to rise, which then cools adiabatically as

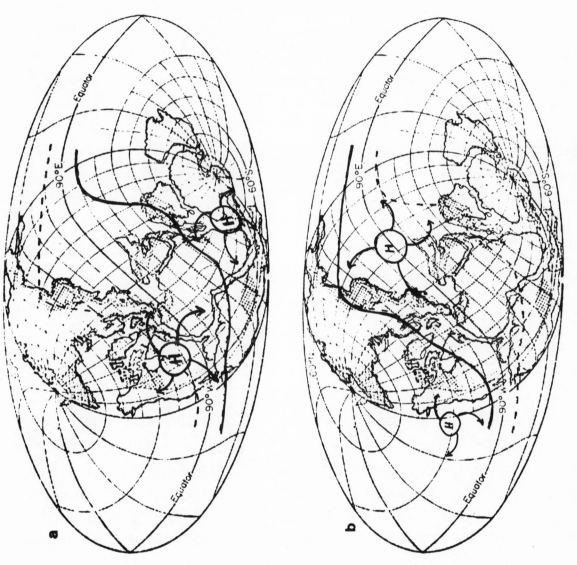

Fig. 21. Sketch of probable course of Intertropical Convergence Zone (heavy line) and probable location of tropical high pressure cells for January (a) and July (b), modified from Robinson, 1973.

it expands (due to a decrease of atmospheric pressure). Since the amount of water vapor that the air can hold depends on the temperature, rising maritime tropical air masses are typically accompanied by condensation and heavy precipitation (rain forest climates), whereas subsiding tropical air masses are typically accompanied by evaporation and desert-like conditions.

As the pressure systems migrate in response to the seasonal migration of the sun, there is a concomitant shift of climatic zones creating a monsoon circulation. Along with the marked wind shift and rainfall changes associated with monsoons, there are also substantial changes in cloud cover, vapor pressure, temperature, evaporation rates, and so forth. Today monsoons are most prominent in the tropics and subtropics, especially in India and southeast Asia, where their effects are strengthened by the presence of the Himalayas and the high plateaus of Mongolia. Considering the size and location of Pangaea and the occurrence of mountainous terrane around the proto-Atlantic, we can infer that monsoon circulation was an important element in the Triassic-Liassic.

Anyone who has traversed a fault basin, or perhaps has skied the slopes of Taos, New Mexico, and then hiked the dried river bed of the Rio Grande, or has eaten fruit from the biblical orchards of Jerusalem or Hebron and then experienced the oppressive heat along the salt flats of the Dead Sea Rift, must have marvelled at the climate extremes. The shoulders of the Dead Sea Rift, for example, receive about 800-1,000 mm of rain per year, while the floor of the basin receives only 5-50 mm of rain per year and yields up to 2,000 mm of water per year through evaporation. The reason for these climatic extremes, which characterize all block-faulted basins and which show up in the stratigraphic record as alternating and interfingering layers of wet and dry climatic indicators, is found in the rift topography (see discussion below and Fig. 22). The orographic effect in the Lower Mesozoic was heightened because of monsoon circulation.

To complete our brief discussion, it is sufficient at this time just to note that the opening of the ocean had a profound effect on the paleoclimatology, because it provided the primary source of water vapor for clouds and rainwater for the streams, lakes and other chemical and physical processes in these basins.

Pressure Systems and Parcels of Air

Let us follow the trajectory of a parcel of air as it crosses north central Pangaea. During the northern winter the proto-Atlantic region was

4-48

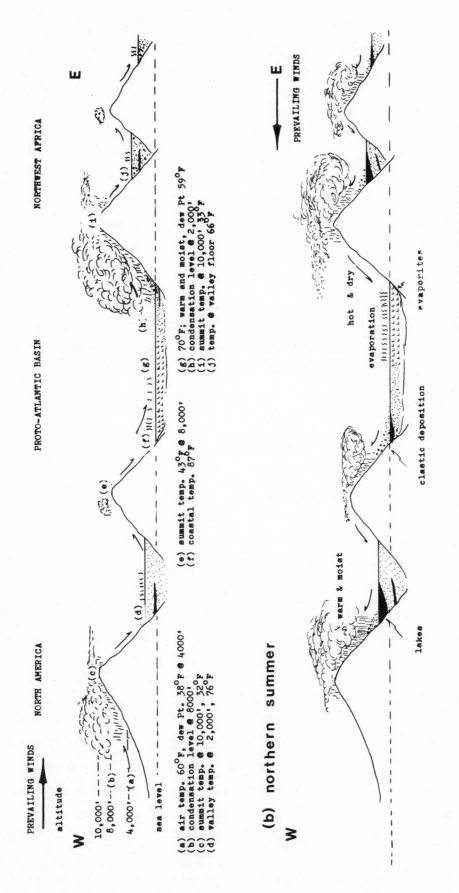

Fig. 22. Sketch of possible cooling and warming trends with subsequent condensation and evaporation as air is forced to rise and fall over mountainous terrane (a) northern winter, (b) northern summer.

dominated by a tropical high pressure cell that was accompanied by moderately warm dry air and prevailing westerly winds (Fig. 21). While the vapor pressure was low and desert-like conditions occurred over most of "North America", the vapor content increased over the northwest coast of Africa as the warm winds blew east across the warm shallow waters of the Tethys tongue that had entered the Atlantic realm (Fig. 21). As evaporites were precipitated in the marine basins, heavy rainfall and clastic deposition occurred in the continental basins to the east (recall the stratigraphic relations of the clastics in the Argana Basin and the evaporites of the Essaouira Basin and the Aaiun Basin, Fig. 1).

Consider now a parcel of air, during the northern winter, coming out of the west at an altitude of 4,000 feet with a temperature of 60°F and a dew point temperature of 38°F (Fig. 22, top left). Condensation will occur at 8,000 feet as cooling proceeds along the dry adiabatic rate of 5.5°F/1,000' (60°F- 4,000' x 5.5°F/1,000'). From 8-10,000' cooling will occur at the wet adiabatic rate of about 3.2°F/1,000' and will be accompanied by limited precipitation. The temperature at the summit will be about 32°F (i.e., 38°F- 2,000' x 3.2°F/ 1,000'). As the air descends on the leeward side of the mountain it warms at the dry rate. If no evaporation occurs on the valley floor, the air temperature will rise to about 76°F (i.e., 32°F + 8,000' x 5.5°F/1,000'). As the parcel of air ultimately descends to the coast, it will be hot and very dry. Evaporation along the shallow shelf will be excessive, resulting in the formation of evaporites and carbonates and the upwelling of deeper ocean waters. Since evaporation is a cooling process, let us assume that the air reaching the "African" coast will be warm (70°F) and very moist with a dew point temperature of 59°F. Condensation, occurring first at the 2,000 foot level, will be followed by heavy rains from 2-10,000 feet and excessive erosion and clastic deposition.

During the northern summer, when the Intertropical Convergence Zone was situated slightly north of the central proto-Atlantic region, the area was dominated by warm moist air from a tropical high pressure located over the warm Tethys Ocean (Fig. 21). As warm moist air blew across the continent it brought heavy rains, lakes and excessive erosion and clastic deposition to the western side of the basins and more arid climate to the eastern sides of the basins (Fig. 22).

HYDROCARBON PROVINCE

Analogs

Wrench-fault tectonics combined with organic-rich lacustrine sediments
make these Triassic-Jurassic pull-apart basins potentially important hydrocarbon
provinces. Yet, except for this brief presentation, almost nothing appears in
the literature about their resource potential, and today they go mainly unexplored. This is not completely surprising, given the prevalent misconceptions
that these basins consist largely of block-faulted continental red beds and, therefore, lack appropriate structures and source rock. Klemme (1980), however, has
shown that: (1) rift basins yield about ten percent of the world's present
resources, provide above average oil recovery per unit volume of sediment, and
are fifty percent productive; and (2) pull-apart basins, while constituting about
eighteen percent of the world's basins, go largely unexplored because of their
inaccessibility offshore. Significant petroleum production today, however, comes
from lacustrine sequences in China, the Rocky Mountains, Europe and Africa (see
Ryder, 1980). Among the most instructive examples from the context of this
course are those basins that formed in a lacustrine setting during the early
faulting phases of the South Atlantic, namely: the Gabon, Cabinda, Congo Brazza-
ville and Angola Basins of the West African Passive Margin (Brice and others,
1980; and Brice and Pardo, 1980), and the Reconcavo Basin of eastern Brazil
(Ghignone and DeAndrade, 1970). While production in these basins is mainly
from Early Cretaceous fluvial-deltaic sandstones and non-marine carbonates
flanking the margins of the basin, organic-rich deep-water lacustrine sediments
provide the source for the hydrocarbons.

Lake Deposits

Organic-rich lacustrine sediments also comprise a major part of the
Triassic and Jurassic sections in Newark-type basins of North America and
Morocco. In some basins lacustrine deposits contain up to eight percent organic
carbon (Manspeizer and others, 1981). Like the producing horizons of the West
African basins, these beds formed in deep-water stratified lakes with anoxic
bottom conditions. Laterally they may interfinger with non-marine shelf carbonates and turbidite-generated sediments from near-shore fan deltas and fluvial-
deltaic complexes. Cyclical lacustrine sequences, recording the expansion and
contraction of perennial lakes, characterize these beds. Like the Green River shales,

micro-laminated sediment with well preserved whole fish from the center of the basin are widespread. Besides numerous species of fish, these lake beds abound with amorphous algal kerogen, zooplankton, pollen and spores, and plant cuticles (Olsen, 1980). These organic-rich micro-laminated sediments are the result of depressed ecological efficiency in a highly productive lake. Perhaps as in the case of Lake Tanganyika, which has a maximum water depth of 5,000 feet and is permanently stratified with anoxic conditions prevailing below 300 feet (Degens and others, 1971), the majority of the organic carbon in the lake sediments is contributed during certain times of the year when dense phytoplanktonic blooms populate the near-shore environment (see Ryder, 1980).

Because of restricted circulation in young basins (e.g., the Mesozoic South Atlantic), anoxic bottom conditions occur along juvenile continental margins. Organic- and phosphate-rich middle Jurassic sediments, attesting to the lack of oxygen in juvenile oceans, was recently reported from the cores of leg 76 of the D.S.D.P. off Florida (Robert E. Sheridan, personal comm.; Geotimes, April 1981). While it is not clear whether anoxic sedimentation of this type results from euxinic bottom conditions or from the transport of detrital organic carbon from surrounding land masses, the high pressure and low temperatures of the outer continental margin sediments are ideal for the formation of methane and related gas hydrates (Curray, 1980). Based on studies of thermal maturation, Robbins (1979) and Robbins and Traverse (1980) have shown that the Triassic-Jurassic sediments of the offshore and onshore basins could have been subjected to petroleum-generated temperatures of 150°F at shallow burial under a regime of high heat flow associated with rifting.

Structure

Having formed in pull-apart basins on the passive margin, these rocks display a variety of structural and stratigraphic traps and should be given serious consideration in future exploration programs. In this regard an understanding of wrench tectonics will be important in their exploration, since sedimentary basins traversed by wrench fault zones ordinarily have the tectonic requisites for a major petroliferous province (Moody, 1973). Where wrench faulting was responsible for the formation and evolution of the basin, individual structures were active contemporaneously with the deposition of organic-rich muds, so that oil and gas accumulation could have been trapped locally. Within the tectonic system, en echelon folds (e.g., the anticlinal traps of the

Los Angeles Basin) are the most important structures for trapping hydrocarbons
(Wilcox and others, 1973). To this, we would add wrench-generated conjugate
strike-slip and normal faults, fracture enhanced brecciated zones, and facies
enhanced stratigraphic traps. Finally, on the continental shelf of the passive
margin, Triassic-Jurassic hydrocarbons may be trapped in the younger drift
sequence by salt diapirs, similar to those in the Baltimore Canyon Trough (Grow,
Fig. 61, 1980). Scotian Shelf (Jansa and Wade, 1974) and the Essaouira Basin of
Morocco (Robb, 1971).

REFERENCES

Amade, E., 1965, Le gisement de potasse Triassique de Khemisset: Maroc Mines et Geologie, no. 23, p. 23-48.

Augier, C., 1967, Quelques éléments essentials de la couverture sédimentaire des Hauts Plateaux: Algerie Service Geol. Bull. 34, p. 47-80.

Bain, G. W., 1941, The Holyoke Range and Connecticut Valley structure: American Jour. Sci., v. 239, p. 261-275.

_____ 1957, Guidebook, geology of northern part - Connecticut Valley: 49th New England Geol. Conf., 56 p.

Bain, G. L., and B. W. Harvey, 1977, Field guide to the geology of the Durham Triassic basin: Carolina Geol. Soc., October, 83 p.

Baker, B. H., P. A. Mohr, and L. M. J. Williams, 1972, Geology of the eastern rift system of Africa: Geol. Soc. America Spec. Paper 136, 67 p.

Ballard, R. D., and E. Uchupi, 1972, Carboniferous and Triassic rifting: A preliminary outline of the tectonic history of the Gulf of Maine: Geol. Soc. America Bull., v. 83, p. 2285-2302.

_____ 1975, Triassic rift structure in Gulf of Maine: AAPG Bull., v. 59, p. 1041-1072.

Barrell, J., 1915, Central Connecticut in the geologic past: Connecticut Geol. Nat. History Survey, Bull. 23, 44 p.

Barss, M. S., and P. A. Hacquebard, 1967, Age and the stratigraphy of the Pictou Group in the Maritime Provinces as revealed by fossil spores: Geol. Assoc. Canada, Spec. Paper 4, p. 267-282.

Beck, R. H., and P. Lehner, 1974, Oceans, new frontier in exploration: AAPG Bull., v. 58, p. 376-395.

Bott, M. H. P., 1980, Problems of passive margins from the viewpoint of the geodynamics project: A review in F. R. S. Kent, A. S. Laughton, D. G. Roberts, and E. W. Jones, organizers, The evolution of passive continental margins in the light of recent deep drilling results: The Royal Society, London, p. 5-15.

Brice, S. E., and G. Pardo, 1980, Hydrocarbon occurrences in non-marine, pre-salt sequence of Cabinda, Angola: AAPG Bull., v. 64, p. 681.

_____, K. R. Kelts, and M. A. Arthur, 1980, Lower Cretaceous lacustrine source beds from early rifting phases of South Atlantic (Abs.): AAPG Bull., v. 64, p. 680.

Brown, R. H., 1980, Triassic rocks of Argana Valley, southern Morocco, and their regional structural implications: AAPG Bull., v. 64, p. 988-1003.

Burke, K., W. S. Kidd, and J. T. Wilson, 1973, Relative and latitudinal motion of Atlantic hot spots: Nature, v. 245, p. 133-137.

Busson, G., 1972, Principes, methodes et resultats d'une étude stratigraphique du Mesozoique Saharien: Mem. Mus. d'Histoire Naturell, NS, Ser. C. T. 26. 442 p.

Carmichael, I. S. E., 1967, The mineralogy and petrology of the volcanic rocks from the Leucite Hills, Wyoming: Contr. Mineralogy and Petrology, v. 15, p. 24-66.

Chapman, C. A., 1968, A comparison of the Maine coastal plutons and magmatic central complexes of New Hampshire, in Zen, E-an, W. S. White, J. B. Hadley, and J. B. Thompson, Jr., eds., Studies in Appalachian geology: Northern and maritime: New York, Interscience Pub., p. 385-396.

Choukroune, P., J. Franchetau, and X. LePichon, 1978, In situ structural obser- vations along transform fault A in the FAMOUS area, mid-Atlantic ridge: Geol. Soc. America Bull., v. 89, p. 1013-1029.

Clarke, R. F. A., 1965, Keuper miospores from Worcestershire, England: Paleon- tology, v. 8, p. 294-321.

Cloos, E., and F. J. Pettijohn, 1974, Southern border of the Triassic basin west of York, Pennsylvania: Fault or overlap?: Geol. Soc. America Bull., v. 84, p. 523-536.

Cornet, B., A. Traverse, and N. G. McDonald, 1973, Fossil spores, pollen, and fishes from Connecticut indicate Early Jurassic age for part of the Newark Group: Science, v. 21, p. 1243-1247.

_____ and A. Traverse, 1975, Palynological contribution to the chronology and stratigraphy of the Hartford Basin in Connecticut and Massachusetts: Geo- science and Man, v. 11, p. 1-33.

Cousminer, H. L., and W. Manspeizer, 1976, Triassic pollen date Moroccan High Atlas and the incipient rifting of Pangaea as Middle Carnian: Science, v. 191, p. 943-945.

Crowell, J. C., 1974, Origin of Late Cenozoic basins in California, in W. R. Dickinson, ed., Tectonics and sedimentation: Soc. Econ. Paleontologists and Mineralogists Spec. Pub. no. 22, p. 190-204.

Curray, J. R., 1980, The Ipod Programme on passive continental margins, in F. R. S. Kent, A. S. Laughton, D. G. Roberts, and E. W. Jones, organizers, The evolution of passive continental margins in the light of recent deep drilling results: The Royal Society, London, p. 17-33.

Daubinger, J., 1974, Etudes palynologiques dans l'Autunien: Rev. Palaeobot. Palynol., v. 17, p. 21-38.

Davis, W. M., 1888, The structure of the Triassic formations of the Connecticut Valley: U.S. Geol. Survey, 7th Ann. Rept. (1885-86), p. 455-490.

DeBoer, J., and F. G. Snider, 1979, Magnetic and chemical variations of Mesozoic diabase dikes from eastern North America: Evidence for a hotspot in the Caro- linas?: Geol. Soc. America Bull., v. 90, Pt. 1, p. 185-198.

Dewey, J. F., W. C. Pitman, W. B. F. Ryan, and J. Bonnin, 1973, Plate tectonics and the evolution of the Alpine system: Geol. Soc. America Bull., v. 84, p. 3137-3180.

Dickinson, W. R., 1974, Plate tectonics and sedimentation, in W. R. Dickinson, ed., Tectonics and sedimentation: Soc. Econ. Paleontologists and Mineralogists Spec. Pub. no. 22, p. 1-27.

Drake, C. L., and H. P. Woodward, 1963, Appalachian curvature, wrench faulting and offshore structures: New York Acad. Sci. Trans., Ser. 2, v. 26, p. 48-63.

Dunay, R. E., and M. J. Fisher, 1974, Late Triassic palynoflorules of North America and their European correlatives: Rev. Palaeobot. Palynol., v. 17, p. 179-186.

Duncan, R. A., N. Petersen, and R. B. Hargraves, 1972, Mantle plumes movement of the European plate, and polar wandering: Nature, v. 198, p. 82-86.

Evans, I., C. G. St. C. Kendall, and J. E. Warme, 1974, Jurassic sedimentation in the High Atlas Mountains of Morocco during early rifting of Africa and North America: Geology, v. 2, p. 295-296.

Faill, R. T., 1973, Tectonic development of the Triassic Newark-Gettysburg basin in Pennsylvania: Geol. Soc. America Bull., v. 84, p. 725-740.

Falvey, D. A., 1974, The development of continental margins in plate tectonic theory: Australian Petroleum Exploration Assoc. Jour., v. 14, no. 1, p. 95-106.

Fischer, A. G., 1975, Origin and growth of basins, in A. G. Fischer and S. Judson, eds., Petroleum and global tectonics, p. 47-79.

Fisher, M. J., 1972, The Triassic palynofloral succession in England: Geoscience and Man, v. 4, p. 101-109.

Foland, K. A., and H. Faul, 1977, Ages of the White Mountain intrusives - New Hampshire, Vermont, and Maine, U.S.A.: American Jour. Sci., v. 277, p. 888-904.

Geiger, M. E., and C. A. Hopping, 1968, Triassic stratigraphy of the southern North Sea basin: Royal Soc. London, Philos. Trans., Ser. B., v. 254, p. 1-36.

Geological Map of Morocco, 1956: Paris, Ministere Production Industrielle et Mines, Div. Geologique Service Carte Geol., Scale 1:500,000, 6 sheets.

Glaeser, J. D., 1966, Provenance, dispersal and depositional environments of Triassic sediments in the Newark-Gettysburg basin: Pennsylvania Geol. Survey, 4th Ser., Bull G43, 168 p.

Grow, J. A., 1980, Deep structure and evolution of the Baltimore Canyon Trough in the vicinity of the East No. B-3 well, in P. A. Scholle, ed., Geological studies of the EAST No. B-3 well, United States mid-Atlantic continental slope area: Geol. Survey Circ. 833, p. 117-132.

Harding, A. G., 1975, The stratigraphic analysis and significance of the Late Triassic to upper Lower Jurassic rocks of the western High Atlas Mountains in southwest Morocco: Master's thesis, Univ. South Carolina, Columbia, 66 p.

Hubert, J. F., A. A. Reed, W. L. Dowdall, and J. M. Gilchrist, 1978, Guide to the red beds of central Connecticut: 1978 Field Trip, Eastern Sec. SEPM, 129 p.

_____ and K. A. Mertz, 1980, Eolian dune field of Late Triassic age, Fundy Basin, Nova Scotia: Geology, v. 8, p. 516-519.

Jansa, L. F., and J. A. Wade, 1975, Geology of the continental margin off Nova Scotia and Newfoundland, in W. J. M. van der Linden and J. A. Wade, eds., Offshore geology of eastern Canada: Canada Geol. Survey Paper 74-30, p. 51-105.

_____, J. P. Bujak, and G. L. Williams, 1980, Upper Triassic salt deposits of the western North Atlantic: Can. Jour. Earth Sci., v. 17, p. 547-559.

King, L. H., and B. MacLean, 1970, Seismic-reflection study, Orpheus gravity anomaly: AAPG Bull., v. 54.

Kinsman, D. J. J., 1975, Rift valley basins and sedimentary history of trailing continental margins, in A. G. Fischer and S. Judson, eds., Petroleum and global tectonics, p. 83-126.

Klaus, W., 1960, Spores der Karnischen stufe der Ostalpinen Trias: Jahrb. Geol. Bundesanstalt (Wien) Sonderbd., v. 5, p. 107-183.

Klein, G. de V., 1962, Triassic sedimentation, Maritime Provinces, Canada: Geol. Soc. America Bull., v. 73, p. 1127-1146.

_____ 1969, Deposition of Triassic sedimentary rocks in separate basins, eastern North America: Geol. Soc. America Bull., v. 80, p. 1825-1832.

Klemme, H. D., 1980, Petroleum basins - classifications and characteristics: Jour. Petroleum Geol., v. 3, p. 187-207.

Lee, C. W., and C. J. Burgess, 1978, Sedimentation and tectonic controls in the Early Jurassic central High Atlas Trough, Morocco: v. 89, p. 1199-1204.

LePichon, X., J. C. Sibuet, and J. Francheteau, 1977, The fit of the continents around the North Atlantic Ocean: Tectonophysics, v. 38, p. 169-209.

Leschik, G., 1955, Die Keuperflora von Neuwelt bei: Basel, Schweiz. Palaeont. Abh. (Separatdrucke), v. 72, p. 1-68.

Lindholm, R. C., 1976, Triassic-Jurassic faulting in eastern North America - A model based on pre-Triassic structures: Geology, v. 6, p. 365-368

Lorenz, J., 1976, Triassic sediments and basin structure of the Kerrouchen basin, central Morocco: Jour. Sed. Petrology, v. 46, p. 897-905.

Manspeizer, W., J. H. Puffer, and H. L. Cousminer, 1978, Separation of Morocco and eastern North America: A Triassic-Liassic stratigraphic record: Geol. Soc. America Bull., v. 89, p. 901-920.

_____ 1980, Rift tectonics inferred from volcanic and clastic structure, in W. Manspeizer, ed., Field studies of New Jersey geology and guide to field trips: New York State Geol. Assoc., p. 314-350.

_____, M. McGowan, P. E. Olsen, and J. J. Renton, 1981, Hydrocarbon occur-
rences in Triassic-Jurassic lacustrine deposits, Newark rift basin, Atlantic
passive margin: Atlantic Margin Energy Conf., Atlantic City, N.J.

Mattauer, M., F. Proust, and P. Tapponnier, 1972, Major strike-slip fault of
Late Hercynian age in Morocco: Nature, v. 237, p. 160-162.

Mattis, A., 1977, Non-marine Triassic sedimentation, central High Atlas Mountains, Morocco: Jour. Sed. Petrology, v. 47, p. 107-119.

May, P. O., 1971, Pattern of Triassic-Jurassic diabase dikes around the North
Atlantic in the context of pre-drift positions of the continents: Geol. Soc.
America Bull., v. 82, p. 1285-1292.

Mayhew, M. A., 1973, Geophysics of Atlantic North America, in D. H. Tarling and
S. K. Runcorn, eds., Implications of continental drift to the earth sciences,
v. I: New York, Academic Press, p. 409-427.

McHone, J. G., 1978, Distribution, orientations and ages of mafic dikes in central New England: Geol. Soc. America Bull., v. 89, p. 1645-1655.

Michard, A., and J. M. Sougy, 1975, L'orogenèse hercynienne à la lisière nord-
ouest de l'Afrique (structure des Chaines primaires du Maroc du Senegal):
Cited in Van Houten, 1976, American Jour. Sci. (see citation below).

Moody, J. D., 1973, Petroleum exploration aspects of wrench-fault tectonics:
AAPG Bull., v. 57, p. 449-476.

_____ and M. J. Hill, 1956, Wrench-fault tectonics: Geol. Soc. America
Bull., v. 67, p. 1207-1246.

Morgan, W. J., 1971, Convection plumes in the lower mantle: Nature, v. 230,
p. 42-43.

_____ 1972, Deep mantle convection plumes and plate motions: AAPG Bull.,
v. 56, p. 203-213.

_____ in press, Hot spot tracks and the opening of the Atlantic and Indian
Oceans, in C. Emiliani, ed., The sea, v. 7: New York, John Wiley & Sons.

Olsen, P. E., and P. M. Galton, 1977, Triassic-Jurassic tetrapod extinctions:
Are they real?: Science, v. 197, p. 983-986.

_____ 1980, Fossil Great Lakes of the Newark supergroup in New Jersey, in
W. Manspeizer, ed., Field studies of New Jersey geology and guide to field
trips: New York State Geol. Assoc., p. 352-398.

_____ 1981, The latest Triassic and Early Jurassic formations of the Newark
basin (eastern North America, Newark supergroup): Stratigraphy, structure and
correlation: Bull. New Jersey Acad. Sci., v. 25, p. 25-51.

_____, A. R. McCune, and K. S. Thompson, in press, Correlation of the
Early Mesozoic Newark supergroup (eastern North America) by vertebrates, especially fishes: American Jour. Sci.

Papezik, V. S., and J. P. Hodych, 1980, Early Mesozoic diabase dikes of the Avalon Peninsula, Newfoundland: Petrochemistry, mineralogy, and origin: Can. Jour. Earth Sci., v. 17, p. 1417-1430.

Pitman, W. C., III, and M. Talwani, 1972, Sea-floor spreading in the North Atlantic: Geol. Soc. America Bull., v. 83, p. 619-746.

Puffer, J. H., and P. Lechler, 1980, Geochemical cross-sections through the Watchung basalt of New Jersey: Geol. Soc. America Bull., v. 91, p. 156-191.

_____, D. O. Hurtubise, F. J. Geiger, and P. Lechler, 1981, Chemical composition of the Mesozoic basalts of the Newark Basin, New Jersey, and the Hartford Basin, Connecticut: Stratigraphic implications: Geol. Soc. America Bull., v. 92, p.

Ratcliffe, N. M., 1980, Brittle faults (Ramapo Fault) and phyllonitic ductile shear zones in the basement rocks of the Ramapo seismic zones, New York and New Jersey, and their relationship to current seismicity, in W. Manspeizer, ed., Field studies of New Jersey geology and guide to field trips: New York State Geol. Assoc., p. 278-311.

Reading, H. G., 1978, Sedimentary environments and facies: New York, Elsevier, 557 p.

Reinemund, J. A., 1955, Geology of the Deep River coal field, North Carolina: U.S. Geol. Survey Prof. Paper 246, 159 p.

Robb, J. M., 1971, Structure of continental margin between Cape Rhir and Cape Sim, Morocco, Northwest Africa: AAPG Bull., v. 55, p. 643-650.

Robbins, E. I., 1979, Geothermal gradients, in P. A. Scholle, ed., Geological studies of the COST CE-1 well, United States South Atlantic Outer Continental Shelf area: U.S. Geol. Survey Circ. 800, p. 72-73.

_____, and A. Traverse, 1980, Degraded palynomorphs from the Dan River (North Carolina)-Danville (Virginia) basin, in V. Price, P. A. Thayer, and W. A. Ranson, eds., Carolina Geol. Soc. Field Trip Guidebook, Geol. Inves. of Piedmont and Triassic rocks, central North Carolina and Virginia, p. B-1 - B-11.

Robinson, P. L., 1973, Paleoclimatology and continental drift, in D. H. Tarling and S. K. Runcorn, eds., Implications of continental drift to the earth sciences, v. I: New York, Academic Press, p. 451-476.

Rodgers, John, 1970, The tectonics of the Appalachians: New York, Wiley Interscience, 271 p.

Russell, W. L., 1922, The structural and stratigraphic relations of the Great Triassic Fault of Southern Connecticut: American Jour. Sci., 5th ser., v. 4, p. 483-497.

Salvan, H. M., 1968, L'évolution du problème des évaporites et ses conséquences sur l'interpretation des gisements marocains: Rabat, Morocco, Mines et Geologie, no. 27, p. 5-30.

_____ 1972, Les niveaux saliferes marocains, leurs caracteristiques et leurs problems, in R. Richter-Berburg, ed., Geologie des depots salins: UNESCO, Sci. Terre, no. 7, p. 147-159.

Sanders, J. E., 1963, Late Triassic tectonic history of Northeastern United States: American Jour. Sci., v. 261, p. 501-524.

Sbar, M. L., and L. R. Sykes, 1973, Contemporary compressive stress and seismicity in Eastern North America: An example of intra-plate tectonics: Geol. Soc. America Bull., v. 84, p. 1861-1881.

Scheuring, B., 1970, Palynologische und palynostratigraphische Untersuchungen des Keupers in Bolchen Tunnel (Solothurner Jura): Basel, Schweiz. Palaeont. Abh 88, p. 1-119.

Schlee, J. S., 1981, Seismic stratigraphy of Baltimore Canyon Trough: AAPG Bull., v. 65, p. 26-53.

Shenk, P. E., 1971, Southeastern Atlantic Canada, Northwestern Africa, and continental drift: Canadian Jour. Earth Sci., v. 8, p. 1218-1251.

Sheridan, R. E., 1973, Atlantic continental margin, in D. H. Tarling and S. K. Runcorn, eds., Implications of continental drift to the earth sciences, v. I: New York, Academic Press, p. 391-407.

Sichler, B., J. L. Olivet, J. M. Auzende, H. Jonquet, J. Bonnin, and A. Bonifay, 1980, Mobility of Morocco: Canadian Jour. Earth Sci., v. 17, p. 1546-1558.

Smith, R. C., II, A. W. Rose, and R. M. Lanning, 1975, Geology and geochemistry of Triassic diabase in Pennsylvania: Geol. Soc. America Bull., v. 86, p. 943-955.

Societe Cherifienne des Petroles, 1966, Le basin du sud-ouest marocain, in D. Reyre, ed., Sedimentary basins of the African Coast: Paris, Assoc. Geol. Africains, p. 5-12.

Sumner, J. R., 1978, Geophysical investigation of the structural framework of the Newark-Gettysburg Triassic basin, Pennsylvania: Geol. Soc. America Bull., v. 88, p. 935-942.

Thayer, P. A., D. S. Kirstein, and R. L. Ingram, 1970, Stratigraphy, sedimentology and economic geology of Dan River basin, North Carolina: North Carolina Geol. Soc. Guidebook, Field Trip, October, 44 p.

Tixeront, M., 1971, Lithostratigraphie et mineralisations cupriferes et uraniferes stratiformes syngenetiques et familieres des formations detritiques Permo-triasiques du couloir d'Argana (Haut-Atlas Occidental, Marve) et possibilitées de recherches: Rabat, Morocco, Service Etudes Gites Mineraux rept. 921, 37 p.

Uchupi, E., K. O. Emery, C. O. Bowin, and J. D. Phillips, 1976, Continental margin off Western Africa: Senegal to Portugal: AAPG Bull., v. 60, p. 809-818.

Van Houten, F. B., 1969, Late Triassic Newark Group, North-Central New Jersey and adjacent Pennsylvania and New York, in S. Subinsky, ed., Geology of selected areas in New Jersey and eastern Pennsylvania: New Brunswick, N.J., Rutgers Univ. Press, p. 314-347.

_____ 1976, Late Variscan non-marine deposits, Northwestern Africa: Implications for pre-drift North Atlantic reconstructions: American Jour. Sci., v. 276, p. 671-693.

_____ 1977, Triassic-Liassic deposits, Morocco and eastern North America: A comparison: AAPG Bull., v. 61, p. 79-99.

Weigand, D. W., and P. C. Ragland, 1970, Geochemistry of Mesozoic dolerite dikes from eastern North America: Contr. Mineralogy and Petrology, v. 29, p. 195-214.

Wessel, J. M., 1969, Sedimentary history of Upper Triassic alluvial fan complexes in North-Central Massachusetts: Amherst, Massachusetts Univ., Dept. Geol., Contr. 2, 157 p.

Wheeler, W. H., and D. A. Tevtoris, 1978, Triassic limestone and chert of playa origin in North Carolina: Jour. Sed. Petrology, v. 48, p. 765-776.

Wilcox, R. E., T. P. Harding, and D. R. Seely, 1973, Basic wrench tectonics: AAPG Bull., v. 57, p. 74-96.

ANCIENT CONTINENTAL MARGINS OF THE TETHYAN OCEAN

Daniel Bernoulli

Geological Institute of the University

4056 Basel, Switzerland

Introduction

From sea-floor spreading and continental drift, it follows that Alpine-type mountain ranges are the result of deformation and elimination of former ocean basins and continental margins (Fig. 1). Such a view was implicit in the mobilistic concepts of Alpine geology since the times when classical nappe theory was developed (Argand, 1924). The opening histories of the Mesozoic-Cenozoic oceans and a related understanding of sedimentary facies in the context of continental margin evolution provide some of the prerequisites for a reconstruction of the paleotectonic and sedimentary evolution of the Mesozoic Tethyan ocean and its margins (Bernoulli and Lemoine, 1980). In this paper I shall discuss some of the problems connected with such paleotectonic reconstructions, and outline the general facies evolution of ancient continental margins of the Mesozoic Tethyan ocean. This short outline is based on earlier publications and owes much to the cooperation of my colleagues, H. C. Jenkyns, O. Kälin, H. Laubscher and M. Lemoine.

Premises and Limitations

1) Our reasoning assumes the mobility of lithospheric plates and accepts plate-kinematic reconstructions derived from the initial fits of continental blocks (Smith and Briden, 1977) and the evolution of magnetic anomaly patterns across accreting plate margins (Pitman and Talwani, 1972). Therefore, we begin with an initial (Triassic) fit between Eurasia, the Americas and Africa (Fig. 2) and with the different kinematic stages of the subsequent dispersal of the continental fragments of Pangea (e.g., Fig. 6). The methodical difficulties of the reconstruction procedures have been discussed by Biju-Duval et al., 1977. Furthermore, we note that inside the Alpine belt the errors in palinspastic restorations are presumably larger than those in palinspastic restoration of the large continental areas: The differing plate-kinematic reconstructions for the Mediterranean part of the Tethys (e.g., Dewey et al., 1973; Biju-Duval et al., 1977; Laubscher and Bernoulli, 1977) reflect many gaps in information and uncertain interpretations within the Alpine megasuture. Such interpretations are complicated by the large-scale allochthony of cover and basement nappes, changing directions of tectonic movements, Alpine metamorphism, uplift and erosion or post-orogenic foundering of large parts of the polyphase nappe edifice in west-Mediterranean and Pannonian-type basins. Although all the different authors respect the same boundary conditions as defined by the overall

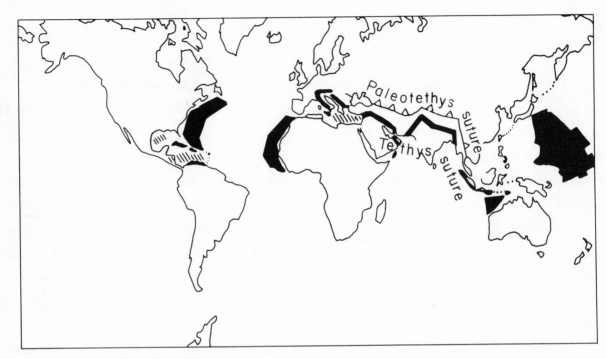

Fig. 1. Present-day distribution of Jurassic oceanic areas (black)
and locations of Paleotethys and Tethys sutures. Dashed
areas (Gulf of Mexico, Caribbean, Eastern Mediterranean)
are possible relics of Jurassic-Early Cretaceous oceans.
After Pitman et al. (1974) and Hsü and Bernoulli (1978).

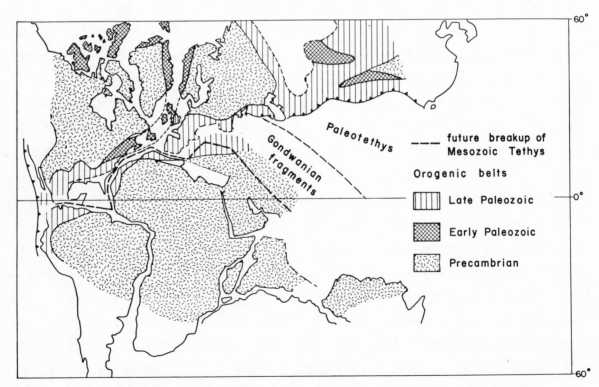

Fig. 2. Tentative restoration of continents in Triassic times,
before the breakup of the Mesozoic Tethys. Outlines of
continents after Smith and Briden, 1977. From Bernoulli
and Lemoine (1980).

movements of the large continental masses of North America, Africa and Eurasia, their results are highly divergent. In contrast to Dewey et al. (1973), we believe that there were only a limited number of continental fragments and oceanic seaways (Biju-Duval et al., 1977; Laubscher and Bernoulli, 1977). The present-day distribution of ophiolite zones and allochthonous continental basement nappes is, in our view, due to complex deformation in oroclines that are related to a combination of north-south compression and right-lateral movement between Africa and Eurasia during the Late Cretaceous and the Tertiary.

2) Whereas the general interpretation of ophiolites as remnants of oceanic crust and lithosphere tectonically emplaced onto former continental margins is now widely accepted, the age of formation of this oceanic crust, the width and palinspastic arrangement of the former oceanic areas, their origin (spreading ridge versus back arc basin) and the time and mode of tectonic emplacement are in most cases still ambiguous. In many cases, however, the association of ophiolites with extensive facies belts characterized by Atlantic-type continental margin sequences, may provide a guiding principle for the definition of former oceanic ridges and continental margins.

3) Seismic and deep sea drilling data from undeformed continental margins provide a basis for comparative anatomy of deformed and undeformed margins (Bernoulli, 1972; Bernoulli et al., 1979b; Graciansky et al., 1979). Particularly the belt of Mesozoic carbonates which can be followed from Morocco through Sicily, the Apennines, the South- and Austro-Alpine units, the internal Carpathians, the external Dinarides and Hellenides to Turkey and beyond, shows striking analogies with Atlantic-type continental margins and is interpreted as the southern margin of the Jurassic-Cretaceous Tethyan ocean. The present-day extent of the southern and northern continental margins of the Tethys and of the major occurrences of ophiolites and associated oceanic sediments is given in Figure 3.

Triassic Paleogeography and Environments

After the Variscan orogeny, the central Atlantic and western Mediterranean areas were part of one continental land mass; no remnants of pre-Jurassic oceanic crust are known from this area and Permo-Triassic deposits are mainly continental with episodic shallow-marine incursions. However, towards the east, the pre-drift configuration (Fig. 2) shows a wedge-shaped wide embayment of Panthalassa into the

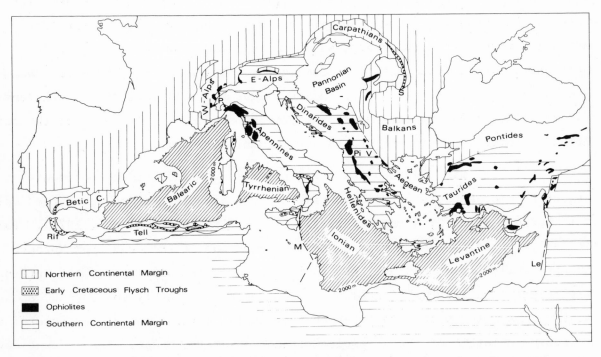

Fig. 3. Occurrences of Tethyan ophiolites with associated oceanic
sediments and of the Mauretanian-Massylian-South Ligurian
Flysch. Also shown is the interpreted extent of the nor-
thern and southern continental margins of the Tethyan
Ocean. Bathymetry of the Mediterranean basins after The
Mediterranean Sea (Defense Mapping Agency, Hydrographic
Center, Washington, D.C., 1972). Important localities:
(L) Ligurian ophiolites; (P) Pennine (Piemonte) ophio-
lites; (Pi) Pindos; (S) Sinaia Flysch; (V) Vardar Zone.
From Laubscher and Bernoulli (1977).

space between Asia and Arabia, with extensive marginal seas that reached into the Mediterranean area. This partly oceanic area has been called Paleotethys (Laubscher and Bernoulli, 1977) to distinguish it from its Jurassic-Early Cretaceous successors; its later disappearance in a "Cimmerian-Indosinian" suture zone extending from the Pontides through Iran to central Asia (Sengör, 1979) is closely linked to the later (? Late Triassic-) Jurassic opening of the Jurassic-Cretaceous Tethys and the northward drift of Gondwanian fragments. Similarly the disappearance of the Mesozoic Tethys is linked to the opening of the Indian ocean and the northward-drift of India (Fig. 1).

Figures 4 and 5 show tentative paleogeographic restorations of the Atlantic-Mediterranean area in Late Triassic times. During the Permian and Triassic, marginal seas of the Paleotethys reached as far west as northern Africa and Sicily. During the Early Triassic, the rapid transgression of a shallow epeiric sea from the east initiated marine conditions over much of the Mediterranean area as far as the internal zones of the Rif and the Betic Cordilleras. Lower Triassic sediments include a preponderance of shallow-marine sandstones, some shales and continental red beds and a few shallow-water carbonates; pelagic limestones of this age are restricted to the eastern Mediterranean area. In the Middle and Upper Triassic, evaporites and neritic carbonate deposits record an increasing marine influence which from time to time extended into the otherwise clastic Germanic facies (Middle Triassic Muschelkalk salt and limestones) and which fed the important Upper Triassic evaporite deposits of the Canadian and Moroccan Basins (Jansa and Wade, 1974). In the central and eastern Mediterranean subsidence rates were of the order of 100 $mm/10^3$ years (d'Argenio, 1974) and thick carbonate build-ups were formed. These shallow-water areas were interspersed with deeper basins in which pelagic limestones; radiolarian cherts; terrigenous, volcanic and carbonate gravity flow and turbiditic deposits, locally associated with submarine volcanics, were deposited. Some of the basins were small and short-lived and eliminated by the reinstallation of a Late Triassic shallow-marine platform (Fig. 5), but others were more extensive and permanent, some persisting throughout the Mesozoic (Sclafani in Sicily and Lagonegro in the Southern Apennines; Budva-Pindos in Greece). Because their submarine morphology appears to be linked to tensional faulting, they were generally interpreted as the result of early rifting. For the southern belt of persisting troughs (Southern Italy, Pindos, Antalya, Cyprus), this interpretation is

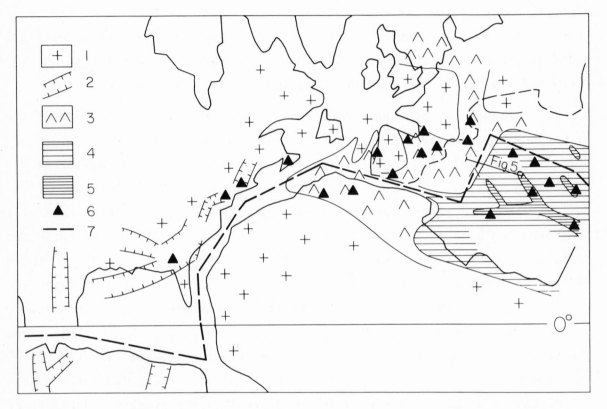

Fig. 4. Tentative palinspastic restoration of the Late Triassic paleogeography in the Caribbean, Central Atlantic and Mediterranean area (after Laubscher and Bernoulli, 1977, and references therein; Bernoulli and Lemoine, 1980).

1. Continental areas with erosion or local continental sediments. 2. Grabens filled with continental clastics. 3. Areas occasionally flooded by marine waters, including important evaporite deposits. 4. Strongly subsiding basins with thick carbonate platform (and evaporite) deposits. 5. Major basins with deep-water facies ("seaways"). 6. Middle to Late Triassic volcanics and intrusives (dikes and sills). 7. Site of breakup along the Jurassic Tethys.

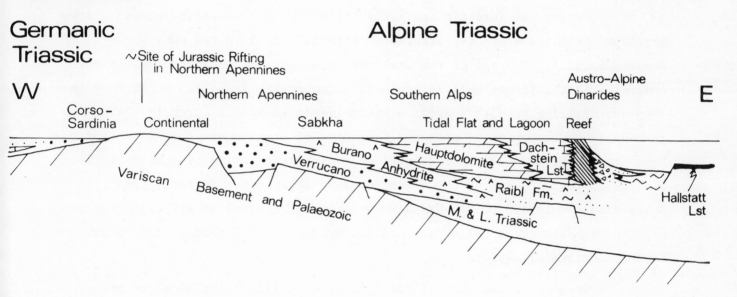

Late Triassic

Germanic Triassic W

Alpine Triassic

~Site of Jurassic Rifting in Northern Apennines

Austro-Alpine Dinarides

Northern Apennines

Southern Alps

E

Corso-Sardinia   Continental   Sabkha   Tidal Flat and Lagoon   Reef

Variscan Basement and Palaeozoic   Verrucano   Burano   Anhydrite   Hauptdolomite   Dachstein Lst   Raibl Fm.   M. & L. Triassic   Hallstatt Lst

Fig. 5. Paleogeographic profile through the Late Triassic deposits of the central Mediterranean area (for location, see
Fig. 4), modified after Bosellini (1973). The section
combines depositional areas now occurring in different
tectonic units into one palinspastic profile in order to
show the general arrangement of facies types (not to
scale). The main feature is a wedge of late Triassic
sediment transgressing westward onto Variscan basement.
From Laubscher and Bernoulli (1977).

supported by the alkaline character of the associated volcanics (Juteau et al., 1973). However, for the more northern occurrences (Southern Alps, internal Dinarides and Hellenides) a calc-alkaline composition of the Middle Triassic volcanics has been claimed (Bébien et al., 1978) and, therefore, a continuation of the Paleotethys subduction zone as far to the west as the Southern Alps has been postulated (Blanchet, 1977; Castellarin and Rossi, 1981).

Kinematics of the Atlantic-Tethyan System
During the Jurassic and Early Cretaceous

During the Jurassic and Early Cretaceous the Atlantic-Tethyan system developed from the stage represented in Figures 3 to 5 to the ones shown in Figures 6 and 7. The age of the earliest appearance of oceanic crust in the central Atlantic is not well determined, but magnetic anomalies combined with deep sea drilling results suggest a Late Liassic to Middle Jurassic age, which is roughly contemporaneous with the formation of oceanic crust in the Liguria-Piemonte ophiolite zone, as indicated by radiometric dating of some ophiolites and the approximate age of the oldest oceanic sediments. In fact, from Early/Middle Jurassic to Mid-Cretaceous times the central Atlantic and the small Liguria-Piemonte ocean followed a similar evolution of spreading and subsidence in the continental margins.

Opening of the central Atlantic also implies relative movements between Africa and Eurasia and a sinistral transcurrent plate boundary from Iberia to the southern Apennines linking the two north-south-trending oceanic areas. This transform boundary seems to have been located in the Mauretanian-Massylian Flysch Trough of the Maghrebian chains and was associated with only minor rifting, documented by sparse occurrences of ophiolites along the base of the oceanic sequences, whereas pelagic conditions were established in the marginal areas of the trough already during the Early Liassic. Another transform margin must have separated the Liguria-Piemonte ocean from the European continent.

To the east the Liguria-Piemonte ocean was bordered by the Apulian margin, which constitutes now the tectonic elements of the external Apennines, Dinarides, Hellenides and Taurides, and the Austro-Alpine nappes of the Eastern Alps and internal Carpathians (Fig. 2). Whether the Apulian block was part of Africa (Channell and Horvath, 1976) or an independent microplate, separated from the African continent by an oceanic Eastern Mediterranean (Biju-Duval et al.,

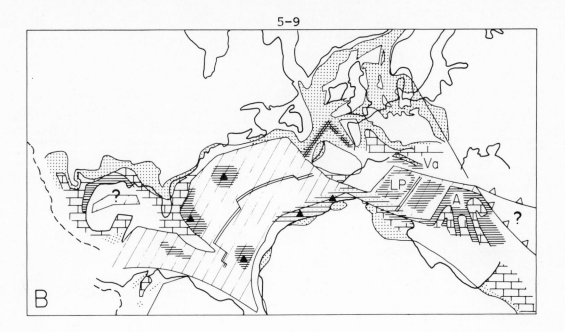

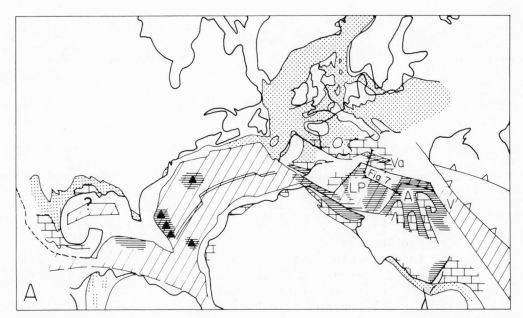

⣿	transitional to shallow marine deposits, sandstones, shales, limestones	⣿	oceanic crust
⣿	carbonate platform deposits (including evaporites)	△△	subduction zones
⣿	deep-water limestones and shales	= =	zones of rifting and spreading
⣿	deep-water clastics	▲	DSDP – sites

Fig. 6. Palinspastic restoration of A: Late Jurassic (Kimmeridgian) and B: Early Cretaceous (approximately Hauterivian) paleogeography of the Mediterranean and central Atlantic area. M-M: Mauretanian-Massylian Flysch Trough. LP: Liguria-Piemonte ocean; Va: Valais Trough; V: Vardar zone; A: Apulian margin. Data from Laubscher and Bernoulli (1977) and references therein; Cook and Bally (1975). Outlines of continents from Smith and Briden (1977).

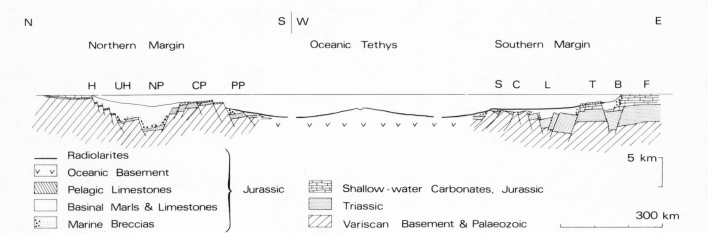

Fig. 7. Palinspastic section through the Liguria-Piemonte Ocean
in the Late Jurassic (Kimmeridgian; for location, see
Fig. 6A). The main features are: (1) Thick "Alpine"
shallow-water sediments in the Triassic of the central
Pennine area (CP) on the northern continental margin.
(2) The Early Jurassic phase of block-faulting in the
embryonic continental margins, well documented by marine
breccia formations in the Ultrahelvetic-North Pennine
(UH and NP) Trough and the southern scarp bordering the
Central Pennine platform (CP), in the Austro-Alpine nappes
and in the Southern Alps. (3) The onlap of pelagic deep-
sea sediments over the deeply submerged continental margins following the initial phase of block-faulting.
(4) The development of Bahamian-type carbonate platforms
along the southern continental margin with adjacent
troughs with pelagic and turbiditic carbonate sedimentation. (5) The development of the Tethys Ocean, documented
by the oceanic ophiolite suite. Its width and shape are
somewhat arbitrary, but 1000 km as a rough figure is con-
sonant with the history of sea-floor spreading in the
Atlantic. Jurassic magmatism in the continental margin
of the Southern Alps and in the North Pennine Trough has
been omitted. (H) Helvetic; (UH) Ultrahelvetic; (NP)
North Pennine; (CP) Central Pennine; (PP) pre-Piemonte
zone; (S) Sesia zone-Dent-Blanche nappe; (C) Canavese
zone; (L) Lombardia zone; (T) Trento zone; (B) Belluno
zone; (F) Friuli zone. From Laubscher and Bernoulli
(1977).

1977), is uncertain (see discussion in Laubscher and Bernoulli, 1977). Whatever
the case, east of the Apulian margin, the kinematic evolution was no longer
determined by the relative movements of Africa and Eurasia alone. Instead, the
kinematic evolution was characterized by the drift of the different smaller
Gondwanian fragments, the opening of the (? Late Triassic-) Jurassic Tethys
(Vardar zone) and the still active Cimmerian-Indosinian suture.

In Mid-Cretaceous times plate motions in the Atlantic-Tethyan system
changed drastically. With the opening of part of the North Atlantic and of the
Bay of Biscay, sinistral and opening movements in the western Tethys were
replaced by dextral and compressive ones leading to the complete elimination of
the western oceanic Tethys between the Late Cretaceous and the Late Eocene.

Early to Middle Liassic: Rifting and
Initial Subsidence of Continental Margins

During the latest Triassic and the Early to Middle Liassic, the areas
which were to become the continental margins of the Tethyan ocean were affected
by tensional block-faulting. These rifting movements were discordant to the
earlier, Triassic, structural elements. In the central Atlantic and western
Mediterranean area earliest rifting occurred in a continental environment and
graben formation was associated with deposition of continental red beds, fluvia-
tile and lacustrine sediments and, later on, with volcanic activity (see Manspeizer, this volume). To the east, in the central and eastern Mediterranean
area, the zones of rifting which eventually led to the opening of the oceanic
Tethys did not follow the complex pattern of Triassic seaways, but occurred
across the marine carbonate belts of the Paleotethyan margin (Fig. 4). As a
consequence, there are hardly any siliciclastic sediments associated with the
Early Jurassic phase of rifting, and evaporite deposits of Jurassic age are con-
spicuously lacking along the rift zone. Traces of volcanic activity are also
extremely scarce along the Jurassic passive margins of the Tethys: Even though
the vertical displacement along deep-seated Early Jurassic fault amounts, in some
cases, to three kilometers and more (Fig. 8), there is hardly any contemporary
volcanicity associated with this phase of breakdown of the future margin. This
general evolution deviates in many respects from the classical evolution of
linear intracontinental rifts such as those preceding the opening of the Red
Sea or the Atlantic ocean, but it closely parallels that of other passive margins
of Atlantic-type, particularly that of the Bay of Biscay (Charpal et al., 1978;
Graciansky et al., 1979).

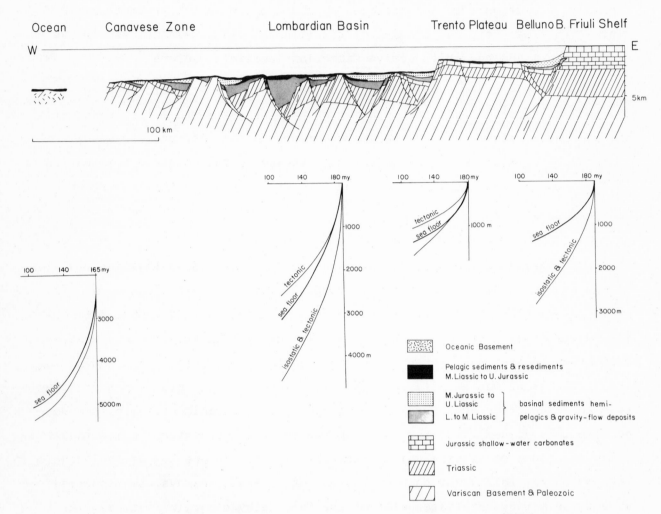

Fig. 8. Palinspastic section across the southern continental margin of the Tethys in the Southern Alps, Late Jurassic
(Kimmeridgian). The section shows the Early Jurassic
rifting phase in the continental margin, which was followed by regional subsidence and pelagic sedimentation
of increasing water depth in the starved distal margin.
The asymmetry of sedimentary syn-rift basins points to
blocks tilted along synsedimentary listric faults. Carbonate platforms in the more proximal margin (Friuli
shelf) are surrounded by prisms of resedimented platform
materials (Vajont and Soccher Limestones of Belluno
Basin). Carbonate platforms, submerged during their
later, Middle Jurassic, evolution (Trento Plateau) are
covered by a thin deepening upward pelagic sequence.
From Bernoulli et al. (1979a). Inferred subsidence
curves from Winterer and Bosellini (1981) (Continental
margin) and Laubscher and Bernoulli (1977) (Liguria-
Piemonte Ocean).

        As a result of Early Jurassic block-faulting, shallow-water carbonate
sedimentation, which reached its widest extension during the Late Triassic, was
interrupted over large areas and only a number of carbonate platforms surrounded
by deeper troughs and plateaus persisted. Beyond the carbonate platforms the
most common type of syn-rift sediments are interbedded grey chert-bearing spicu-
litic limestones and marls. This facies, which has a variety of local names
(Fleckenkalk, Medolo, Corniola, Siniais Limestone) is very widespread and occurs
from southern Spain through the Apennines and Alps into the Carpathians and
Hellenides. Formational thickness locally amounts to 1000 meters and more (more
than 3500 meters in the Early Jurassic Generoso section in the Southern Alps,
Fig. 8), and associated gravity flow deposits and turbidites suggest, together
with the expanded nature of these sediments, that this facies has been deposited
in basins, bounded by active faults. The high sedimentation rates (>100 mm/10^3 y)
in these Early Jurassic basinal deposits also suggests that, although calcareous
nannoplankton is abundant, much of the carbonate lutum is peri-platform ooze
derived from still active carbonate platforms (Kälin et al., 1979). The Southern
Alps of northern Italy probably preserve the most complete and least disturbed
record of a late Mesozoic passive continental margin of the Tethys (Winterer and
Bosellini, 1981). There the existence of synsedimentary normal faults is established by rapid changes of facies and formational thickness of the syn-rift
sediments across the fault zones and by the existence of pronounced fault scarps
that were the source areas for gravity flow deposits and carbonate turbidites in
the adjacent basins (Fig. 8). The incorporation of turbidites into later slump
deposits points also to repeated rejuvenation of the sea-floor topography.

        Subsidence rates were highest during this early phase of disintegration
of the margin and varied widely between the different fault blocks. Some of the
blocks that were submerged only in the course of the Late Liassic to Middle
Jurassic became submarine highs and plateaus on which only limited amounts of
pelagic sediments accumulated (e.g., Trento plateau, Fig. 8). With the onset of
spreading and the formation of oceanic crust in the Liguria-Piemonte ocean in
the late Early to Middle Jurassic, subsidence rates decreased and were more
evenly distributed over the margin.

        Depositional geometry of the syn-rift sediments in the Lombardian Basin
of the Southern Alps (Fig. 8) and elsewhere suggests listric faulting as a possible mechanism of crustal thinning (Bally et al., 1981). Tilting of fault

blocks is suggested by the asymmetry of certain troughs reflected by the pattern of formational thicknesses of the basinal syn-rift sediments. Deposition matches approximately the rates of <u>differential</u> subsidence and results in approximately horizontal layering at the end of the rifting phase. There is no unconformity at the base of the basinal syn-rift sequences, but lensing out of packages of strata and local unconformities are ubiquitous <u>within</u> the sequences, and locally stacks of strata are observed that have been rotated along synsedimentary listric growth faults. The formation of tilted fault blocks, contemporaneous with sedimentation, is also suggested by troughs and half-grabens bounded along one side by steep fault scarps, documented by coarse proximal resediments and by a much smoother topography along the other (Fig. 8; cf. Kälin and Trümpy, 1977). Along the uplifted flanks of tilted blocks angular unconformities are observed locally (Fig. 9). These intra-basinal highs were restricted in size and characterized by first subaerial, then submarine erosion. Shallow-water mounds with stalked crinoids, brachiopods, calcareous sponges and occasional ahermatypic corals are overlain by pelagic limestones, indicating the eventual sinking of the entire margin after breakup and initiation of spreading. Tectonic activity is documented here by polyphase breccias and neptunian dikes in the Triassic shallow-water substratum.

The depositional geometry of the syn-rift sediments of the Southern Alps compares well with that of the corresponding formations of the Iberian (Formation 4, Groupe Galice, 1979) and of the Armorican margin (Montadert et al., 1979). In the Southern Alps, the Early Jurassic basins measure some 25 to 40 kilometers across; this is in accordance with the observations along the Iberian and Armorican margins, where fault blocks from a few to 30 kilometers across are observed. Likewise, the throw of some individual fault zones is in the same order with a maximum of 3 to 4 kilometers; this corresponds to the throw reconstructed for the Early Jurassic Lugano fault (Fig. 8). Size and areal extension of the larger fault blocks suggest that the major fault zones sole in the pre-Triassic basement.

In the Iberian and Armorican margins a polarity of the listric faults towards the axis of the rift zone is observed. In the Southern Alps it appears that rifting started in the central zone of the Lombardian basin with the stepwise foundering of new fault-blocks to the east and to the west during the Middle

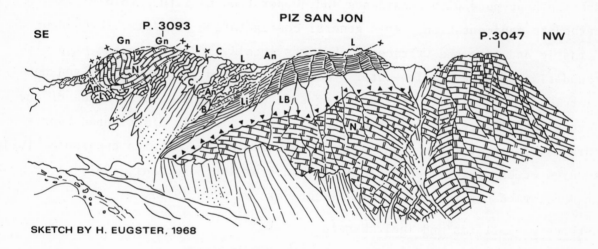

SKETCH BY H. EUGSTER, 1968

Fig. 9. Angular unconformity between tilted pre-rift sediments
        (Upper Triassic shallow-water Hauptdolomite Formation)
        and late syn-rift sediments (? Late Liassic breccias and
        dark gray marls) of the southern Tethyan margin.
        Triassic sediments and crystalline basement rocks in the
        southeast were overthrusted during Alpine orogeny. Gn:
        crystalline basement rocks; B: Lower Triassic clastics;
        An and L: Middle Triassic carbonates; C: Upper Triassic
        dolomites, marls and rauhwackes; N: Upper Triassic
        (Norian) Hauptdolomite Formation; LB: Liassic breccias;
        Li: Liassic dark gray marls. Piz San Jon, Austro-Alpine
        Scharl Nappe, Graubünden, Switzerland. From Eugster, in
        Bally et al. (1981).

to Late Liassic (Fig. 7). In the Late Liassic to Middle Jurassic finally the axis of rifting was somewhat shifted, and breakup and spreading occurred some hundred kilometers to the north and west.

Late Liassic to Early Cretaceous: Prolonged Subsidence of the Continental Margins

During the Early to Middle Liassic, initial block-faulting and subsidence in the embryonic continental margins of the western Tethys had led to the submergence of many former carbonate platform areas and to the morphological differentiation of the margins into Bahamian-type platforms where carbonate production kept pace with subsidence and deeper troughs with turbiditic and pelagic carbonate sedimentation. This general configuration persisted throughout the Jurassic and into the Cretaceous, but was locally modified by the step-wise foundering of some shallow-water areas which turned into seamounts and submarine plateaus (Fig. 8). With the onset of spreading in the oceanic areas of the Tethys, subsidence rates decreased and were more evenly distributed over the margins; during drifting, the subsidence curve of the margins apparently followed a curve of exponential decay (Fig. 7, Winterer and Bosellini, 1981) as observed in undeformed continental margins (Montadert et al., 1979).

Carbonate Platforms and Their Margins

During the rifting stage of the Early Jurassic, the almost continuous belt of Upper Triassic shallow-water carbonates was disintegrated into isolated carbonate platforms separated by areas of deep water. Of all the Tethyan carbonate platforms, those along the Apulian margin displayed the most remarkable longevity, persisting up to the Late Cretaceous and Early Tertiary and resulting in sedimentary piles several kilometers thick (Fig. 10). The analogies between these carbonate platforms and the Bahamian margin with its irregular belts of shallow and deep water comprise not only carbonate facies, but also size and shape of the platforms, rates of subsidence and the like (Bernoulli, 1972; d'Argenio, 1974).

The largest platforms are more than 200 kilometers across and up to 1000 kilometers long. The internal parts of the platforms are characterized by well-bedded, often cyclically arranged shallow subtidal to inter- and supratidal flat deposits, by marsh sediments including occasional coal and by subtidal

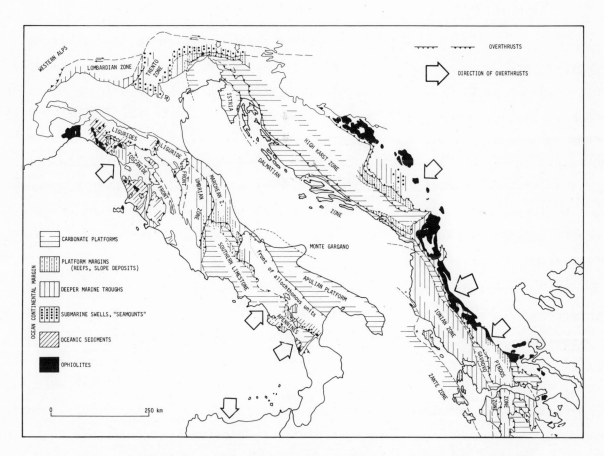

Fig. 10. Distribution of carbonate platforms, platform margins,
deeper marine basins and submarine swells (plateaus and
seamounts) along the Apulian (south Tethyan) margin.
Late Jurassic. The Alpine tectonic units have not been
arranged palinspastically. For a simplified palinspastic
map, see Figure 6A. From Bernoulli (1972).

micritic and pelletal limestones with a poorly diversified fauna and flora. Biomicrites with porcellaneous and agglutinating foraminifera, green algae, gastropods, bivalves were deposited in environments with less restricted circulation. Along the platform margins, belts of high water energy are documented by oolite bars, bioclastic sands and massif reefs (cf. Bosellini and Broglio Loriga, 1971; d'Argenio, 1974).

Off the carbonate platforms thick prisms of resedimented platform material were deposited (e.g., Cantelli et al., 1978; Bosellini et al., 1981). During the Early to Middle Liassic rifting stage the platform margins were fault-controlled, and along the active fault scarps huge slide scars, filled by olistoliths and gravity emplaced megabreccias occur (Fig. 11; Cantelli et al., 1978). Basinward these deposits grade into debris flows and proximal turbidites intercalated with chert-bearing fine-grained limestones. Again the high sedimentation rate of these basinal limestones during the phases of step-wise foundering of carbonate platforms suggests that much of the fine carbonate material is platform-derived peri-platform ooze.

Later, after faulting decreased and throughout the Jurassic and the Cretaceous, coarse channelized debris flow deposits and proximal turbidites with penecontemporaneously displaced shallow-water particles and skeletal fragments of neritic organisms were deposited along the slope and foot of the carbonate platforms. Occasional organization in thickening upward cycles suggests redeposition in prograding and overlapping sandstone lobes (Bosellini et al., 1981). Basinwards these deposits grade into more distal turbidites intercalated with pelagic limestones. Close analogies between these deposits and those deposited in the deep Bahamian channels have also been established (Bernoulli, 1972; Bosellini et al., 1981).

During the Jurassic and the Cretaceous subsidence rates of the carbonate platforms decreased from about 100 $mm/10^3$ y in the Late Triassic to about 10 $mm/10^3$ y in the Late Cretaceous (d'Argenio, 1974). Interferences between subsidence and eustatic sea level changes repeatedly led to episodic emersions with bauxite formation (e.g., Early Cenomanian) or transgressions followed by progradation of the platform margins and the platform derived resediments (Oxfordian transgression, Bosellini et al., 1981). Climatic variations may be reflected by platform margins dominated by oolite deposition during the Early and Middle

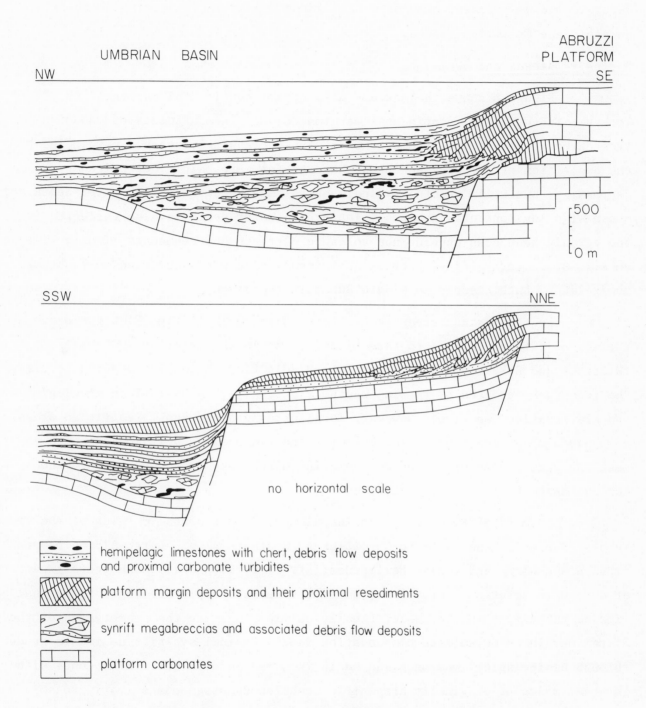

hemipelagic limestones with chert, debris flow deposits
and proximal carbonate turbidites

platform margin deposits and their proximal resediments

synrift megabreccias and associated debris flow deposits

platform carbonates

Fig. 11. Simplified palinspastic sections through the platform
margin of the Abbruzzi platform of the Southern Apennines.
Note fault controlled margin during early (rifting) stage
of platform evolution followed by upbuilding and progradation of platform margin and resediment prism during
subsequent subsidence. From Cantelli et al. (1978) and
Castellarin et al. (1978).

Jurassic and extensive growth of coral/hydrozoan and rudist reefs during Late Jurassic and Cretaceous times.

Basins, Plateaus and Seamounts

Figure 8 shows the anatomy of a sunken continental margin of the Tethys. In the distal continental margins, beyond the influence of Bahamian-type carbonate platforms, submergence of the increasingly starved margin led to the deposition of pelagic sequences whose facies were mainly determined by decreasing, but still ongoing synsedimentary faulting, increasing water depth and ocean-wide environmental changes. Increasing water depth is also reflected in the pelagic sequences capping non-volcanic plateaus and seamounts (Trento Plateau on Fig. 8; western Sicily, Umbrian Apennines) which were submerged only during their later, Late Liassic to Middle Jurassic evolution.

In the basinal areas (e.g., Lombardian Basin on Fig. 8) water depth at the end of rifting (Middle to Late Liassic) was in the order of 1000 meters (Winterer and Bosellini, 1981), and from Middle Liassic to Middle Jurassic times the topography created by rifting was nearly levelled by basinal, hemipelagic and gravity-flow deposits. However, local stratigraphic gaps, restricted areas of condensed and shallower pelagic facies and redeposited pelagic sediments suggest the persistence of a subdued submarine morphology in the basin throughout the Jurassic and the Early Cretaceous.

In many of the starved basins along the continental margins of the Tethys (Subbetic Zone of Betic Cordilleras, Southern Alps, Austro-Alpine nappes, Umbrian Apennines and Ionian Hellenides; cf. Figs. 12 and 13), the overall pattern of carbonate solution facies observed in the pelagic sediments suggests gradual sinking throughout the Jurassic, finally culminating with the submergence of the distal margin below calcite compensation depth: Basinal syn-rift sediments grade through hemipelagic limestones and marls into red nodular marly limestones with internal molds of originally aragonitic cephalopod phragmocones (marly Rosso Ammonitico facies of Middle to Late Liassic age), which are in turn overlain by nannofossil limestones with pelagic bivalves and radiolarians but without traces of aragonitic fossils, and finally by siliceous calcilutites and carbonate-free bedded radiolarian cherts of Late Jurassic age. Some of these Jurassic facies, particularly the red marly limestones (Rosso Ammonitico, Late Jurassic Rosso ad Aptici) are very similar indeed to Late Jurassic oceanic sediments of the central Atlantic (Cat Gap Formation, Jansa et al., 1979; Bernoulli, 1972).

 5-21

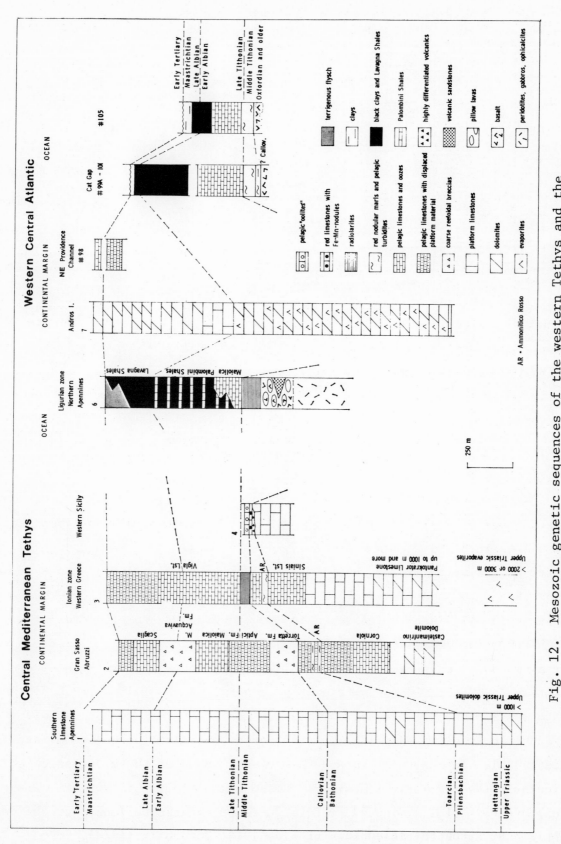

Fig. 12. Mesozoic genetic sequences of the western Tethys and the western central Atlantic. From Bernoulli and Jenkyns (1974).

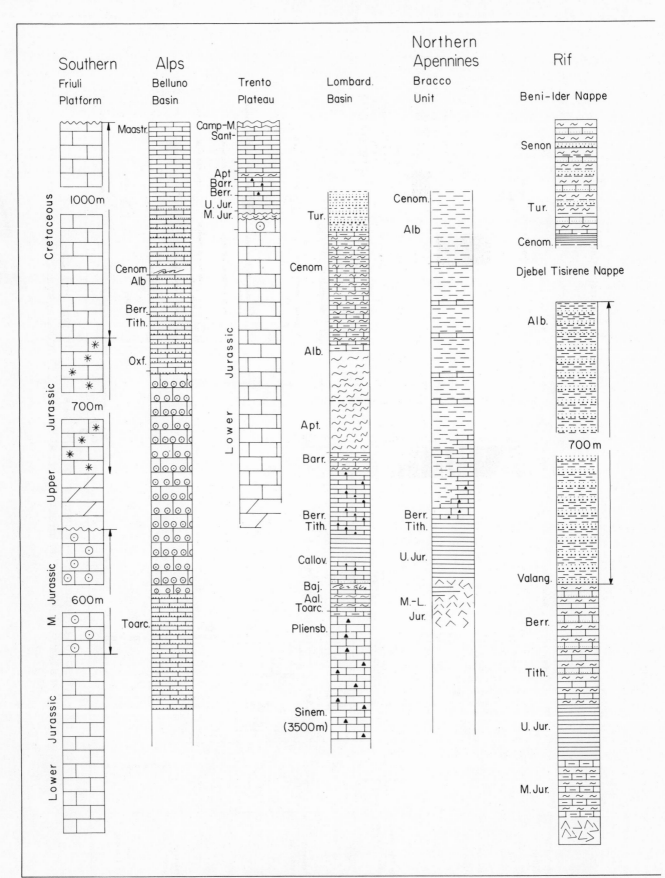

Fig. 13. Mesozoic genetic sequences of the western Tethys and the
a & b   central Atlantic. From data in: Bernoulli (1972), Ber-
         noulli and Jenkyns (1974), Bosellini et al. (1981), Jansa
         et al. (1979), Robertson and Bernoulli (1981), and Winterer
         and Bosellini (1981).

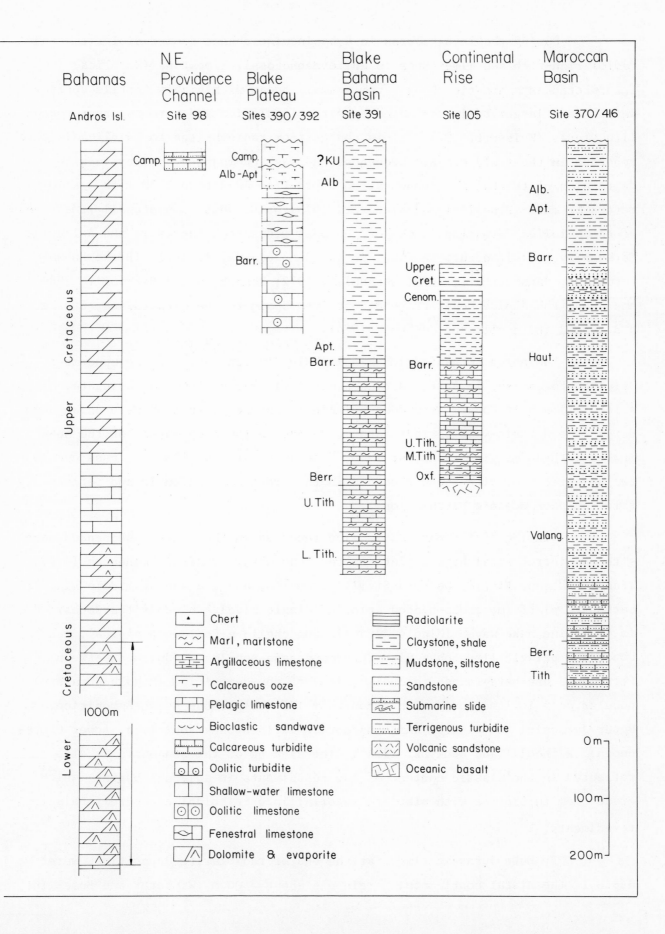

During the latest Jurassic a basin-wide change from radiolarites and radiolarian-rich red limestones to white nannofossil limestone (Maiolica) is interpreted as a drastic change from a small ocean with highly fertile surface waters to a larger basin dominated by gyre-circulation and more tolerant coccolith floras (Weissert, 1979). This change from radiolarites to Maiolica is also recorded in the truly oceanic sequences and was accompanied by a basin-wide depression of the calcite compensation depth from less than 2500 m to 4 kilometers or more (Bosellini and Winterer, 1975). The white nannofossil limestone of the Maiolica Formation is one of the most widespread facies in the Atlantic-Tethyan System: It occurs in Cuba, in the deep central Atlantic (Blake-Bahama Formation, Jansa et al., 1979; Bernoulli, 1972; Robertson and Bernoulli, 1981), and along the Alpine Mediterranean belt from Spain to the Carpathians, Greece and beyond (Bernoulli and Jenkyns, 1974).

Laminated, organic-rich black shales intercalated in the uppermost Maiolica Formation, in Aptian-Albian hemipelagic marls (Scaglia variegata, Marne a fucoidi) and in Upper Cretaceous pelagic limestones (Cenomanian-Turonian boundary) record basin-wide periodic anoxic events in the deep waters of the submerged Tethyan margins (Jenkyns, 1980; Graciansky et al., 1981). These events can be correlated with those recorded in the Cretaceous Atlantic and reflect times of poor oceanic circulation.

Sinking of the margins is also recorded in the pelagic sequences deposited on intrabasinal highs, plateaus and seamounts. Typical sequences (e.g., Trento Plateau, Fig. 8, western Sicily) comprise, above a sunken Middle Liassic carbonate platform, cross-bedded crinoid/pelagic bivalve biosparites deposited in submarine sand-waves (Middle Jurassic Lumachella a Posidonia alpina), red condensed pelagic limestones with ferromanganese nodules sandwiched between ferromanganese hardgrounds recording times of non-deposition (Middle Jurassic), nodular pelagic limestones with ammonite molds (calcareous Rosso Ammonitico, Upper Jurassic) and finally white nannofossil limestones (Maiolica, Lower Cretaceous) (Bernoulli and Jenkyns, 1974). The sinking of the seamounts is also reflected in the clastic content of the resediments in adjacent basins, which grade from turbidites with platform material into crinoidal and purely pelagic resediments.

By Late Jurassic times, at the end of radiolarite deposition, water depth in the distal continental margin was about 2500 m (Winterer and Bosellini,

1981). Circumstantial reasoning (Bosellini and Winterer, 1975; Bernoulli et al., 1979b; Winterer and Bosellini, 1981) suggests that calcite compensation depth was close to this depth during the Late Jurassic. This may be due to the circulation pattern of the small ocean basin, high organic productivity in the surface waters and to the fact that much calcium carbonate was bound in Bahamian-type carbonate platforms, with a probably significant influence on the carbonate budget.

During the Early Cretaceous the distal continental margin sank to a few kilometers water depth, as shown by the encroachment of deep oceanic facies onto the most oceanward parts of the margin. The occurrence of Early Cretaceous black shales, believed to be deposited below calcite compensation depth, in tectonic units derived from the most distal parts of the margin (Palombini shales) suggests water depth in the order of 4 kilometers. Isostatic sinking of the starved continental margin to this depth strongly suggests crustal thinning and cooling; there are, however, until now only very limited petrologic and radiometric data to support this.

Oceanic Sediments

Following rifting and parallel to the submergence of the distal continental margin, formation of oceanic crust and lithosphere occurred in the western Tethys. The oldest oceanic sediments in the Liguria-Piemonte ocean are generally radiolarian cherts and siliceous mudstones, which are interlayered along their base with pillow lavas and ophiolitic sandstones. The age of the radiolarites is poorly established; however, a (? late) Middle to Late Jurassic age is suggested by Late Liassic to Middle Jurassic radiometric ages in the ophiolites and by the overlying Berriasian to Valanginian nannofossil limestones (Maiolica). These Early Cretaceous nannofossil limestones, which obviously record a basin-wide lowering of the calcite compensation depth pass upwards and laterally into a sequence of argillites and siliceous (redeposited) limestones (Palombini shales, Berriasian to Albian). Sedimentary melanges, olistostromes with large olistoliths of ophiolitic rocks and turbidites intercalated with the Middle to Late Cretaceous Val Lavagna shales reflect the passage to a structural regime governed by subduction and compression (Fig. 12).

There is good evidence that the ophiolites of the Liguria-Piemonte ocean accreted along a slow spreading ridge of Atlantic-type. The sedimentary metalliferous deposits along the base of the Ligurian radiolarites show clear affinities to hydrothermal deposits associated with modern spreading centers (Bonatti et al., 1976). During the Jurassic the spreading ridge was transsected by a number of transform faults, as is suggested by the cataclastic structure of some ophiolites, the scarcity of indications of a layered peridotite-gabbro-basalt complex and by uplifted blocks or ultramafic and gabbroic rocks: In places radio-larites, Maiolica or Palombini shales directly overlay serpentinites or gabbros which are fractured in situ and cut by a network of dikes filled with alternating submarine calcite cement and red recrystallized limestone, forming complex breccias (ophicalcites) with different generations of fracturing and infill. The highs were also the source areas for breccias composed of fragments of pillow lava, foliated gabbro, amphibolite, chert and ophiolitic sandstone, deposited along the foot of submarine fault scarps (Lemoine, 1980, and references therein).

In some areas of the western Tethys, terrigenous turbidites were depo-sited as early as during the latest Jurassic and Early Cretaceous (e.g., Mauretanian-Massylian Flysch, Fig. 6B). These "flysch" deposits are associated with Middle Jurassic deep-water marls and limestones and Upper Jurassic radio-larites; some slivers of ophiolites along their base probably represent relics of oceanic crust. The turbiditic sequences are likely to be the lateral equiva-lents of the Upper Jurassic-Lower Cretaceous deep-sea sands of the Moroccan Basin and of the Canary Islands and are related to relative uplift and erosion along the northwest African margin rather than to incipient Alpine orogeny (Robertson and Bernoulli, 1981).

Transform Margins

From the Early Jurassic up to the time of opening along the Iberian margin and the Bay of Biscay, Africa has moved east by about 2000 kilometers with respect to Europe. These sinistral movements took place along major plate boun-daries along the Mauretanian-Massylian Flysch Trough, and to the north of the Liguria-Piemonte ocean (Fig. 6). There are at present no studies available which deal in detail with the north African segment in terms of a transcurrent margin, but many new observations in the western and central Alps suggest transcurrent movements during the evolution of the Tethyan Ocean (Homewood, 1977; Kelts, 1981).

Movements along the northern margin of the Liguria-Piemonte ocean apparently were distributed over a belt a few hundred kilometers across which

now constitutes the North and Central Pennine units of the western and central
Alps (Fig. 7). To the north of the ocean there was a basement high, the Central
Pennine Briançonnais Ridge which had a complex history of Early to Middle
Jurassic fragmentation, tilting and uplift, followed by differential subsidence
and shallow-water to pelagic carbonate sedimentation during the Late Jurassic
and the Cretaceous (Bourbon et al., 1977). Jurassic to Cretaceous marine breccia
formations (e.g., Breccia Nappe, Prepiemontais Zone, Fig. 7) point to long-lived
fault scarps along both margins of the Briançonnais Ridge.

To the north, the Briançonnais Ridge was sheltered from terrigenous
influx from the European continent by the North Pennine Valais Trough (Figs. 6
and 7). This trough contains a sequence of (now greenschist-grade metamorphic)
gray calcareous mica slates associated with redeposited quartzose and calcareous
layers, all known under the names of Schistes lustrés or Bündnerschiefer. The
total thickness of the Early Jurassic to Middle Cretaceous section is estimated
to be more than 5 kilometers, corresponding to a sedimentation rate of
> 80 mm/10^3 y. These sediments do not conform well with the facies types encoun-
tered in the normal oceanic sequences of the Tethyan Ocean or its submerged
rifted continental margins, and there are only a limited number of isolated serpentinite bodies and some massif intrusions, dikes, sills and submarine extru-
sions of mafic rocks associated. The close juxtaposition of uplifted blocks and
down-faulted basins, of compressional and tensional movements throughout the
Jurassic and Cretaceous suggest a broad region of transcurrent rifting with possible minor oblique spreading with intrusion of ultramafic and mafic igneous
rocks (Laubscher, 1975; Homewood, 1977; Kelts, 1981, and references therein).

Source Beds

Potential source beds for hydrocarbons occur in different paleotectonic settings in the Alpine-Mediterranean Mesozoic. Triassic occurrences are
closely associated with carbonate platforms along the Paleotethys continental
margins, whereas late Mesozoic organic-rich sequences are connected with basin-
wide anoxic events in the Atlantic and Tethyan oceans and their submerged continental margins. Bituminous hemipelagic carbonate rocks also occur in thick
basinal formations of the Early Jurassic rifting stage, but their importance as
oil source rocks has not been assessed as yet.

Paleotethys Continental Margin

Triassic bituminous sequences are always horizontally and vertically linked to shallow-water carbonate complexes and, therefore, included in a general carbonate platform environment. The sequences typically consist of alternations of cm- to some dm-bedded dolomites, in which light colored slightly coarser laminae alternate with darker, finer, clay and organic-rich ones, and of mm- to cm-thick black bituminous shales. The organic carbon content is usually between 5 and 10 percent in the black shales, but in fresh samples values up to 30 percent and more are determined. Depending on the formational thicknesses of the enclosing shallow-water carbonates, the thicknesses of these alternations may vary between 10 m (Upper Anisian Grenzbitumenzone, Southern Alps) and more than 100 m (Filettino Formation of the central Apennines; Hauptdolomite Forma-tion of the Southern Alps, both Upper Triassic); locally several hundred meters are reported (Seefeld Shales, Upper Triassic, Austria). In the thinner sequences the black shales may make up 10 percent or more of the sequence, whereas in the more expanded series the black shales constitute one percent or a little more.

Still more expanded bituminous sequences consist mainly of bituminous limestones and dolomites with only thin shale partings (Calcare di Zorzino, Upper Triassic, Southern Alps). The bituminous sequences of the Middle and Late Triassic are thought to have been deposited in subaqueous low-energy environ-ments with poor water circulation and conditions unfavorable for animal life, as suggested by the total absence of bioturbation. Although the deposits are laterally linked to shallow platforms, water depth was important enough for the development of stratified water masses, as suggested by the occasional occur-rence of planktonic (radiolaria), pseudoplanktonic (Daonella) and nektonic faunas (ammonites, vertebrates).

Syn-rift Sediments

Bituminous hemipelagic limestones occur in basinal deposits of the Early Jurassic syn-rift stage, e.g., in the Southern Alps (Fig. 7; Lombardian Siliceous Limestones) and basinal deposits rich in organic matter and pyrite are associated with rifted basins of transform margins (Schistes lustrés of the Valais Trough), but published geochemical data are virtually non-existent. Higher concentrations of bituminous matter are particularly frequent in the Early Toarcian section of late syn-rift sediments in the Austro-Alpine nappes

(Allgäuschiefer-Fleckenmergel Group, Bitterli, 1962) and similar sequences; they coincide, however, with a basin-wide anoxic event recorded over much of epi-continental Europe and in the pelagic sediments of the Tethys (Jenkyns, 1980).

Carbonate Platforms

Within the thick expanded sequences of the Jurassic-Cretaceous carbonate platforms bituminous sequences are rare. They comprise local occurrences of bituminous calcilutites and marls, a few tens of meters thick and laterally and vertically linked to carbonate platform deposits. The sequences contain diagenetic chert nodules and planktonic (radiolaria) and nektonic (ammonites, vertebrates) faunas suggesting deeper lagoons with stratified water masses within the general platform setting (Upper Jurassic Lemeš Beds, Yugoslavia; Barremian to Albian Pietraroia Formation of the Southern Apennines).

Pelagic Sequences

Bituminous sequences are intercalated at different levels in the deeper marine pelagic sequences. Several time envelopes can be identified during which bituminous mudstones, shales or marls were deposited in the Tethyan Ocean and along its submerged margins: Early Toarcian, Barremian to Albian, the Cenomanian-Turonian boundary and to a lesser extent, the Coniacian-Santonian (Jenkyns, 1980). These times can be correlated with major transgressions and, in the case of the Cretaceous, with worldwide oceanic events during which oceanic waters were poorly oxygenated and deposition of organic matter from both terrestrial and planktonic sources was widespread. Deposition of organic-rich sediments occurred over a wide variety of deep-sea environments. During the Toarcian bituminous argillites seem to be restricted to the deepest depressions of the continental margin ("Posidonia"-Beds of the Ionian Hellenides, the Umbrian Apennines and the Southern Alps) which were flanked by areas of non-deposition or of Rosso Ammonitico sedimentation.

In oceanic settings, black organic-rich shales occur over much of the Cretaceous period: In the Liguria-Piemonte ocean the Early Cretaceous is represented by expanded sequences of carbonate-free black shales (Palombini and Val Lavagna Shales), and black manganiferous shales are frequent in Late Cretaceous oceanic flysch sequences (Helminthoid Flysch of northern Apennines and western Alps, Graciansky et al., 1981). In basinal continental margin settings cyclic alternations of foram-nanno marlstones and bituminous marls and shales rich in terrestrial organic matter occur in the Barremian to Albian interval (Maiolica, Marne a fucoidi, Scaglia variegata, etc.). The Cenomanian-Turonian event was of very short duration in the margins: in the purely pelagic sequences of the Umbrian Apennines, e.g., it is recorded by a two meters thick intercalation of black bituminous argillite (Livello Bonarelli) with up to 25 percent of organic carbon. Finally, the lateral association of these bituminous sequences with carbonate (grainstone) turbidites and marginal reefs may provide the scenario for hydrocarbon migration and accumulation under favorable geothermal conditions (Arthur and Schlanger, 1979).

Conclusions

In the western Tethys, rifting and subsequent sea-floor spreading were discordantly superimposed on the earlier Paleotethys margin and did not closely follow the sites of Middle Triassic subsidence and volcanicity which are generally interpreted as a phase of abortive rifting. During the Early Jurassic, the areas which were to become the continental margins were affected by block-faulting. As a consequence, shallow-water carbonate sedimentation was interrupted over large areas and only a limited number of Bahamian-type platforms, surrounded by deeper troughs and plateaus, persisted throughout the Mesozoic. In the basins bordering the platforms coarse platform derived debris flow deposits, carbonate turbidites and peri-platform oozes were deposited.

Subsidence rates were highest during the early phase of disintegration of the margin and varied widely between the different fault-blocks. The asymmetry of certain syn-rift basins and "break-up unconformities" on local highs suggest crustal attenuation and associated listric normal faulting. Size and shape of the different fault blocks and depositional geometry of the syn-rift sediments recall the evolution of rifted Atlantic-type margins like the Iberian margin or the Bay of Biscay (Fig. 14). With the onset of spreading and the formation of oceanic crust during the latest Liassic to Middle Jurassic, subsidence rates decreased and were more evenly distributed over the margins. Through time, the submerged distal margins became increasingly starved and only pelagic sediments whose facies were determined by subdued synsedimentary faulting, increasing water depth and basin-wide environmental changes were deposited. Of these changes, the Middle Cretaceous anoxic events may be of particular importance for the hydrocarbon potential of the Tethyan margins.

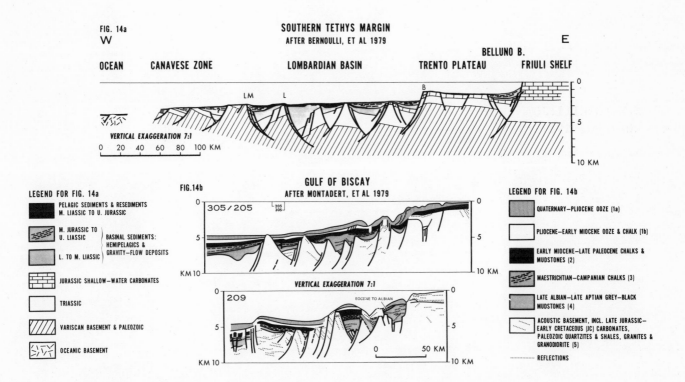

Fig. 14. Comparative sections through the southern continental
margin of Tethys (Late Jurassic) and the undeformed continental margin of Bay of Biscay. From Bernoulli et al.
(1979a) and Montadert et al. (1979), in Bally et al.
(1981).

From Early Jurassic to Middle Cretaceous times, the evolution of the western Tethys and of the central Atlantic were kinematically linked and both oceans and their margins followed a similar paleotectonic and sedimentary evolution. However, in the western Tethys a turn from passive continental margins of the Atlantic-type to margins governed by compression and subduction occurred in the Middle Cretaceous when Atlantic plate boundaries were rearranged and sinistral movements in the Tethyan system were replaced by dextral ones.

D.Bernoulli:JC
June 30, 1981

REFERENCES

Argand, E., 1924, La tectonique de l'Asie: Congr. Géol. Int. (13e Session), fasc. 1, Liège, Vaillant-Carmanne, p. 171-372.

Arthur, M. A., and S. O. Schlanger, 1979, Cretaceous "oceanic anoxic events" as causal factors in development of reef-reservoired giant oil fields: AAPG Bull., v. 63, p. 870-885.

Bally, A. W., D. Bernoulli, G. A. Davis, and L. Montadert, 1981, in press, Lisric normal faults: Paris, Oceanologica Acta.

Bébien, J., R. Blanchet, J. P. Cadet, J. Charvet, J. Chorowicz, H. Lapierre, and J. P. Rampnoux, 1978, Le volcanisme triasique des Dinarides en Yougoslavie: sa place dans l'évolution géotectonique péri-méditerranéenne: Tectonophysics, v. 47, p. 159-176.

Bernoulli, D., 1972, North Atlantic and Mediterranean Mesozoic facies: a comparison, in C. D. Hollister, J. I. Ewing et al.: Init. Rept. Deep Sea Drill. Proj., v. 11, p. 801-871: Washington, D.C., U.S. Govt. Printing Ofc.

_____ and H. C. Jenkyns, 1974, Alpine, Mediterranean and central Atlantic Mesozoic facies in relation to the early evolution of the Tethys, in R. H. Dott and R. H. Shaver, eds., Modern and ancient geosynclinal sedimentation: Soc. Econ. Paleont. Mineral. Spec. Pub. 19, p. 129-160.

_____, C. Caron, P. Homewood, O. Kälin, and J. van Stuijvenberg, 1979, Evolution of continental margins in the Alps: Schweiz. Mineral. Petrog. Mitt., v. 59, 1965-170.

_____, O. Kälin, and E. Patacca, 1979, A sunken continental margin of the Mesozoic Tethys: The northern and central Apennines: Assoc. Sédimentol. franç., Pub. spéc. 1, p. 197-210.

_____ and M. Lemoine, 1980, Birth and early evolution of the Tethys: The overall situation: Paris, 26th Internat. Geol. Cong., Coll. C-5, p. 168-179.

Biju-Duval, B., J. Dercourt, and X. LePichon, 1977, From the Tethys Ocean to the Mediterranean Seas: A plate tectonic model of the evolution of the western Alpine system, in B. Biju-Duval and L. Montadert, eds., Internat. Symp. Struct. Hist. Mediterranean basins, Split (Yugoslavia), 1976: Paris, Editions Technip, p. 143-164.

Bitterli, P., 1962, Studien an bituminösen Gesteinen aus Oesterreich und benachbarten Gebieten: Erdoel-Z., 1962, p. 405-416.

Blanchet, R., 1977, Bassins marginaux et Tethys alpine: De la marge continentale au domaine océanique dans les Dinarides, in B. Biju-Duval and L. Montadert, eds., Internat. Symp. Struct. Hist. Mediterranean basins, Split (Yugoslavia), 1976: Paris, Editions Technip, p. 47-72.

Bonatti, E., M. Zerbi, R. Kay, and H. Rydell, 1976, Metalliferous deposits from the Apennine ophiolites: Mesozoic equivalents of modern deposits from oceanic spreading centers: Geol. Soc. America Bull., v. 87, p. 83-94.

Bosellini, A., 1973, Modello geodinamico e paleotettonico delle Alpi Meridionali durante il Giurassico-Cretacico. Sue possibili applicazioni agli Appennini, in Moderne vedute sulla geologia dell'Appennino, Roma: Accad. naz. Lincei, p. 163-213.

_____ and C. Broglio Loriga, 1971, I "calcari grigi" di Rotzo (Giurassico Inferiore, Altipiano d'Asiago) e loro inquadramento nella paleogeografia e nella evoluzione tettono-sedimentaria delle Prealpi Venete: Ann. Univ. Ferrara, Sec. 9, Sci. Geol. Paleont., v. 5, p. 1-61.

_____ and E. L. Winterer, 1975, Pelagic limestone and radiolarite of the Tethyan Mesozoic: A genetic model: Geology, v. 3, p. 279-282.

_____, D. Masetti, and M. Sarti, 1981, in press, A Jurassic "Tongue of the Ocean" infilled with oolitic sands: the Belluno Trough, Venetian Alps, Italy: Mar. Geology.

Bourbon, M., J. M. Caron, P. Ch. de Graciansky, M. Lemoine, J. Mégard-Galli, and D. Mercier, 1977, Mesozoic evolution of the Western Alps: Birth and development of part of the spreading oceanic Tethys and of its European continental margin, in B. Biju-Duval and L. Montadert, eds., Internat. Symp. Struct. Hist. Mediterranean basins, Split (Yugoslavia), 1976: Paris, Editions Technip, p. 19-34.

Cantelli, C., A. Castellarin, and A. Praturlon, 1978, Tettonismo giurassico lungo l'"Ancona-Anzio" nel settore Monte Terminillo-Antrodoco: Geologica Romana, v. 8, p. 85-97.

Castellarin, A., R. Colacicchi, and A. Praturlon, 1978, Fasi distensive, trascorrenze e sovrascorrimento lungo la "linea Ancona-Anzio", dal Lias Medio al Pliocene: Geologica Romana, v. 8, p. 161-189.

_____ and P. M. L. Rossi, 1981, The Southern Alps: an aborted Middle Triassic mountain chain?: Eclogae Geol. Helv., v. 74, p. 313-316.

Channell, J. E. T., and F. Horvath, 1976, The African/Adriatic promontory as a paleogeographical premise for Alpine orogeny and plate movements in the Carpatho-Balkan region: Tectonophysics, v. 35, p. 71-101.

Charpal de, O., P. Guennoc, L. Montadert, and D. G. Roberts, 1978, Rifting, crustal attenuation and subsidence in the Bay of Biscay: Nature, v. 275, no. 5682, p. 706-711.

Cook, T. D., and A. W. Bally, 1975, Stratigraphic Atlas of North and Central America: Princeton, N.J., Princeton Univ. Press, 272 p.

D'Argenio, B., 1974, Le piattaforme carbonatiche periadriatiche: una rassegna di problemi nel quadro geodinamico mesozoico dell'area mediterranea: Mem. Soc. Geol. Ital., v. 13, Supp. 2, p. 137-159.

Dewey, J. F., W. C. Pitman, W. B. F. Ryan, and J. Bonnin, 1973, Plate tectonics and the evolution of the Alpine system: Geol. Soc. America Bull., v. 84, p. 3137-3180.

Graciansky de, P. Ch., M. Bourbon, P. Y. Chenet, O. de Charpal, and M. Lemoine, 1979, Gènese et évolution comparées de deux marges continentales passives: Marge ibérique de l'Océan Atlantique et marge européenne de la Tethys dans les Alpes Occidentales: Bull. Soc. Géol. France, s. 7, v. 21, p. 663-674.

_____, M. Bourbon, M. Lemoine, and J. Sigal, 1981, The sedimentary record of Mid-Cretaceous events in the western Tethys and central Atlantic Oceans and their continental margins: Eclogae Geol. Helv., v. 74, p. 353-367.

Groupe Galice, 1979, The continental margin off Galicia and Portugal: Acoustical stratigraphy, dredge stratigraphy, and structural evolution, in J. C. Sibuet, W. B. F. Ryan et al.: Init. Rept. Deep Sea Drill. Proj., v. 47, Pt. 2: Washington, D.C., U.S. Govt. Printing Ofc., p. 633-662.

Homewood, P. W., 1977, Ultrahelvetic and North-Penninic flysch of the Prealps: A general account: Eclogae Geol. Helv., v. 70, p. 627-641.

Hsü, K., and D. Bernoulli, 1978, Genesis of the Tethys and the Mediterranean, in K. J. Hsü, L. Montadert et al.: Init. Rept. Deep Sea Drill. Proj., v. 42, Pt. 1: Washington, D.C., U.S. Govt. Printing Ofc., p. 943-949.

Jansa, L. F., and J. A. Wade, 1974, Geology of the continental margin of Nova Scotia and Newfoundland: Geol. Surv. Canada Paper, v. 2, p. 51-105.

_____, P. Enos, B. E. Tucholke, F. M. Gradstein, and R. E. Sheridan, 1979, Mesozoic-Cenozoic sedimentary formations of the North America Basin, western North Atlantic, in M. Talwani, W. Hay, and W. B. F. Ryan, eds., Deep drilling results in the Atlantic Ocean: Continental margins and paleoenvironment: Maurice Ewing Ser. 3, Amer. Geophys. Union, p. 1-57.

Jenkyns, H. C., 1980, Cretaceous anoxic events: from continents to oceans: Jour. Geol. Soc., v. 137, p. 171-188.

Juteau, T., H. Lapierre, A. Nicolas, J. F. Parrot, L. E. Ricou, G. Rocci, and M. Rollet, 1973, Idées actuelles sur la constitution, l'origine et l'évolution des assemblages ophiolitiques mésogéens: Bull. Soc. Géol. France, s. 7, v. 15, p. 476-493.

Kälin, O., and D. M. Trümpy, 1977, Sedimentation und Paläotektonik in den westlichen Südalpen: Zur triasisch-jurassischen Geschichte des Monte Nudo-Beckens: Eclogae Geol. Helv., v. 70, p. 295-350.

_____, E. Patacca, and O. Renz, 1979, Jurassic pelagic deposits from Southeastern Tuscany; aspects of sedimentation and new biostratigraphic data: Eclogae Geol. Helv., v. 72, p. 715-762.

Kelts, K., 1981, Comparison of aspects of the translational tectonics and sedimentation in the Gulf of California and along the Mesozoic Northern Pennine margin: Eclogae Geol. Helv., v. 74, p. 317-338.

Laubscher, H. P., 1975, Plate boundaries and microplates in Alpine history: American Jour. Sci., v. 275, p. 865-876.

_____ and D. Bernoulli, 1977, Mediterranean and Tethys, in A. E. M. Nairn, W. H. Kanes, and F. G. Stehli, eds., The ocean basins and margins, 4A: New York, Plenum Press, p. 1-28.

Lemoine, M., 1980, Serpentinites, gabbros and ophicalcites in the Piemonte-Ligurian domain of the western Alps: Possible indicators of oceanic fracture zones and of associated serpentinite protrusions in the Jurassic-Cretaceous Tethys: Arch. Sci., v. 33, p. 103-115.

Montadert, L., D. G. Roberts, O. de Charpal, and P. Guennoc, 1979, Rifting and subsidence of the northern continental margin of the Bay of Biscay, in L. Montadert, D. G. Roberts et al.: Init. Rept. Deep Sea Drill. Proj., v. 48: Washington, D.C., U.S. Govt. Printing Ofc., p. 1025-1060.

Pitman, W. C., and M. Talwani, 1972, Sea-floor spreading in the North Atlantic: Geol. Soc. America Bull., v. 83, p. 619-646.

_____, R. L. Larson, and E. M. Herron, 1974, The age of the ocean basins: Geol. Soc. America

Robertson, A. H. F., and D. Bernoulli, 1981, Stratigraphy, facies and significance of Late Mesozoic and Early Tertiary sedimentary rocks of Fuerteventura (Canary Islands) and Maio (Cape Verde Islands), in U. von Rad, K. Hinz, M. Sarnthein, E. Seibold, and J. Wiedmann, eds., Geology of the Northwest African continental margin: Berlin, Heidelberg, New York, Springer-Verlag.

Sengör, A. M. C., 1979, Mid-Mesozoic closure of Permo-Triassic Tethys and its implications: Nature, v. 279, no. 5714, p. 590-593.

Smith, A. G., and J. C. Briden, 1977, Mesozoic and Cenozoic paleocontinental maps: Cambridge Earth Science Series, Cambridge, Univ. Press, 63 p.

Weissert, H., 1979, Die Paläoozeanographie der südwestlichen Tethys in der Unterkreide: Mitt. Geol. Inst. Eidg. Techn. Hochsch. Univ. Zürich, N.F. 226, 174 p.

Winterer, E. L., and A. Bosellini, 1981, Subsidence and sedimentation on a Jurassic passive continental margin (Southern Alps, Italy): AAPG Bull., v. 65, p. 394-421.

EVAPORITES, CARBONATES, AND OIL

by

B. Charlotte Schreiber

Dept. of Earth and Environmental Sciences

Queens College (C.U.N.Y.), Flushing, NY   11367

and Lamont-Doherty Geological Observatory

Palisades, NY   10964

Stephen Marshak

Lamont-Doherty Geological Observatory

and Dept. of Geological Sciences, Columbia University

Palisades, NY   10964

INTRODUCTION

Evaporite and carbonate rocks are known to be important components
of many oil fields. The processes by which these rock types originate,
evolve, and deform are relatively complex, and thus, these rocks can be
involved in the genesis and entrapment of petroleum in diverse and sometimes
unique ways. Research carried out in the last few years has documented or
discredited many long-held beliefs concerning the development of evaporite
deposits. In particular, there is new information concerning rates of
deposition, organic content, facies development, and geochemistry. An extensive data base on carbonates has long been available, so recent work has
concentrated on synthesizing this data to permit tectonic interpretations.

The purpose of this outline is first, to summarize features of
evaporite and carbonate deposits which should be considered when evaluating
their role in the creation of an oil field, and second, to point out what
information these deposits may hold which might be of use in guiding exploration. With this latter goal in mind, we will present a discussion of
the evaporites and carbonates found in recent drillholes of the continental
margin off the eastern United States. This outline concentrates on evaporites
because less information is currently available on evaporites than on
carbonates.

BACKGROUND DATA ON EVAPORITES

Evaporite Compositions

Evaporites are sedimentary rocks composed primarily of minerals
deposited by chemical precipitation from concentrated natural brines.

They may develop wherever the evaporation rate of water exceeds the influx rate of water. Evaporites contain a diverse population of minerals of which the most common are gypsum ($CaSO_4 \cdot 2H_2O$), anhydrite ($CaSO_4$), halite (NaCl), calcite ($CaCO_3$), aragonite ($CaCO_3$), dolomite ($CaMg(CO_3)_2$), magnesite ($MgCO_3$), sylvite (KCl), carnallite ($KMgCl_3 \cdot 6H_2O$), and poly-halite ($K_2Ca_2Mg(SO_4)_4 \cdot 2H_2O$) (c.f. Stewart, 1963; Holser, 1979). These minerals are salts which, when dissolved in water, exist as disassociated ions. Table 1 lists the principal ions of typical seawater. Seawater in the open oceans contains about 3.5% salt by weight, of which 78% is halite. Evaporite minerals can occur either as grains dispersed in a host rock of non-evaporite composition or in layers which contain only a minor component of non-evaporite material.

TABLE 1

Principal Dissolved Ions in Seawater

Anions	Wt%	Cations	Wt%
chloride (Cl^-)	55.04	sodium (Na^+)	30.61
sulfate (SO_4^{-2})	7.68	magnesium (Mg^{+2})	3.69
bicarbonate (HCO_3^-)	0.41	calcium (Ca^{+2})	1.16
bromine (Br^-)	0.19	potassium (K^+)	1.10
		strontium (Sr^{+2})	0.03
		boron (B^{+2})	0.01

Order of Deposition of Evaporite Minerals

Evaporite minerals precipitate from solution when the solution becomes oversaturated. Thus, the order in which they precipitate is

controlled by their relative solubilities; the least soluble salts precipitate first. Usiglio (1849; see Dean, 1978, p. 75), by observing the
products obtained from evaporating seawater, determined the relative
volumes and the order of deposition of evaporite minerals (Table 2).
Such studies were repeated in greater detail by Van't Hoff and his co-
workers (1896 to 1908; see references in Harvie et al, 1980). Seawater
must be concentrated to about 3.35 times its starting composition before
gypsum precipitates. Because halite is much more soluble, seawater must
be reduced to one-tenth its original volume before halite precipitates.
Clearly, the composition of an evaporite deposit is, in part, a consequence of the brine concentration that is maintained in the depositional
area.

TABLE 2

Order of Precipitation from Seawater

Order	Mineral	Formula	Volume % (approx.)*
First	calcite	$CaCO_3$	2
	gypsum	$CaSO_4 \cdot 2H_2O$	4
	halite	$NaCl$	77
	epsomite	$MgSO_4 \cdot 7H_2O$	4
	sylvite	KCl	5
Last	bischofite	$MgCl_2 \cdot 6H_2O$	8

*Volume % refers to percent of total volume of salt that
precipitates from seawater.

If evaporite deposits formed by simple evaporation of seawater, a
worldwide average evaporite composition would contain minerals in the
proportions shown by Table 2. But in actuality, average evaporites are
quite different; an average evaporite is composed of approximately 63%
(by volume) NaCl, 4% KCl, and 33% $CaSO_4$ interbedded with biogenic carbonate.
Calcium sulfate deposits are volumetrically much more extensive worldwide
than would be the case if evaporites formed by complete evaporation of
seawater bodies. The excess of calcium sulfate can be explained, in
part, by the fact that evaporites commonly form in areas where there is
some circulation and interaction with freshwater or with normal seawater.
Thus, concentrations appropriate for precipitation of calcium sulfate
develop and are maintained, but concentrations high enough to precipitate halite do not.

Recently, Harvie et al. (1980) pointed out that the systems in
which evaporites precipitate are more complicated and variable than
previously realized. Brine solutions change composition while they are
moving through a depositional basin because of mineral precipitation
and additional evaporation. Thus, for example, as brines move over
the seaward side of a basin they are relatively dilute and precipitate
calcium sulfate, but by the time they have reached the landward side
of the basin, they have lost their gypsum and have been so concentrated
by additional evaporation that they precipitate predominantly halite.
Furthermore, reactions between early precipitates and residual brines
constantly occur, and these reactions can alter the gross mineralogy
of the deposits.

Another problem concerning the origin of evaporites pertains to
the degree of hydration of calcium sulfate. Experimental and field data
indicate that gypsum is the usual form of calcium sulfate to precipitate
from brines in the subaqueous environment. The only environment in which
primary anhydrite forms was thought to be the vadose zone (the zone above
the water table) of soil in hot, arid regions such as the Persian Gulf.
Yet most ancient deposits of calcium sulfate are composed of anhydrite.
It is generally thought that the bulk of this anhydrite is not a consequence
of primary precipitation; but rather that it develops by the dewatering of
gypsum after burial (Murray, 1964). Hardie (1967) studied the thermodynamics
of this process. Observation of anyhydrite pseudomorphs of gypsum crystals
in the subsurface (as observed in cores) is direct evidence for the burial
transformation of gypsum to anhydrite. Such pseudomorphs are not common
in outcrop because exhumation usually results in rehydration and consequent
destruction of the original morphologies.

Recently, Cody and Hull (1980) have shown that the presence of
organic compounds such as maleic and polyacrylic acid can suppress the
nucleation of gypsum in very saline brines and can permit primary anhydrite
to form. Thus, while it is certain that much anhydrite is secondary, it
is possible that in certain deposits, a component of the anhydrite is
primary.

Evaporite Facies

Evaporation leading to oversaturation of brine with respect to
its dissolved salts occurs at the air-water interface; the interface can
occur either at the surface of a standing body of water or in the vadose

portion of the soil. Conditions conducive to the development of over-saturation occur in a variety of geologic settings each of which produces a distinctive facies. The characteristics of these facies are described below. Evaporite facies are complex because, in part, there are rapid fluctuations in the water level of evaporite basins, and because diagenesis of evaporites is extremely rapid.

Continental Evaporites: Chemical precipitates which are deposited in regions of interior drainage are generally referred to as continental evaporites. These deposits form in four interrelated settings: 1) lakes, 2) playas, 3) continental sabkhas, and 4) the vadose zone of the subsurface. The mineralogy of these deposits depends on the ionic composition of the water from which they were derived. Ionic compositions are highly variable because the dissolved salts are derived by the percolation of meteoric water through a variety of materials including pre-existing evaporites (as is the case in the Dead Sea region; Neev and Emery, 1967), soils, weathered rocks, and volcanic ejecta. Thus, continental evaporites can be composed of a simple assemblage like carbonate + sulfate + halite, just like marine deposits (though the halite of non-marine deposits is lower in bromine than the halite of marine deposits), or of complex ones which include accumulation of exotic minerals like mirabilite ($Na_2SO_4 \cdot 10H_2O$), trona ($Na_2CO_3 \cdot NaHCO_3 \cdot 2H_2O$), and gaylussite ($Na_2CO_3 \cdot CaCO_3 \cdot 5H_2O$). Evaporite deposits formed on lake floors are composed predominantly of algal carbonates with varying admixtures of calcium sulfate and, less commonly, other salts. Continental evaporites also include a proportion of silicic clastic detritus which was transported into the basin both by

by wind and water. Large quantities of borate minerals commonly occur
in continental evaporites.

Discriminating between continental and marine evaporites is not
always an easy task. As noted above the same mineral assemblages can
form in both environments. For example, the Paleogene non-marine
crystalline gypsum beds of the Paris Basin and of the Mormoiron Basin
in France are very similar in appearance to many marine gypsum deposits
(compare the descriptions in Truc, 1978 with those in Ogniben, 1957 or
in Schreiber et al., 1976). Nodular sulfates occurring in the silicic
or calcareous sands and muds of continental playas and sabkhas look
and form exactly as do those in marine margin deposits (compare the
descriptions in Tucker, 1978 with those in Kinsman, 1969). Continental
evaporite deposits are most readily distinguished by their association
with certain distinctive sedimentary features or deposits including:
1) alluvial, mud flat, and wind-blown deposits (c.f. Hanford, in
press), 2) lake deltas and lake-bottom turbidites (Picard and High,
1972), 3) marked soil horizons, caliche development, plant debris, and
animal footprints and remains, and 4) poor stratigraphic continuity.
Most sediments of continental deposits are reddish-brown in color.

Continental Margin Evaporites: These deposits develop adjacent to
seas in arid regions and are the arid region equivalent of a salt water
marsh. Typically sabkhas occur along such margins, and locally there may
be shallow intermittent hypersaline ponds or lagoons (Hanford, in press).
The products of deposition on a continental margin are very sensitive to
fluctuations in water level. A progradational depositional cycle is

composed, starting at the base, of various shallow water sediments (principally carbonate), grading up into laminar algal carbonates which interfinger upwards with evaporites. The evaporites are sometimes overlain by terrestrial clastics (silicic and/or carbonate) which are frequently composed of eolian transported sand. The sequence of laminar algal carbonates and over- lying nodular evaporites is typical of the sabkha cycle. Frequently, any gypsum in the evaporite transforms into nodular or bedded anhydrite, and in some cases it may be interlayered with halite. Carbonate components are generally extensively dolomitized due to interaction with hypersaline and/or meteoric water.

Sabkha sequences are typically 1-2 m thick (Shearman, 1971; 1978), but some continental margins, particularly those which are a consequence of recent rifting, subside rapidly enough to permit development of 12-15 m thick sabkha sequences. If subsidence is too slow to keep pace with deposi- tion or if the margin is not broad enough to permit extended progradation, the sabkha deposit will rapidly cover and fill the available margin and the top of the cycle will be marked by a pronounced hiatus. The Late Permian Bellerophon Formation of the Italian Dolomites (Bosellini and Hardie, 1973) and the uppermost Jurassic deposits of the Persian Gulf (Murris, 1980) are representative sabkha deposits.

Basinal Evaporites: Basinal evaporites are those evaporites which accumulate in marine areas that have restricted circulation. Evaporite deposits of basins can occur in three facies groupings: 1) Along the margins of the basin sabkha evaporites develop which are identical in appearance and composition to those which develop along continental margins adjacent to the open sea. 2) Further offshore, shallow water

subaqueous deposits develop which are characterized by the presence of

high energy sedimentary structures and the development of algal structures.

These deposits occur as even-bedded banks composed of gypsum sands and

silts intercalated with algal carbonate. Because of the harshness of the

environment, fossil populations are very restricted. 3) The evaporite

deposits which develop in deeper water are composed of laminar beds of

fine-grained gypsum or anhydrite mixed with micritic carbonate that is formed

by the action of anaerobic bacteria on early formed gypsum. Laminar halite

beds have also been observed. The laminar beds often are continuous for great

distances. Anderson et al. (1972) documented laminar evaporites in the

Delaware Basin which could be correlated for great distances. Turbidite

and debris flow deposits are sometimes intercalated with the laminar evaporites

(Schreiber et al., 1976; Schlager and Boltz, 1977; Meier, 1977).

The processes by which deep water evaporites crystallize is not

totally understood. It is possible that they crystallize in shallow water

along the basin margin and are transported to depth, as is surely the case

for the turbidites. Alternatively, dense saline water may form at the

margin and then sink to the basin floor, where the evaporites precipitate

(c.f. Sloss, 1969; Schmalz, 1969) while surface waters remain at near normal

salinity. Finally, it may be that high salinities are reached at the

surface and that evaporites crystallize there and subsequently sink to the

floor through the water column.

In order for thick basinal evaporite deposits to form, the requisite

salinity in the restricted sea must be maintained for a long time. This requires a delicate balance between evaporation and the influx of new seawater. If the influx is too slow, the restricted sea would dry up. If the influx is too fast, salinities that are high enough to permit evaporite nucleation might never be achieved. The delicate balance is only possible in non-humid climates, such as occur in the belt between 40°N and 40°S latitude.

A second prerequisite to the development of a thick basinal evaporite deposit is that the basin of deposition must be rapidly subsiding. Otherwise, because of the high rate of evaporite deposition, the basin would soon fill. Loading caused by the weight of the low density evaporite sediment (such as halite and potash) can account for about 65% of the necessary subsidence, whereas loading by anhydrite, which has a higher density, can account for 80% of the subsidence. Thus, there must be an additional, tectonic component of subsidence. Requisite subsidence occurs in at least four tectonic settings:

1) Rift Basins. During the late stages of rifting, just before commencement of sea-floor spreading, subsidence rates are very high. Incursions of the sea may begin, but circulation is restricted. Examples of evaporites developed in this setting are the Middle Miocene deposits of the Red Sea region and the Triassic-Jurassic deposits of eastern North America.

2) Interior Basins. For reasons that are not totally understood, certain regions of cratonic interiors have subsided to form roughly circular basins. Epeiric seas fill these basins, and carbonate deposits develop around their rims, ultimately restricting the influx of new

seawater. With the consequent increase in salinity, evaporite precipitation can begin. An example of evaporites developed in this setting are the Upper Silurian deposits of the Michigan Basin.

3) Tectonically Isolated Seas. Ocean basins, such as the Mediterranean Sea, may sometimes be isolated from the world ocean because of regional tectonism. During such times, if the climate is arid, evaporation can increase salinity sufficiently to cause precipitation of extensive evaporites. This situation happened in the Mediterranean Sea during Messinian (Late Miocene) time.

4) Back Arc Basins. It is possible that a back arc basin could be isolated if volcanic activity and tectonism block its connection to the ocean. Back arc basins have been known to become euxinic, but evaporite deposits in them have not been documented.

Rates of Deposition

The extremely high rates at which evaporite deposits form have been determined only recently. Under certain conditions, accumulation rates of evaporites are over an order of magnitude greater than those of other sediments. In a geologic time frame, it is possible for an evaporite to fill a basin instantaneously. For example, 2 km of salt were deposited in a span of 250,000 to 500,000 years in the Mediterranean Sea during the Messinian (Schreiber and Hsü, 1980). Typical rates of deposition, determined from field observations of presently forming evaporite deposits, are listed in Table 3. As indicated by the table, depositional rates are higher for shallow water environments because the surface area of the air-water interface per unit volume of water is greater.

TABLE 3

Rates of Deposition of Marine Evaporites*

Sediment Type	Area of Formation	Observed Rates of Deposition
Anhydrite and carbonate	Sabkha	1m/1000 yr, with 1 km progradation/1000 yr
Gypsum	Solar Ponds (subaqueous)	1-40 m/1000 yr, over entire basin
Halite	Solar Ponds (subaqueous)	10-100 m/1000 yr, over entire basin

*Data from Schreiber and Hsü (1980); Kinsman (1969).

Structural Associations of Evaporites

Evaporites are among the most ductile rocks known. As a consequence they are generally the weakest member of a sedimentary sequence, and commonly become zones of detachment along which large-scale thrust sheets may travel. Müller and Hsü (1980) suggested that many of the detachment horizons of the Jura are marked by anhydrite beds. Locally, evaporites may be squeezed up along ramps or other faults. The property of high ductility permits evaporites to flow under very low pressure-temperature conditions; salt will flow down slope, as rock glaciers, even at the surface of the earth (Kent, 1970).

As noted earlier, many evaporite units are composed of alternating layers of evaporite and carbonate. When such units deform, the evaporite layers flow coherently, but the carbonate layers break into fragments which become displaced and may rotate as deformation progresses.

Evaporites such as halite, carnallite, and sylvite are also among
the least dense rocks known. This property, along with their high ductility,
makes evaporites susceptible to diapirism. Large-scale salt diapirs commonly
occur along continental margins. But evaporites can rise diapirically only
if the overlying material is essentially unconsolidated; either the
buoyant forces must be able to exceed the strength of the overlying material
or there must be pre-existing vertical planes of weakness (Bishop, 1978).
Indeed, the style of structures in evaporites is strongly dependent on
the strength of the overlying rock (c.f. Watkins et al., 1978; Humphries,
1978). Rapidly prograding clastic wedges may cover an evaporite, but the
clastics will take a long time to lithify. Thus, diapiric rise of evaporites
into clastic wedges is common. The movement of a salt substrate may change
the morphology of the clastic wedge and thus affect the distribution of
subsequent sediments. Carbonate rocks lithify much more quickly than clastics
and thus inhibit diapirism of underlying salt; only gentle swells and arches
may develop. The salt layers may also act as glide planes along which blocks
of carbonate or other sediments can slide. Thus, flow of evaporites permits
tilting of large blocks of the sedimentary prism along continental margin.
Mullins and Lynts (1977) view salt movement as the major cause of tilting
along the Bahama platform.

Organic Content of Evaporites

Although many oil fields contain considerable deposits of evaporites,
most ancient evaporites have little or no organic material (less than

0.2-0.5%) (Sloss, 1959). It was thought that evaporitic environments were too harsh to support substantial numbers of organisms. But it has been shown recently that evaporites which have not been deeply buried or extensively altered do contain substantial amounts of organic material (up to 15%) (Palmer et al., 1980; Kirkland and Evans, 1980; 1981). The organic material is not incorporated within individual crystals (Barcelona and Atwood, 1978; 1979), but rather it is dispersed througnout gypsiferous marls and diatomites. This organic material is composed largely of the remains of halophytic plants (e.g., Salicornia sp.), blue-green and green algae, halophyllic bacteria, brine shrimp (Artimis sp.), and other crus-tacea that are adapted to highly saline waters. The remains of these organ-isms transform into liptinitic (fat) accumulations.

Migration of the organic material in evaporites appears to take place in two phases. The first phase occurs very early, at shallow depths and at low levels of thermal maturity. Indeed, in Sicily, organic material (asphaltic oils) is presently migrating out of Messinian evaporite deposits that are now buried to depths of only one-half to one kilometer below the surface (Schreiber and Palmer, 1979, unpub. data). The action of bacteria on the organic and evaporitic material results in the development of sulfur deposits in these seep areas. The second phase of migration occurs under temperatures at which anhydrite commences to flow (150°-180°C). The propensity for migration of organic material out of evaporites may explain why ancient evaporites have such low organic contents.

ROLE OF EVAPORITES IN OIL FIELDS

Evaporites, because of their unique properties and compositions, play a distinctive role in the development of oil fields. Though they are not important as reservoirs, they may be important traps, may be important sources, may affect the structure and composition of adjacent reservoir rocks, and may provide information on environments of deposition that may be useful in guiding exploration.

Evaporites as Seals

In addition to being very ductile and buoyant, evaporites are almost always impermeable and non-porous. Thus, if they overlie a reservoir rock they may act as an effective seal. Because evaporites are often associated with good reservoir rocks, there are many examples where evaporites act as seals, in both stratigraphic straps and fault traps. Evaporites are deposited so rapidly that they can cover the underlying source rocks before the organic material of the source rocks can migrate.

Evaporites as Sources

Thick evaporite deposits, particularly those which form in basinal settings, have high initial organic contents, and thus may serve as source rocks. Migration of the organic material out of the evaporite frequently occurs very early, before the rock has been buried very deeply. Unfortunately, therefore, much of this organic material may be lost before it can be trapped in a reservoir unless subsidence rates are rapid enough that reservoir rocks are deposited on top of the evaporite before migration is complete or unless pre-existing reservoirs are already in place. Requisite rates of subsidence may be achieved in certain tectonic settings such as late stage rift basins. In such settings biogenic carbonate deposits or thick clastic wedges may rapidly cover an organic-rich evaporite and can provide reservoirs for the migrating organics.

Reaction of Evaporites with Other Rocks

The presence of evaporites in a sedimentary section can affect the composition of adjacent carbonate rocks. The highly saline waters associated with evaporites have high Mg/Ca ratios. These magnesium-rich waters react with pre-existing calcite to produce dolomite. The decrease in volume which results from this reaction can result in the creation of secondary porosity. Evaporites may occlude porosity, however, by precipitating in primary pore spaces of both carbonate and silicic clastic rocks.

Evaporites as Environmental Indicators

Commonly when core is taken during the drilling of a well, the presence of evaporites is noted, for they are useful marker beds, but they are not studied. This is unfortunate, because an understanding of the evaporite facies encountered may help to determine the facies of adjacent reservoir rocks. Such information may help guide further drilling. For example, knowledge of evaporite facies in the Michigan Basin changed thinking on the distribution of reservoir deposits.

Michigan Basin: A Case Study

The Michigan Basin existed as an intracratonic low from Cambrian (Catacosines, 1973) through Mississippian time. By Upper Silurian time, a substantial carbonate bank had built up around the rim of the basin.

Around the interior edge of the bank there was a marginal platform on
which pinnacle reefs grew. In Upper Silurian time the interior of the
basin filled with a succession of carbonates and evaporites. This succession, which has been analyzed using drilled core and geophysical data,
is illustrated in Table 4.

Until recently, two contrasting depositional models had been proposed
to account for the stratigraphic succession in the basin. The first is that
the sequence of the basin interior was deposited entirely in a deep water
basin separated from the surrounding epeiric sea by a barrier bar (Bischof,
1875; Ochsenius, 1877). The second is that the basin essentially dried out
so that the evaporites developed in desert or desiccated sabkha conditions
(Walther, 1903; Grabau and Sherzer, 1910; Friedman, 1972). But neither of
these theories could account for the complexity of the succession. One
factor that inhibited further understanding was that no one could be sure
of the environment in which the evaporite facies were created. By the
mid-1970's, however, following studies of modern-day evaporite depositional
settings, it became possible to interpret the evaporite facies on the basis
of their bedding characteristics and sedimentary structures, as well as on
their mineral associations. Using this information, Nurmi and Friedman
(1977) proposed that the Michigan Basin succession was the product of
varying water depths. The laminar deposits at the base of the succession
in the basin center were laid down in deep water, whereas the complex
deposits in the upper parts of the section were deposited in shallow-
water subaqueous or sabkha environments. In this model, the Michigan
Basin is principally a carbonate basin which periodically became restricted

TABLE 4

Succession of Evaporites and Carbonates in the Michigan Basin*

Stratigraphic Position	Unit Name	Lithologic Description	Areal Distribution
Top of Succession	C	green-grey dolomitic shale	covers entire basin and extends well beyond
	B	massive highly recrystal-lized halite, with local anhydrite and dolomite stringers	covers entire basin and extends well beyond
	A-2C	lime mudstone, lower part argillaceous, upper part dolomitic; local stromato-lites and pebble conglomer-ates; many erosion surfaces	covers basin interior and the rimming reef
	A-2E	halite with intercalated dolomite and nodular anhy-drite; widespread desicca-tion cracks, oscillation ripples and algal struc-tures; near basin edge sabkha cycles occur	covers basin interior, covers most of pinnacle reefs, laps around rimming reef
	A-1C	fetid dark lime mudstone; near basin edge there are intercalated beds of anhy-drite; local erosional surfaces	covers basin interior up to the interior edge of the rim reefs; surrounds pinnacle reefs and fills gaps in rim reefs
	A-1E	laminated black limestone and anhydrite, massive an-hydrite; halite lenses near top; beds continuous for great distances	basin interior
Base of Succession	A-O	laminar micritic carbonate; high organic content	basin interior

*Adapted from Nurmi (1975); Nurmi and Friedman (1977)

and thus precipitated evaporites. During the times of evaporative draw-down, the reefs along the rim of the basin, especially the pinnacle reefs, were exposed and underwent dolomitization, thus creating secondary porosity (Huh et al., 1977).

This new depositional model, along with new information on the rates of deposition of evaporites and on their potential as source rocks, has important implications for oil exploration. In particular, it points to the barrier and especially the pinnacle reefs on the rim of the basin as the most likely reservoirs. They developed porosity early on, because of evaporative drawdown and exposure, and thus could act as reservoirs for the early migrating organic content of the evaporites and carbonates in the basin center. This oil was trapped by the rapidly deposited impermeable evaporites that overstepped the basin rim.

BACKGROUND DATA ON CARBONATES

Introduction

The processes of carbonate sedimentation and diagenesis have been studied in great detail over the past thirty years. Excellent reviews of the subject have been written (c.f. Bathurst, 1971; Wilson, 1975; Walker, 1978) so it is not appropriate to enter into a detailed discussion here, as was done with evaporites. After a brief summary of carbonate compositions, structures, and facies, presented primarily to clarify our terminology, we will consider some aspects of the Mesozoic evaporites and carbonates of the Atlantic continental margin of North America, with emphasis on their petroleum potential.

Carbonate Compositions and Facies

Carbonate lithologies are highly variable as a consequence of three factors: 1) carbonate sediment can come from a variety of sources, 2) this sediment can be deposited in a variety of sedimentary environments, and 3) the process of diagenesis of this sediment can follow a variety of paths. In fact, the only requirement that a rock needs to meet in order for it to be classified as a carbonate is that it contain greater than 50% calcite and/or dolomite.

There are two basic types of carbonate rocks (c.f. Pettijohn, 1975). Autochthonous carbonates are those which grow in place either by the action of carbonate secreting organisms or by direct precipitation from seawater. Autochthonous carbonates are composed principally of fragments of carbonate fragments which have been transported to the site of deposition. The carbonate fragments, which are cemented together by sparite or embedded in a matrix of micrite, include skeletal materials, micrite grains, pellets, oolites, and intraclasts. As noted, up to 50% of a carbonate rock can be composed of non-carbonate material, such as quartz, clay, organic remains, and evaporites. Because of the diversity of carbonates, it has become necessary to develop fairly elaborate classification schemes. The most commonly used schemes are those of Dunham (1962) which is based on textures, Folk (1959) which is based on origin of constituent grains, and Choquette and Pray (1970) which is based on the nature of the pore space.

Carbonate sediments can be deposited in diverse environments ranging from deep ocean basins to fresh water lakes. Several facies can occur in each of these settings. A list of the most important marine facies is presented as Table 5. Within each facies, compositions may vary depending on the influx of evaporites and terrestrial sediments and on the degree of diagenesis.

Structural Associations of Carbonates

Carbonate rocks are much less ductile than evaporites. Thus, under shallow crustal conditions, carbonate rocks are susceptible to faulting and to flexural slip folding. Certain carbonate rocks will also undergo pressure solution in response to both vertical loading stresses and non-vertical tectonic stresses. Solution processes can affect the porosity of a carbonate reservoir, can permit stratigraphic thinning, and can accommodate layer-parallel shortening. The latter two processes may change the shape of carbonate reservoirs (Dunnington, 1967). Recently, there has been renewed interest in pressure-solution phenomena, and this interest resulted in the convening of a Geological Society of America Penrose Conference on the subject (Engelder, Geiser, and Alvarez, 1981).

Carbonates as Reservoirs

Carbonate rocks are frequently excellent reservoir rocks because of their high porosity. High primary porosity occurs in framework autochthonous carbonates and in lime grainstones. Many limestones appear to undergo diagenesis without extensive compaction, so, unless filled with spar, primary porosity can be maintained. Secondary porosity can develop in all carbonate rocks as a consequence of dolomitization (and resultant volume loss), mechanical fracturing, and dissolution.

TABLE 5

Facies of Marine Carbonate Rocks*

Facies Name	Components
Tidal Flat	extensively bioturbated lime mud and micritized allochems, nodular anhydrite and dolomite, varying terrestrial admixtures, intermittent storm deposits, mudcracks.
Restricted Platform (lagoonal)	locally laminated dolomitized bioclastic wacke-stone, lime mud, channelized cross-bedded lime sands, algal laminated stromatolites; variable terrigenous input.
Open Platform	well-bedded lime sands, wackestones, and mud-stones; variable terrigenous input, localized bioherms, variable textures.
Platform Edge	cross-bedded shoal lime sands (well-sorted grainstones), oolite banks and shoals.
Reef	boundstone with pockets of grainstone, framework structure pervasive.
Slope and Slope Base (fore-reef)	bedded fine-grained sediments with intercalated talus aprons, slumps and debris flow deposits; proximal turbidites.
Open Epeiric Sea (continental basement)	fossiliferous limestones interbedded with marls, planktonic remains, turbidites.
Open Ocean (oceanic basement)	evenly bedded lime mudstones composed of pelagic faunal remains, turbidites. Carbonate may be partially dissolved upon sinking below CCD.

*Modified from Wilson (1975); Pettijohn (1975).

Carbonates as Sources

Most primary carbonate forms by biogenic processes which occur in oxygenated water. If this carbonate material is also deposited in oxygenated conditions, much of the associated organic material will be oxidized and lost. Thus, only those carbonate rocks deposited in waters that are low in oxygen will contain significant amounts of organic material which may ultimately be transformed into oil. Geologic settings where low oxygen waters or euxinic conditions can occur include 1) restricted depositional basins, 2) hypersaline lagoons, and 3) deep ocean basins.

The Carbonates of the Atlantic Continental Margin

The Atlantic continental margin of North America was created in Early Jurassic time after rifting and subsequent sea-floor spreading separated North America from the rest of Pangea. The rifting episode created fault-bounded grabens along the margin which filled with thick terrestrial redbeds, lake deposits, and locally, evaporites. After rifting, which was not completely synchronous along the margin, subsidence continued and the deposits characterisitc of a passive continental margin began to build up. The first deposits were marine evaporites of several facies. The thickness of these evaporites varies along the strike of the margin as a consequence both of variations in depositional rates and in the amount of movement of the evaporites subsequent to deposition in response to loading by overburden. Shallow marine carbonates of many facies, some of which have local intercalations of evaporites, succeeded the evaporites. Carbonate deposition has continued to the present day south of the Blake Platform, resulting in a 5 km thick build up. But to the north, the carbonates have been buried beneath a wedge of clastic detritus. In the subsurface of the Nova Scotia

Shelf, for example, the 1 km thick Late Jurassic Abenaki Formation, which is

composed of a variety of carbonate lithologies, is sandwiched between salts

of the Argo Formation and clastic deltaic deposits of the Missisauga Forma-

tion (Eliuk, 1978; Jansa and Wade, 1975).

The carbonates of the Atlantic margin are of interest to the petro-

leum industry because they may contain extensive reservoirs. This petroleum

potential is a consequence of two factors; first, carbonate rocks can have

high porosities and permeabilities, and second, in places they are buried

deeply enough so that the organic material in them and in the adjacent source

rocks could have matured into oil or gas. The evaporites that are associated

with these carbonates could have played a role as both source and seal,

and also by reacting with the carbonates to produce dolomite. The silicic

clastic rocks which overlie the carbonates have not been buried deeply

enough in most places for their organic content to have matured to oil.

Jansa (in press) discussed the factors which control the variability

of carbonate buildups along the strike of the margin. He proposed that there

are six morphological types of carbonate platforms (Fig. 1). The morphology

of carbonate platforms is a function of many variables including: 1) struc-

ture of the underlying basement, 2) rate of subsidence of the margin,

3) volume of clastic influx, 4) water quality (temperature, oxygen content,

turbidity), 5) strength of nearby ocean currents, 6) occurrence of tectonic

activity, 7) atmospheric conditions (cloudiness), and 8) amount of movement

of underlying evaporite.

Platforms prograde seaward when the carbonate deposition rate is high

MORPHOLOGICAL TYPES OF CARBONATE PLATFORMS

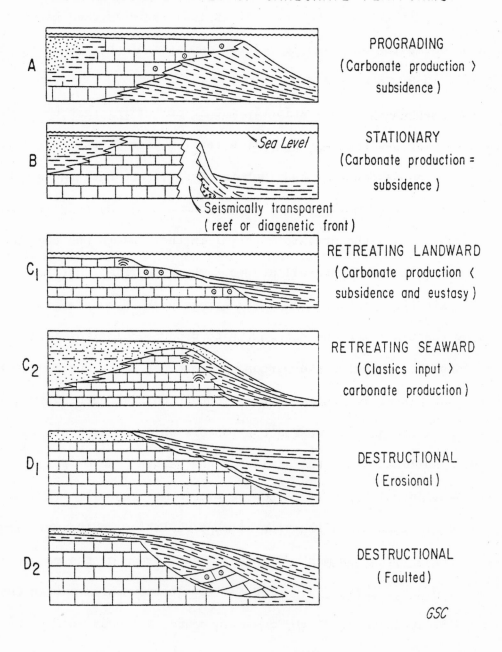

FIGURE 1. Schematic presentation of the morphological types
of carbonate platforms seen on the East Coast Continental Margin
(taken from Jansa, in press).

and the seaward slope is gentle, so that the platform can build out over its own talus. Landward retreat occurs when the deposition rate of carbonate cannot keep pace with the rate of subsidence or of sea-level rise. The platform maintains its position and builds vertically when deposition rate is high, but the seaward slope is too steep for seaward progradation to occur. The requisite steep slopes can be maintained by slumping or by erosion. Platform morphology affects both the facies of carbonate rocks that occur in stratigraphic section, and the facies of bounding units (Fig. 2), and thus can affect the distribution of oil.

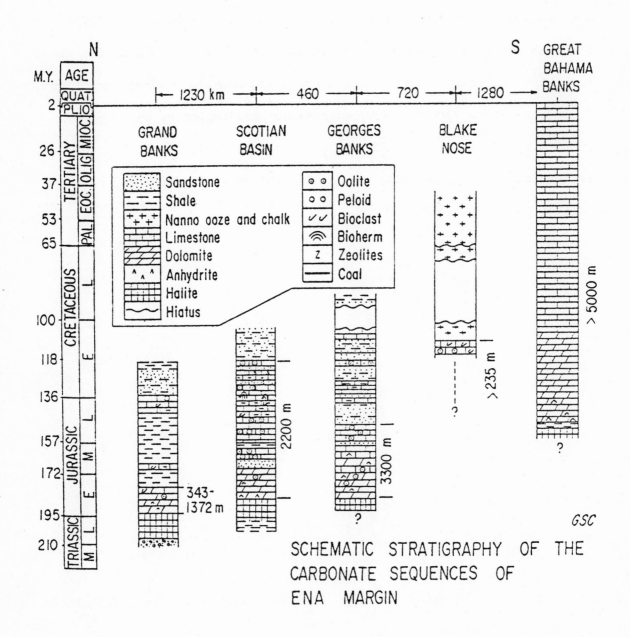

Figure 2: Lithology and stratigraphic position of strata enclosing the carbonate sequences on the eastern North American margin. Note the North-South diachronism in the initiation and termination of the shallow water carbonate deposition (taken from Jansa, in press).

REFERENCES

Anderson, R.Y., W.E. Dean, D.W. Kirkland, and H.I. Snider, 1972, Permian Castile varved evaporite sequence, West Texas and New Mexico: Geol. Soc. Am. Bull., v. 83, p. 59-86.

Barcelona, M.J., and D.K. Atwood, 1978, Gypsum-organic interactions in natural seawater: Effect of organics on precipitation kinetics and crystal morphology: Marine Chemistry, v. 6, p. 99-115.

_____, 1979, Gypsum-organic interactions in the marine environment: Sorption of fatty acids and hydrocarbons: Geochemica et Cosmochimica Acta, v. 43, p. 47-53.

Bathurst, R.G.C., 1971, Carbonate sediments and their diagenesis: Amsterdam, Elsevier, 620 pp.

Bishof, F., 1865, Die Steinsalzwerke der Stassfurt: Halle, Pfeiffer, 2nd ed., 95 pp.

Bishop, R.S., 1978, Mechanism for emplacement of piercement diapirs: A.A.P.G. Bull., v. 62, p. 1561-1583.

Bosellini, A., and L. Hardie, 1973, Depositional theme of a marginal marine evaporite: Sedimentology, v. 20, p. 5-27.

Catacosines, P.A., 1973, Cambrian lithostratigraphy of Michigan Basin: A.A.P.G. Bull., v. 57, p. 2404-2418.

Choquette, P.W., and L.C. Pray, 1970, Geologic nomenclature and classification of porosity in sedimentary carbonates: A.A.P.G. Bull., v. 54, p. 207-250.

Cody, W.G., and A.B. Hull, 1980, Experimental growth of primary anhydrite at low temperatures and water salinities: Geology, v. 8, p. 505-509.

Dean, W.E., 1978, Theoretical versus observed successions from evaporation of seawater (Ch. 4). Trace and minor elements in evaporites (Ch. 5) in Dean, W.E., and B.C. Schreiber (eds), Marine Evaporites: S.E.P.M. Short Course Notes #4, p. 74-85; 86-104.

Dunham, R.J., 1962, Classification of carbonate rocks according to depositional texture, in Ham, W.E. (ed.), Classification of carbonate rocks: A.A.P.G. Mem. 11, Tulsa, Oklahoma, p. 108-121.

Dunnington, H.V., 1967, Aspects of diagenesis and shape change in stylolitic limestone reservoirs: Proc., 7th World Petroleum Cong., Mexico, p. 339-352.

Eliuk, L.S., 1978, The Abenaki Formation, Nova Scotia Shelf, Canada--A depositional and diagenetic model for a Mesozoic carbonate platform: Bull. Canadian Petroleum Geology, v. 26, p. 424-514.

Engelder, T., P.A. Geiser, and W. Alvarez, 1981, Penrose conference report: Role of pressure solution and dissolution in geology: Geology, v. 9, p. 44-45.

Folk, R.L., 1959, Practical petrographic classification of limestones: A.A.P.G. Bull., v. 43, p. 1-38.

Friedman, G.M., 1972, Significance of Red Sea in problem of evaporites and basinal limestones: A.A.P.G. Bull., v. 59, p. 1072-1086.

Grabau, A.W., and W.H. Sherzer, 1910, The Monroe Formation of Southern Michigan and adjoining regions: Michigan Geological and Biological Survey, Publication No. 2, Geol. Ser. 1, 248p.

Hanford, C.R., in press, Facies anatomy of a Halocene continental sabkha: Bristol Dry Lake, California: A.A.P.G. Bull., v. 65.

Hardie, L.A., 1967, The gypsum-anhydrite equilibrium at one atmosphere pressure: Amer. Mineralogist, v. 52, p. 171-200.

Harvie, C.E., J.H. Weare, L.A. Hardie, and H.P. Eugster, 1980, Evaporation of seawater: Calculated mineral sequences: Science, v. 208, p. 498-500.

Holzer, W.T., 1979, Mineralogy of evaporites (Ch. 8). Trace elements and isotopes in evaporites (Ch. 9) in Burns, R.G. (ed.), Marine Minerals: Mineralogical Society of America, Short Course Notes, v. 6, p. 211-294; 296-346.

Huh, J.M., L.J. Briggs, and D. Gill, 1977, Depositional environments of pinnacle reefs, Niagara and Salina Groups, northern shelf, Michigan Basin, in J.H. Fisher (ed.), Reefs and evaporites-- concepts and depositional models: A.A.P.G., Studies in Geology, no. 5, p. 1-22.

Humphries, C.C. Jr., 1978, Salt movements on continental slope, northern Gulf of Mexico, in Bouma, A.H., G.T. Moore, and J.M. Coleman (eds.), Framework, facies and oil-trapping characteristics of the upper continental margin: A.A.P.G., Studies in Geology, no. 7, p. 69-86.

Jansa, L.F., in press, Mesozoic carbonate platforms and banks of the eastern North American margin: Marine Geol.

Jansa, L., and J.A. Wade, 1975, Geology of the continental margin off Nova Scotia and Newfoundland, in Offshore geology of eastern Canada: Geol. Surv. Can., Paper 74-30, v. 2, p. 51-105.

Kent, P.E., 1970, The salt plugs of the Persian Gulf region: Leicester Literary and Phil. Soc., p. 56-88.

Kinsman, D.J.J., 1969, Modes of formation, sedimentary associations and diagnostic features of shallow water and supratidal evaporites: A.A.P.G. Bull., v. 53, p. 830-840.

Kirkland, D.W., and R. Evans, 1980, Source-rock potential of the evaporitic environment (abs.): A.A.P.G. Bull., v. 64, p. 733.

_____, 1981, Source-rock potential of evaporitic environment: A.A.P.G. Bull., v. 65, p. 181-190.

Meier, R., 1977, Turbidite und Olisthostrome--Sedimentationsphänomene des Werra-Sulfats (Zechstein 1) am Osthang der Eichsfeld-Schwelle im Gebiet des Südharzes: Veröffentlichungen des Zentralinstituts für Physik der Erde, Nr. 50, 45 p.

Müller, W.H., and K. Hsü, 1980, Stress distribution in overthrusting slabs and mechanics of Jura deformation: Rock Mechanics, Supp. v. 9, p. 219-232.

Mullins, H.T., and G.W. Lynts, 1977, Origin of the northwestern Bahama Platform: Review and reinterpretation: Geol. Soc. Am. Bull., v. 88, p. 1447-1461.

Murray, R.C., 1964, Origin and diagenesis of gypsum and anhydrite: Jour. Sedimentary Petrology, v. 34, p. 512-523.

Murris, R.J., 1980, Middle East: Stratigraphic evolution and oil habital: A.A.P.G. Bull., v. 64, p. 597-618.

Neev, D., and K.O. Emery, 1967, The Dead Sea Bulletin #41 (Depositional processes and environments of evaporites): State of Israel, Ministry of Development, Geol. Survey, 147 pp.

Nurmi, R.D., 1975, Stratigraphy and sedimentology of the lower Salina Group (Upper Silurian) in the Michigan Basin: Unpub. Ph.D. dissertation, Rensselaer Polytechnic Institute, 279 pp.

_____, and G.M. Friedman, 1977, Sedimentology and depositional environments of basin-center evaporites, lower Salina Group (Upper Silurian), Michigan Basin, in Fisher, J.H. (ed.), Reefs and evaporites--concepts and depositional models: A.A.P.G., Studies in Geology, v. 5, p. 23-52.

Ogniben, L., 1957, Petrographia delle Serie Solfifera siciliana e considerazioni geologiche relative: Mem. Descr. Carta Geol. Italia, v. 33, 275 pp.

Ochsenius, C., 1877, Die Bildung der Steinsalzlager und ihrer Mutterlaugensalze: Halle, C.E.M. Pfeiffer, 172 pp.

Palmer, S., J.E. Zumberge, and B.C. Schreiber, 1980, Organic geochemistry of evaporite deposits in Sicilian Basin, Sicily: Abs. International Palynological Conference, Cambridge, England (6/29/80).

Pettijohn, E.J., 1975, Sedimentary rocks: New York, Harper & Row, 628 pp.

Picard, M.D., and L.R. High, 1972, Criteria for recognizing lacustrine rocks, in Rigby, J.K., and W.K. Hamblen (eds.): Spec. Publ. Soc. Econ. Paleont. Mineral, v. 16, p. 108-145.

Schlager, W., and H. Bolz, 1977, Clastic accumulation of sulfate evaporites in deep-water: Jour. Sed. Petrology, v. 47, p. 600-609.

Schmalz, R.F., 1969, Deep-water evaporite deposition: A generic model: A.A.P.G. Bull., v. 53, p. 798-823.

Schreiber, B.C., and H.J. Hsü, 1980, Evaporites, in Hobson, G.D., Developments in petroleum geology--2: Berking, Essex, Applied Science Publishers Ltd., p. 87-138.

Schreiber, B.C., G.M. Friedman, A. Decima, and E. Schreiber, 1976, Depositional environments of Upper Miocene (Messinian) evaporite deposits in the Sicilian Basin: Sedimentology, v. 23, p. 729-760.

Shearman, D.J., 1971, Marine evaporites: The calcium sulfate facies: A.S.P.G. Seminar, University of Calgary, 65 pp.

_____, 1978, Evaporites of coastal sabkhas, in Dean, W.E., and B.C. Schreiber (eds.), Marine Evaporites: S.E.P.M. Short Course Notes #4, p. 6-42.

Sloss, L.L., 1959, The significance of evaporites: Jour. Sed. Petrology, v. 23, p. 143-161.

_____, 1969, Evaporite deposition from layered solutions: A.A.P.G. Bull., v. 53, p. 776-789.

Stewart, F.W., 1963, Data of geochemistry, Chapter Y, Marine evaporites: U.S.G.S. Professional Paper, 440-Y.

Tucker, M.E., 1978, Triassic lacustrine sediments from South Wales: Shore-zone clastics, evaporites and carbonates, in Matter, A., and M.E. Tucker (eds.): I.A.S., Special Publ. No. 2, p. 203-222.

Truc, G., 1978, Lacustrine sedimentation in an evaporite environment: The Ludian (Paleogene) of the Mormoiron Basin, southeastern France, in Matter, A., and M.E. Tucker (eds.), Modern and ancient lake sediments: I.A.S., Special Publ. No. 2, p. 203-222.

Usiglio, J., 1849, Analyse de l'eau de la Mediterranée sur les cotes de
    France: Annalen der Chemie, v. 27, p. 92-107; 172-191.

Walker, R.G., 1978 (ed.), Facies models: Toronto, Geological Association
    of Canada, 211 pp.

Walther, J., 1893, Einleitung in die Geologie als historische Wissenschaft:
    Jena, Verlag von Gustav Fischer, 1055 pp.

Watkins, J.S., J.W. Ladd, R.T. Buffler, F.J. Shaub, M.H. Houston, and
    J.L. Worzel, 1978, Occurrence and evolution of salt in deep Gulf
    of Mexico, in Bouma, A.H., G.T. Moore, and J.M. Coleman (eds.),
    Framework, facies and oil-trapping characteristics of the upper
    continental margin: A.A.P.G., Studies in Geology, no. 7, p. 43-66.

Wilson, J.L., 1975, Carbonate facies in geological history: New York,
    Springer Verlag, 471 pp.

PETROLEUM GEOCHEMISTRY OF THE ATLANTIC MARGIN

John M. Hunt
Woods Hole Oceanographic Institution
Woods Hole, Massachusetts 02543

PETROLEUM GEOCHEMISTRY OF THE ATLANTIC MARGIN

John M. Hunt[1]
Woods Hole Oceanographic Institution
Woods Hole, Massachusetts 02543

How much oil and gas will be discovered on the North Atlantic Margin? The petroleum geochemists can assist in answering this question from analyses of organic matter in the cores and cuttings of the first wildcat wells. Even without such data, rough estimates can be made of hydrocarbon potential providing the volume of fine-grained rocks within the oil window can be estimated. For example, world-wide, the average shale contains about 1% organic matter of which 10% is generated as bitumen (Fig. 1). After the bitumen is generated, possibly 10% of it migrates as oil of which possibly 50% is collected in traps. If these assumptions are correct, then the quantity of hydrocarbons in traps on the North Atlantic Margin is equal to 5×10^{-5} times the weight of presumed source rock.

Unfortunately such estimates are off by several orders of magnitude because of the tremendous variation in both the quantity and quality of organic matter in sedimentary basins. The three most important factors for determining the amount of petroleum generated in a basin are the (1) quantity, (2) type and (3) maturation state of the organic matter. At one time it was thought that high biologic productivity during deposition would result in a high content of organic matter. However, as Demaison and Moore (1980) have pointed out, productivity is much less important than the preservation of the organic matter. Areas of high productivity like the Grand Banks of Newfoundland and the northeastern Brazilian Shelf have relatively little organic carbon in their bottom sediments because of poor preservation.

[1]WHOI Contribution No. 4919. This work was supported by the Office of Basic Energy Sciences, Department of Energy, Contract No. EG-77-S-02-4392.

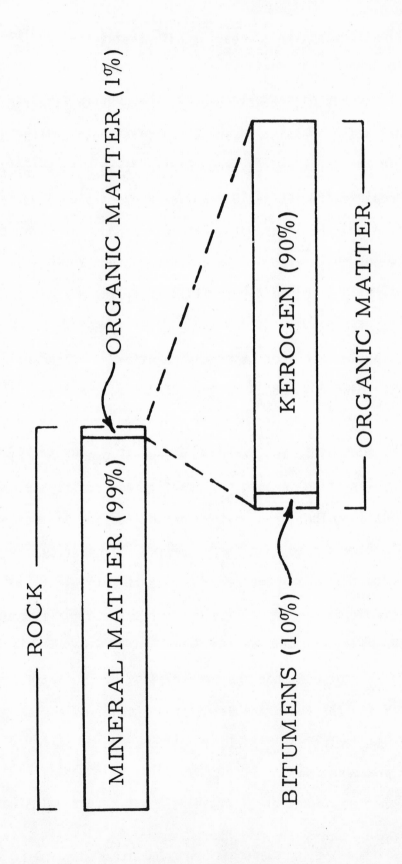

1. Relationship of weight per cent extractable bitumen to total rock.

Preservation is directly related to the oxic-anoxic conditions of deposition. In 1958 Ronov reported the analysis of organic carbon in several hundred samples of upper Devonian shale throughout the Russian Platform from Kiev in the west to Ufa in the east. Ronov also determined the ratios of ferric to ferrous iron in the sediments, a measure of the state of oxidation or reduction. He found that the ferric to ferrous ratios in the west were about 10 (strongly oxidizing) and the organic carbon values of the same samples were less than 0.25% by weight. Going east there was a gradual decrease in the ferric/ferrous ratio from 10 to 5 toward the central part of the platform and from 5 to 1 in the east and southeast. The corresponding organic carbon values changed from 0.25 to 0.5 to 5%. The highest values of from 2 to 5% organic carbon occurred where the ferric/ferrous ratio fell below 1. This was the most highly reducing environment at the time of deposition of the upper Devonian shale on the Russian Platform.

This difference betweeen oxic and anoxic depositional environments is more clearly shown in Figures 2 and 3 from the Demaison and Moore (1980) paper. In the oxygenated environment, the organic matter is partially degraded as it falls through the water column. An additional percentage of the carbon is consumed by benthic fauna on the seabottom after which worms and other burrowing organisms work it over in the sediments. Bioturbation caused by these organisms introduces oxygen into the sediments resulting in a high level of destruction of the less inert forms of carbon.

In contrast, the anoxic environment frequently has hydrogen sulfide in the water column just above the ocean bottom. This effectively kills all benthic organisms so that no oxidation of organic carbon occurs. Instead, bacterial sulfate reduction leading to more hydrocarbon-like biomasses, is common. Under

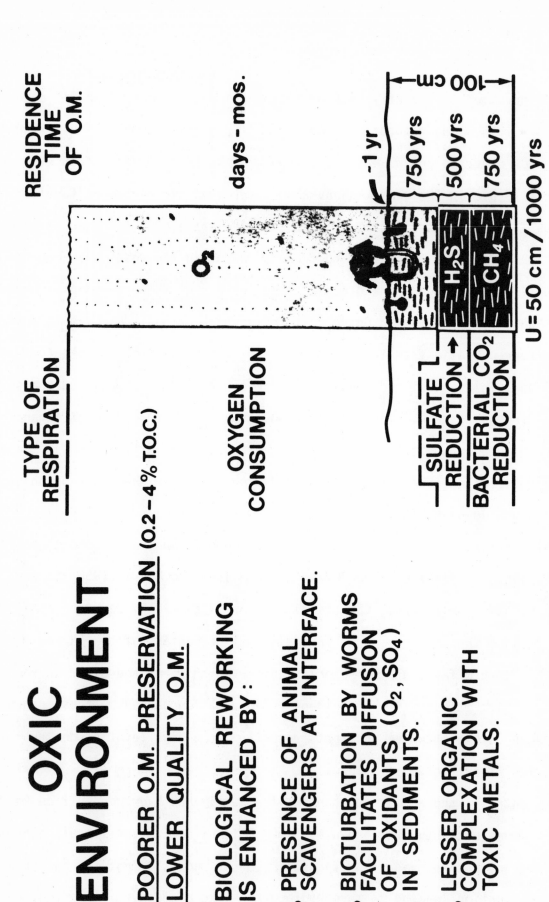

OXIC ENVIRONMENT

POORER O.M. PRESERVATION (0.2 – 4 % T.O.C.)

LOWER QUALITY O.M.

BIOLOGICAL REWORKING IS ENHANCED BY:

- PRESENCE OF ANIMAL SCAVENGERS AT INTERFACE.

- BIOTURBATION BY WORMS FACILITATES DIFFUSION OF OXIDANTS (O_2, SO_4) IN SEDIMENTS.

- LESSER ORGANIC COMPLEXATION WITH TOXIC METALS.

TYPE OF RESPIRATION

OXYGEN CONSUMPTION

RESIDENCE TIME OF O.M.

days – mos.

~1 yr

750 yrs

500 yrs

750 yrs

O_2

H_2S

CH_4

SULFATE REDUCTION

BACTERIAL CO_2 REDUCTION

100 cm

U = 50 cm / 1000 yrs

2. Degradation of organic matter in water column and surface sediments containing oxygen (Demaison and Moore, 1980).

Anoxic Environments

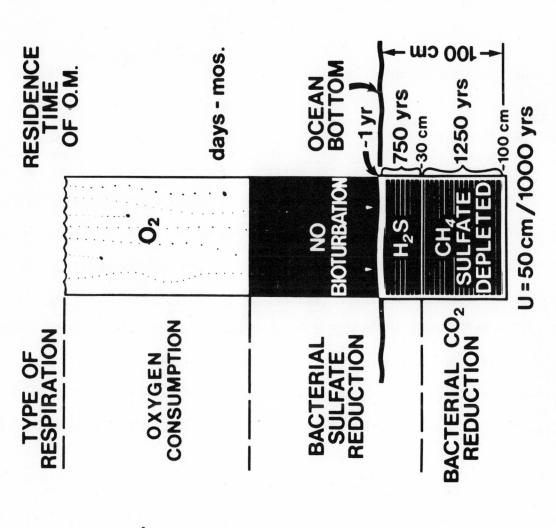

ANOXIC ENVIRONMENT

BETTER O.M. PRESERVATION-
(1-25% T.O.C.)
HIGHER QUALITY O.M.

BIOLOGICAL REWORKING
IS SLOWED BY:

- THE ABSENCE OF
  ANIMAL SCAVENGERS.

- RESTRICTED DIFFUSION OF
  OXIDANTS (SO_4) INTO
  UNDISTURBED SEDIMENT.

- LESSER UTILIZATION
  OF LIPIDS BY
  ANAEROBIC BACTERIA.?

3. Degradation of organic matter in water column and surface sediments
   containing hydrogen sulfide (Demaison and Moore, 1980).

such conditions the organic carbon content of the rock may exceed 25% by weight. Demaison and Moore (1980) believe that oxygen contents of less than 0.5 ml per liter of water result in good organic matter preservation.

It has long been known that the world's oceans contain an oxygen minimum layer where the oxygen content of the water is inadequate to meet the biochemical oxygen demands. The depth of this layer varies but is frequently in the range from about 400 to 1,000 meters. When this oxygen minimum layer impinges on a coastline it results in the creation of anoxic conditions. Examples of this are shown in Figures 4 and 5 from the Demaison and Moore (1980) paper. In both of these areas upwelling results in high productivity thereby creating a high oxygen demand which results in an oxygen minimum. The anoxic sediments, deposited where oxygen concentrations are less than 0.5 ml/l of water, cause organic carbon contents of the sediments to be as high as 26%.

The quality or type of organic matter in a sediment is as important as the quantity in the sense that it determines whether oil, gas or neither will be generated. Basically there are two types of organic matter in sediments, the high hydrogen sapropelic material and low hydrogen humic material (Figure 6). The term sapropelic refers to decomposition and polymerization products of fatty, lipid organic materials such as spores and planktonic algae deposited in subaquatic muds (marine or lacustrine) usually under oxygen-restricted conditions. Sapropelic organic matter initially has hydrogen to carbon ratios in the range from 1.3 to 1.7. Extremely organic rich sapropelic deposits undergo maturation to form boghead coals and oil shales. The term humic refers to products of peat formation, mainly land plant material either deposited in swamps or carried out to sea and deposited in basins under oxygenated conditions. Peat has a hydrogen to carbon ratio of less than 1 so it is not an

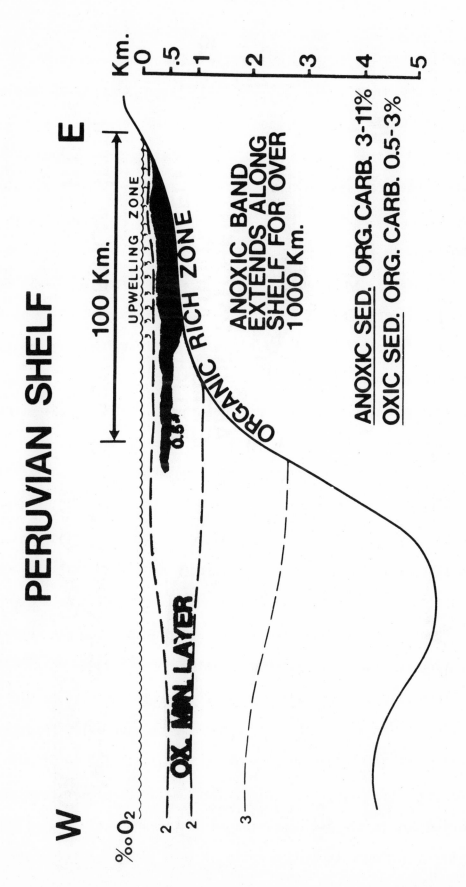

4. Organic rich anoxic sediments off Peru. Oxygen content in ml/l sea water shown by dashed lines (Demaison and Moore, 1980).

Anoxic Environments

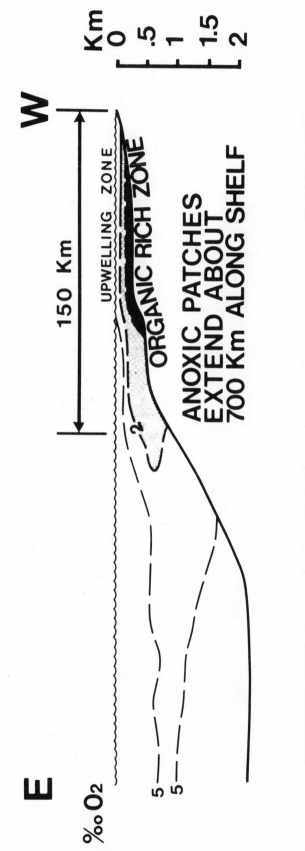

S.W. AFRICAN SHELF

ANOXIC SED. ORG. CARB. 3–26%
OXIC SED. ORG. CARB. <3%

SIMILAR SETTING: **PERU**

5. Organic rich anoxic sediments off S.W. Africa. Black area is less than

0.5 ml O$_2$/1H$_2$O (Demaison and Moore, 1980).

SAPROPELIC   H/C > 1

FATS, OILS, RESINS, WAXES, PIGMENTS

HUMIC   H/C < 1

PRODUCTS OF PEAT FM. LIGNIN, CELLULOSE, TANNINS, CHARCOAL

6. Oil forming organic matter is high in hydrogen and becomes gas forming when H/C drops much below 1.

important progenitor of oil. Sapropelic material will form oil until the hydrogen to carbon ratio drops much below 1 after which it forms gas. Humic material generally forms only gas.

Sapropelic and humic materials have been defined in visual kerogen terms by the palynologist, in coal maceral terms by the coal petrographer and in kerogen type (chemical) terms by the chemists (Figures 7 and 8).

Marine organic matter is usually amorphous-algal material in the liptinite (type I-II) category. In the marine environment it generates oil and in the lacustrine environment it is responsible for both oil and oil shales. During maturation, H/C and O/C ratios decrease as shown in Figure 7. Waxy oils are derived from the herbaceous exinite materials (spores, pollen, cutin) which are land derived. The woody, vitrinite material yields gas on maturation while inertinite yields either a little gas or nothing. The only difference between coal macerals and the organic matter (kerogen) of sedimentary rocks is that the latter are more diluted with inorganic mineral matter. Many oil company geochemists prefer the simple coal maceral terminology of liptinite (oil and gas forming), vitrinite (gas forming), and inertinite (no hydrocarbons) for defining the organic matter of sedimentary rocks. Figure 9 shows how these three major organic types plot on an H/C-O/C Krevelen (1961) diagram. Shown on the diagram are the evolutionary pathways of organic matter in the Jurassic of the Paris Basin, the Devonian of the Western Canada Basin and Cretaceous of the Douala Basin that resulted in the generation of oil and gas. The Paris Basin source rocks produce oil, the Douala Basin on land produces gas and the W. Canada Basins both oil and gas.

This leads to the third important factor for evaluating source rocks, the state of maturation. Oil and gas are formed within specific time-temperature

SAPROPELIC		
VISUAL KEROGEN		
ALGAL	AMORPHOUS	HERBACEOUS
COAL MACERALS		
ALGINITE	LIPTINITE (EXINITE) AMORPHOUS	SPORINITE CUTINITE RESINITE
KEROGEN TYPE		
I	II	
H/C		
1.6 TO 0.3	1.3 TO 0.3	
O/C		
0.1 TO 0.02	0.2 TO 0.02	
SOURCE		
MARINE AND LACUSTRINE	CONTINENTAL	

7. Classification of sapropelic kerogen (Hunt, 1979, p. 279).

	HUMIC	
VISUAL KEROGEN	WOODY	COALY
COAL MACERALS	VITRINITE	INERTINITE
KEROGEN TYPE	III	IV
H/C	1.0 TO 0.3	0.45 TO 0.3
O/C	0.4 TO 0.02	0.3 TO 0.02
SOURCE	CONTINENTAL AND RECYCLED	

8. Classification of humic kerogen (Hunt, 1979, p. 279).

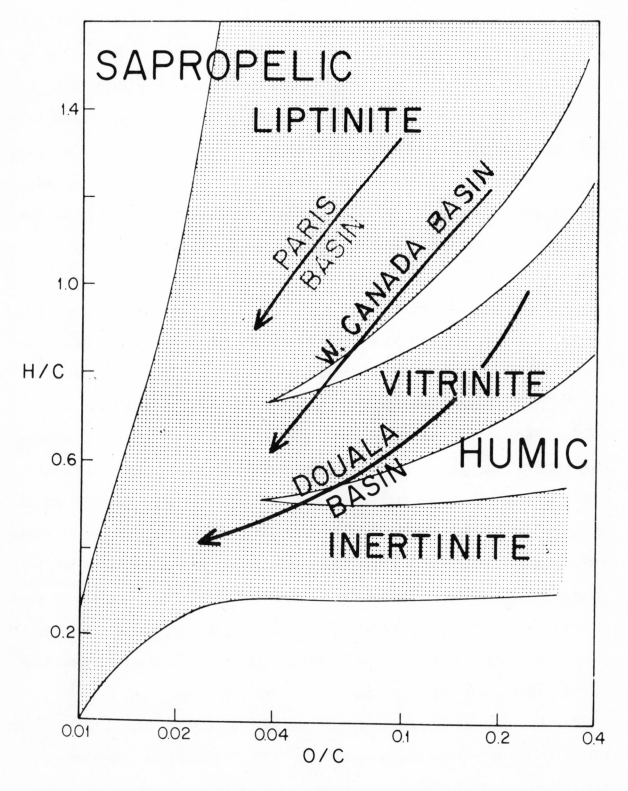

9. Maturation pathways of the major kerogen types (Hunt, 1979, p. 341).

conditions which are discussed in more detail in Hunt, (p. 131-147, 1979). Due
to the nature of this process, oil and gas tends to be generated in the crust
of the earth within a temperature range from 50 to 200°C (Fig. 10). This has
sometimes been referred to as the oil window or kitchen where the cooking of
the organic matter takes place. During organic genesis, at temperatures below
50°C, biogenic methane and heavy hydrocarbons of biological origin are present. As temperatures increase, the catagenesis stage results in the cracking of
organic matter with the formation of wet gas (ethane, propane, butanes), gasoline, kerosene, and diesel oil (C_4-C_{14}) plus increasing amounts of lubrica-
ting oils and residuum (C_{15} to C_{40}). By the end of the catagenic stage
around 200°C, only methane is present in significant quantities. As oil and
gas are generated, the hydrogen to carbon and oxygen to carbon ratios of the
organic matter decrease along the evolutionary pathways shown in Figure 9.

The critical question regarding the hydrocarbon potential of the North
American Margin then becomes an evaluation of the quantity, type and maturation state of the organic matter in fine-grained sediments associated with
potential reservoirs. Initial studies of the organic matter were limited to
holes drilled by the Deep Sea Drilling Project on the outer continental rises
and abyssal plains. These initial results were not very encouraging but later
studies of COST wells drilled on the continental shelf showed pockets of organic matter with a favorable potential for oil and gas. In general, however, the
organic geochemistry studies to date do not indicate that the North American
Atlantic Margin will ever be comparable to the North Sea.

The Jurassic and Cretaceous formations of the Atlantic Margin have the best
potential for petroleum source rocks. In 1980, Tissot et al. published a detailed evaluation of the paleoenvironment and petroleum potential of middle

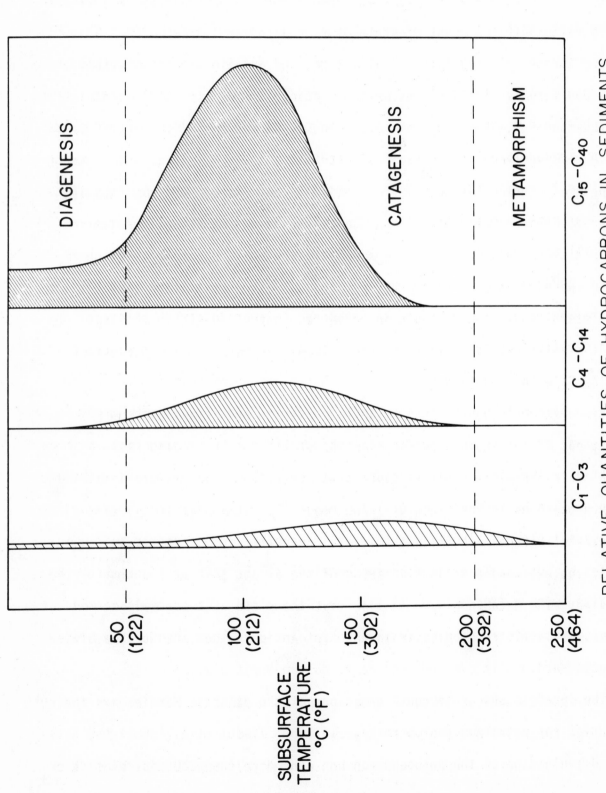

RELATIVE QUANTITIES OF HYDROCARBONS IN SEDIMENTS

10. Hydrocarbon distributions in fine-grained rocks. Areas under curve are proportional to masses as carbon (Hunt, 1979, p. 146).

Cretaceous black shales in Atlantic basins based on Deep Sea Drilling Project results. They found a significant difference between the quantity and type of organic matter off the coast of Africa compared to North America (U.S.A.) and Southern Europe. During Aptian/Albian time, the organic matter deposited off Africa was largely liptinitic material of planktonic origin. In contrast, the outer continental margins of both Southern Europe and the U.S. coast of North America received large percentages of vitrinitic material and degraded inertinite, both of continental orgin. The study did not include the continental margins of Canada, Greenland and the United Kingdom. It also was found that the depositional environments were more strongly reducing along the African coast compared to the other coastlines through most of the Cretaceous (Figure 11). Intermittant anoxic conditions resulted in the deposition of large quantities of liptinitic planktonic organic matter in the deepest parts of both the Cape and Angola Basins.

This difference between the Atlantic coasts of Africa and North America are brought out in one example of the quantity of light hydrocarbons that has been generated in the sediments to a depth of about 1,400 meters as shown in Figure 12. Hydrocarbons in the light gasoline range (C_4-C_7) are generated at the beginning of catagenesis (Figure 10). The quantity formed even at the beginning of the oil window is an indication of the amount that will ultimately be generated. The data in Figure 12 show that the yield of these hydrocarbons at 1200 meters is 100 times greater in the African basins compared to the Blake-Bahama Basin.

A further comparison of these areas based on organic carbon and hydrocarbon source potential by pyrolysis is shown in Figures 13 and 14 from the Tissot et al. (1980) paper. The Angola Basin contains more than 200 meters of black

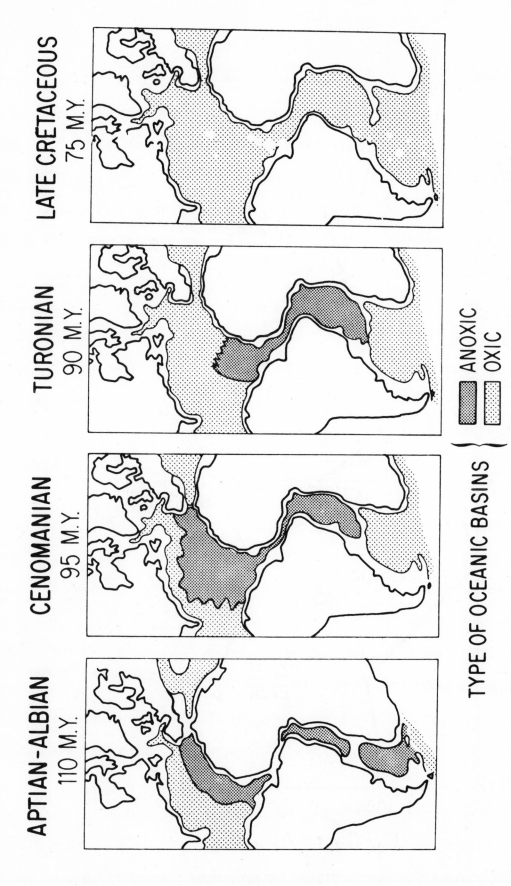

TYPE OF OCEANIC BASINS { ANOXIC / OXIC

11. Generalized depositional environments through Cretaceous time in Atlantic basins. Localized variability between oxic and anoxic conditions probably occurred (Tissot, et al, 1980).

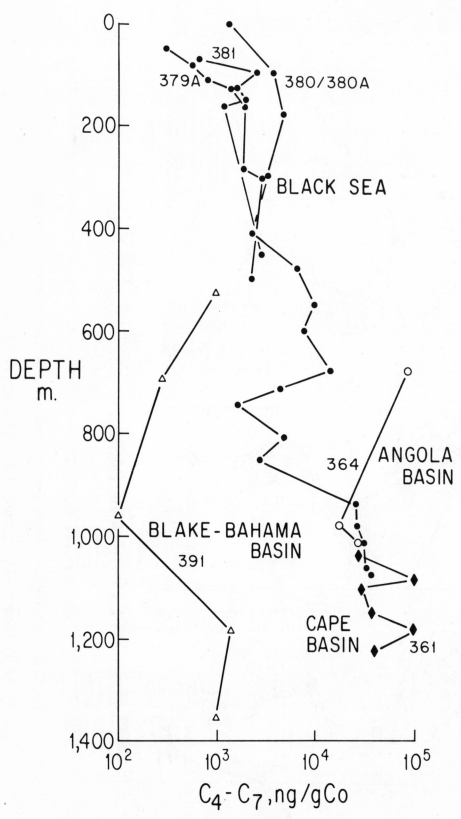

12. Yield of butanes through heptanes in nanograms/gram of organic carbon in Atlantic basin sediments (Hunt and Whelan, 1978).

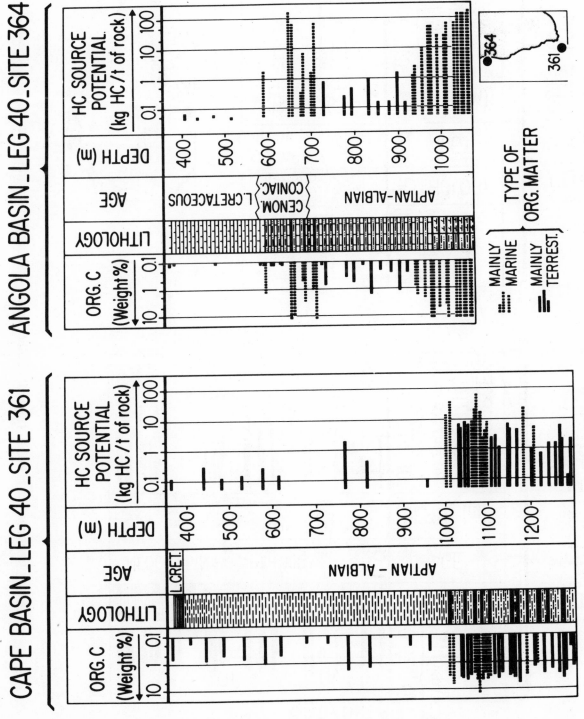

13. Geochemical well logs showing organic carbon and hydrocarbon yield by pyrolysis at DSDP Sites 361 and 364. Yields are in kilograms of hydrocarbon per metric ton of rock (Tissot et al, 1980).

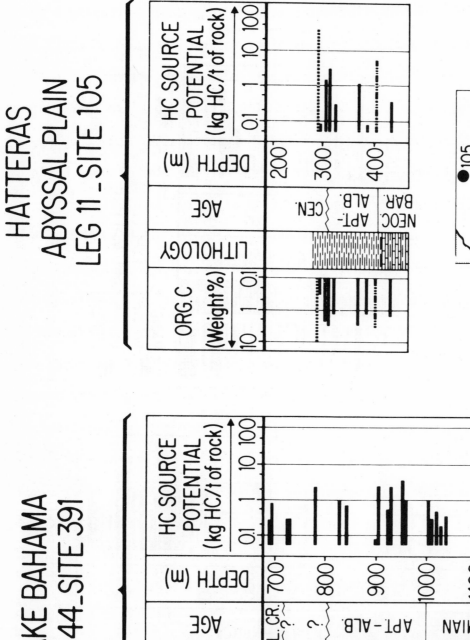

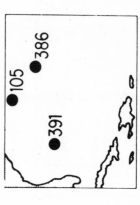

14. Geochemical well logs of DSDP Sites 391 and 105 (Tissot et al, 1980).

Cretaceous shales with over 10% liptinitic marine organic matter having a potential oil yield as high as 100 kilograms of hydrocarbon per ton of rock. In contrast, most Cretaceous samples from Site 391 in the Blake-Bahama Basin had terrestrial organic matter with an oil yield of 0.5 to 5 kg HC/ton rock. Although the Cape Basin contains more terrestrial organic matter than the Angola Basin, it still has a significantly higher yield than the Blake-Bahama Basin based on Site 391. However, three analyses from Sites 105 and 391 near the U.S. coast suggest that there are pockets of high organic carbon with high hydrocarbon source rock potential, that is more than 5 kilograms of hydrocarbon per ton of rock (1 kg oil/ton rock is approximately equal to 20 barrels of oil/ acre-foot or 1,000 ppm). The hydrocarbon source potential shown in Figures 13 and 14 is the quantity that hypothetically could be generated if the rocks were buried clear through the oil window. It does not represent the quantity present in the rocks today or potentially available for migration and accumulation.

Additional data obtained by several geochemical laboratories at DSDP Site 391 in the Blake-Bahama Basin is summarized in Figure 15 (Hunt, p. 529, 1979). The organic matter in the Miocene in this well is about 75% liptinitic. However this decreases in the Cretaceous and Jurassic where land derived material becomes more dominant. Vitrinite reflectance and thermal alteration indices indicate that the oil generation range was just being approached in the 1,400 to 1,600 meter depth interval in this well. Unfortunately, this deeper section contains primarily continental derived humic materials such as vitrinite and inertinite. Dow (1978) identified two populations of recycled vitrinite in the Cretaceous and Jurassic formations. The conclusion of several laboratories was that the Cretaceous in this part of the western Atlantic would be capable of generating gas with little or no oil if it is found in a higher

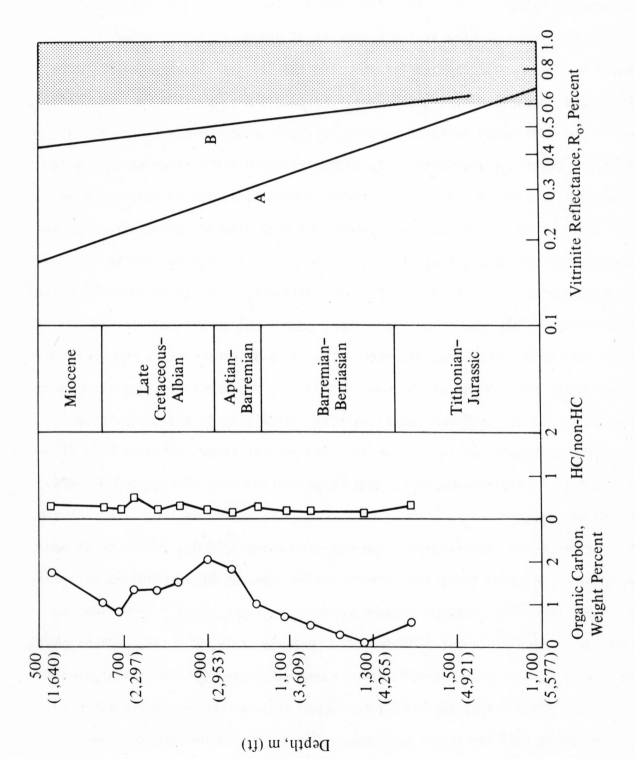

15. Geochemical data on cores from DSDP Leg 44, Site 391 (Hunt, 1979, p. 529).

temperature regime.

The COST Atlantic B-2 well was drilled to 16,043 feet in the Baltimore Canyon offshore eastern United States (Scholle, 1980). Total organic carbon content of the sediments in this well was low, generally less than 1% down to a depth of about 9500 feet. From here to 14,000 feet there was a marked increase in organic carbon with some values ranging above 6% and the mean being around 2%. At greater depths the organic carbon decreased abruptly with the mean around 0.3%. Over half the kerogen was described as liptinitic with amorphous marine derived material dominating in the upper sections and herbaceous continental derived material in the lower sections. The threshhold of intense hydrocarbon generation (beginning of the oil window) appeared to be around 9,500 feet based on a sharp increase in light hydrocarbon and C_{15} extraction data. Also, the vitrinite reflectance values at the beginning of oil generation (R_o = 0.5 to 0.6%) are reached around 10,000 feet (Figure 16). Since the organic type in the oil window was largely herbaceous, it was concluded that this interval would yield primarily gas or wet gas, with possibly a small amount of waxy oil.

Further north, the Georges Bank area (Amato and Simonis, 1980) is the site of the COST G-2 well which bottomed at 21,874 feet in Middle Jurassic to Early Jurassic sediments. Organic carbon contents were low, usually less than 1% down to 10,000 feet and less than 0.5% from there to total depth. The kerogen types were rather evenly distributed throughout the well. About half the kerogen was liptinitic (30% marine amorphous and 20% continental herbaceous) while the remaining half was humic continental derived vitrinite and inertinite. Hydrogen to carbon ratios of the kerogen in practically all well samples was reported to be less than 0.9 indicating mainly a gas-prone source section.

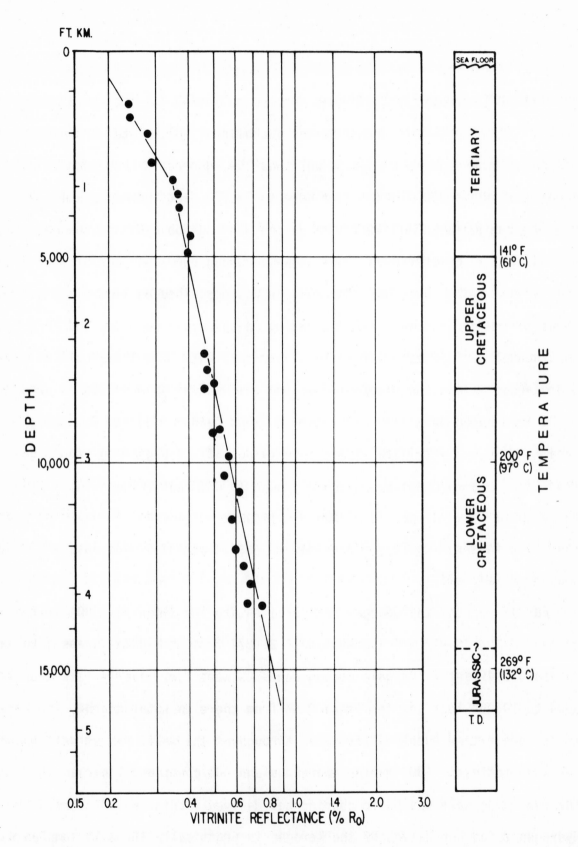

16. Kerogen maturation profile for Baltimore Canyon, B-2 COST well (Dow, 1978).

Bitumen (extract) yields were generally less than 450ppm (0.5 kg oil/ton of rock) which is generally considered below the level (700-1,000ppm) required to initiate oil migration. The threshold of intense oil generation appeared to be around 9,000 feet based on the thermal alteration index and vitinite reflectance. However, since the H/C ratio indicated the sediments could not generate oil, the gas window starting around 12,000 feet becomes more important than the oil window. In summary, gas or condensate from Middle to Late Jurassic source rocks appears to have the best potential on Georges Bank based on the COST G-2 well.

The principle exploration areas off eastern Canada have been the Scotian Basin, Grand Banks, East Newfoundland Basin and the Laborador Shelf. Geochemical studies in these areas have shown a variety of quantities and types of organic matter. Some areas appear to be gas prone, others prospective for large amounts of oil (Bujak et al, 1977, Powell and Snowdon, 1980, Purcell et al, 1979, 1980, Swift and Williams, 1980 and Rashid et al, 1980). Tertiary and Upper Cretaceous rocks in the Scotian Basin contain mostly liptinitic material about half amorphous marine derived and the rest exinite (herbaceous land derived). This kerogen is an excellent source of oil when mature but it is too shallow to account for most of the discoveries on the Scotian Shelf. In Cretaceous and Jurassic rocks the liptinite drops to about half the total kerogen and most of this is land derived exinite (spores, cuticles, and resins). Purcell, et al (1979) recognized the threshhold of intense oil generation as occurring at about 2500 meters on the Scotian Shelf which identifies the Cretaceous Missisauga and the Jurassic Micmac and Verrill Canyon formations as probable source rocks for the light oils and condensates found in the basin. Some accumulations on the shelf are associated with high relief piercement salt diapirs. The high heat conductivity of salt (bringing up heat from the diapir source) has resulted in local heat anomalies causing enhanced maturation of the sediments immediately overlying the salt diapirs.

The Grand Banks area to the east was intensively explored by Amoco Canada without commercial success (39 dry holes). Geochemical studies indicated that the quantity and type of organic matter in the mature formations drilled was adequate for commercial accumulations of petroleum. Unfortunately, however, the Avalon Uplift, an early Cretaceous tectonic feature, deeply eroded both potential source rocks and reservoirs (Swift and Williams, 1980). Several oil and gas shows were encountered but nothing of commercial significance. Maps of source rock maturity and organic carbon times formation thickness indicated that a more prospective area to explore would be the deeper parts of the south Whale and Jeanne d'Arc Basins to the southwest and northeast respectively. Subsequently, this prediction proved correct when Mobil Oil Canada Ltd. made a major oil discovery on the Hibernia structure northeast of Amoco's area. Bujak et al (1977) had previously noted that Jurassic sediments on the Grand Banks generally contained more liptinitic amorphous marine material than that on the Scotian Shelf.

Although the Grand Banks area east of Newfoundland appears to have a high oil potential based on the geochemical studies, the picture becomes more murky moving northwest along the Laborador coast. Rashid et al (1980) analyzed the kerogen in canned cuttings from a series of wells extending from the Grand Banks to the northern tip of Labrador. The amorphous type of organic matter continued to represent more than a third of the total kerogen but the hydrogen to carbon atomic ratio of the latter was found to be surprising low, generally less than 1. Rashid et al suggested that this was either due to the admixture of low H/C terrestrial humic material or that the amorphous material was actually degraded terrestrial kerogen. In any event, these few analyses suggest that the entire coast off Labrador is more apt to produce gas or condensate than oil.

The range of H/C and O/C ratios for the kerogen from several of these basins along the North Atlantic Margin are plotted in Figure 17 on a Van Krevelen diagram along with data from the Atlantic Margin of Africa. This may be compared with Figure 9. The kerogen of Cretaceous shales from DSDP Sites 367 and 368 near the Cape Verde Islands is definitely liptinitic (oil forming) type II with H/C ratios ranging from 1.1 to 1.4 (Deroo et al, 1978). The few samples that have been analyzed from DSDP Sites 105 and 391 off the U.S. Coast are clearly vitrinitic (gas forming). Likewise, the samples from the COST wells in the Baltimore Canyon (B-2) and on Georges Bank (G-2) are of the vitrinitic, type III kerogen as are the samples from the Labrador Shelf (Rashid et al, 1980).

The data in Figure 17 imply that the North American Atlantic Margin is a gas prone area within the maturity zone. Obviously, this is not entirely the case as attested by the many oil shows encountered by Amoco Canada on Grand Banks and the subsequent discoveries by Mobil Canada at Hibernia. The problem is that the Atlantic Margin covers millions of square miles and the only pub-lished data on the organic matter is from a few DSDP Sites, COST wells and some Canadian oil company wells. These results show a large area off the coast where maturities are adequate for the generation and migration of oil (Figure 18, Dow, 1978). The kerogen, however, in areas south of Grand Banks is mainly the vitrinitic gas forming type III material in the few samples studied. The liptinitic oil forming type II kerogen is present along most of the North

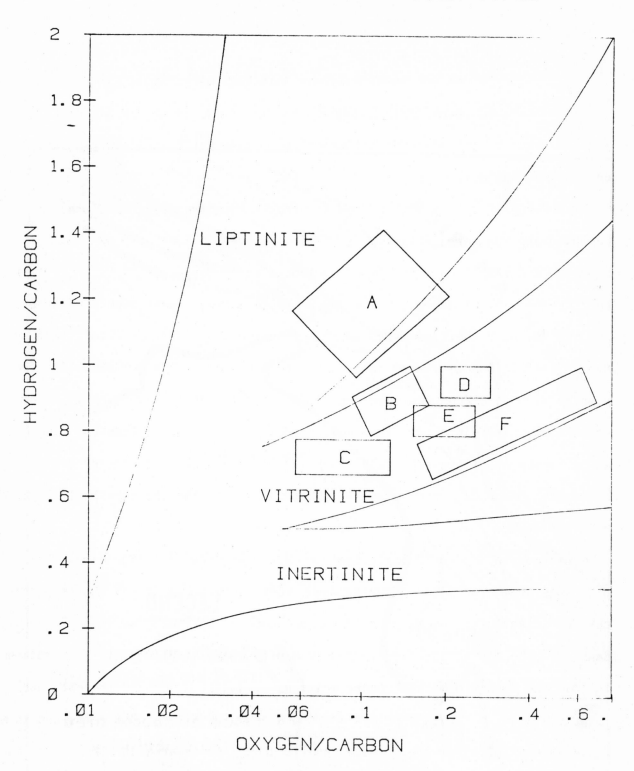

ATLANTIC MARGIN KEROGEN TYPES

17. Kerogen types based on elemental analysis:
   A. Cretaceous, DSDP Site 367, Cape Verde Basin (Deroo et al, 1977
   B. Cretaceous, 6,000 to 13,000 ft., Baltimore Canyon COST B-2 well
       (Scholle, 1977).
   C. Jurassic below 10,000 ft., Georges Bank Cost G-2 well (Amato
       and Simonis, 1980).
   D. Cretaceous, DSDP Site 105, Hatteras (Tisst et al, 1980).
   E. Cretaceous, DSDP Site 391, Blake-Bahama (Deroo et al, 1978).
   F. Labrador Shelf (Rashid et al, 1980).

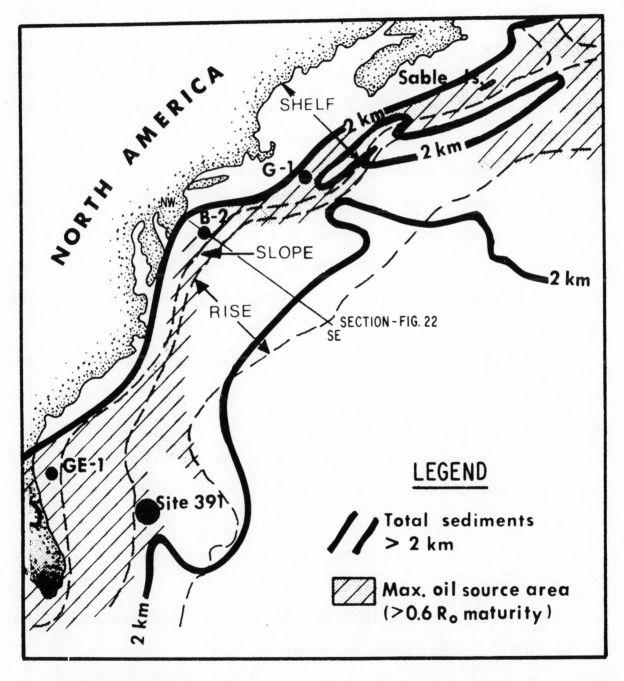

18. Map showing probable extent of area (shaded) containing sediments mature
    enough to generate oil (Ro 0.6) providing liptinitic organic rich
    sediments are present (Dow, 1978).

American margin, but in deeper mature sediments it appears to be dominant only in the Cretaceous and Jurassic sediments of the Grand Banks area. The Iroquois, Verrill Canyon, Logan and Dawson Canyon formations and their equivalents have oil source rock characteristics in localized areas rather than in a broad area running several hundred miles as does the Jurassic Kimmeridgian source rock of the North Sea. This suggests that gas and condensate will continue to be the principal petroleum found on the North American margin, with oil occuring where pockets of liptinitic organic matter are deposited.

Gas hydrates, which are crystalline structures containing methane, ethane and occasionally some non-hydrocarbons, in a cubic lattic of water molecules, are common in continental margin sediments (Kvenvolden, 1981). They have been intriguing economically because near the surface they can contain several times the volume of methane compared to a conventional reservoir (Hunt, 1979, p. 156-162). Unfortunately, there is no way to produce them economically so most drillers case off hydrate zones and drill for the free gas that is frequently found beneath the hydrates. As a seal, gas hydrates are probably comparable to evaporites. However, it is not yet known to what extent they exist continuously over large structures in which commercial gas accumulations may be trapped.

REFERENCES CITED

Amato, R.V. and E.K. Simonis, 1980, Geologic and operational summary, COST No. G-2 well: USGS Open File Report 80-269.

Bujak, J.P., Barss, M.S. and Williams, G.L., 1977a, Offshore East Canada's organic type and color and hydrocarbon potential, Part I: Oil and Gas J., v. 75, No. 14, p. 198-202.

Bujak, J.P., Barss, M.S. and Williams, G.L., 1977b, Offshore East Canada's organic type and color and hydrocarbon potential. Part II: Oil and Gas J., v. 75, no. 15, 96-100.

Demaison, G.J. and Moore, G.T., 1980, Anoxic environments and oil source bed genesis: Bull. AAPG, v. 64, p. 1179-1209.

Deroo, G., et al, 1977, Organic geochemistry of some Cretaceous black shales from Sites 367 and 368, Leg 41, eastern North Atlantic: Initial Rept. Deep Sea Drilling Project, v. 41, p. 865-873.

Deroo, G., et al, 1978, Organic geochemistry of some Cretaceous claystones from Site 391, Leg 44, western North Atlantic: Initial Rept. Deep Sea Drilling Project, v. 44, p. 593-598.

Dow, W.G., 1979, Petroleum source beds on continental slopes and rises: AAPG, v. 62, No. 9, p. 1584-1606.

Hunt, J.M., 1979, Petroleum geochemistry and geology: W.H. Freeman, San Francisco, 617 pp.

Hunt, J.M. and J. Whelan, 1978, Light hydrocarbons in sediments of DSDP Leg 44 holes: Initial Rept. Deep Sea Drilling Project, v. 44, p. 651-652.

Kvenvolden, K.A., 1981, Hydrates of natural gas in continental margins:

Powell, T.G. and L.R. Snowdon, 1980, Geochemical controls on hydrocarbon generation in Canadian sedimentary basins: Canad. Soc. Petrol. Geol. Memoir 6, p. 421-446.

Purcell, L.P., Umpleby, D.C. and Wade, J.A., 1980, Regional geology and hydro-carbon occurrences off the east coast of Canada: Cand. Soc. Petrol. Geol. Memoir 6, p. 551-566.

Rashid, M.A., Purcell, L.P. and Hardy, I.A., 1980, Source rock potential for oil and gas of the east Newfoundland and Labrador Shelf areas: Canad. Soc. Petr. Geol. Memoir No. 6, p. 589-608.

Ronov, A.B., 1958, Organic carbon in sedimentary rocks (in relation to the presence of petroleum). Geochem., no. 5, pp. 497-509.

Scholle, P.A., 1980, Geological studies on the COST No. B-2 well, United States Mid-Atlantic Outer Continental Shelf area: U.S. Geological Survey Circ. 750.

Swift, J.H. and Williams, J.A., 1980, Petroleum source rocks: Grand Banks area: Canad. Soc. Petr. Geol., Memoir No. 6, p. 567-588.

Tissot, B., G. Demaison, P. Masson, J.R. Delteil and A. Combaz, 1980, Paleoenvironment and petroleum potential of Middle Cretaceous black shales in the Atlantic basins: AAPG Bull., v. 64, p. 2051-2063.

Van Krevelen, D.W., 1961, Coal. New York, Elsevier Pub. Co., 514 p.